by

Heart

by Heart

Recipes to Hold Near and Dear

Hailee Catalano

Publisher Mike Sanders
Art & Design Director William Thomas
Editorial Director Ann Barton
Senior Editor Olivia Peluso
Senior Designer Jessica Lee
Illustrator Maxine McCrann
Photographer Emily Hawkes
Food Stylist Tiffany Schleigh
Prop Stylist Julia Rose
Recipe Tester Rebecca Firkser
Copyeditor Christy Wagner
Proofreaders Hannah Matuszak & Mira S. Park
Indexer Louisa Emmons

First American Edition, 2025
Published in the United States by DK Publishing
1745 Broadway, 20th Floor, New York, NY 10019

The authorized representative in the EEA is Dorling Kindersley
Verlag GmbH. Arnulfstr. 124, 80636 Munich, Germany

A catalog record for this book
is available from the Library of Congress.
ISBN 978-0-5938-4265-2

DK books are available at special discounts when purchased
in bulk for sales promotions, premiums, fund-raising, or
educational use. For details, contact SpecialSales@dk.com

Printed and bound in China

www.dk.com

This book was made with Forest
Stewardship Council™ certified
paper – one small step in DK's
commitment to a sustainable future.
Learn more at
www.dk.com/uk/information/sustainability

To my dear parents, Cindy and Frank,
who have always reminded me that
"wherever you go, there you are."

Contents

At the Heart of It

To know something "by heart" is to know it from memory, to remember a recipe so well that you can make it with barely any reference. When you make a well-loved recipe over and over, it becomes a part of who you are. My grandma's stuffed artichoke recipe is that for me. I've made and eaten those artichokes so many times that the recipe is basically a part of my personality at this point. That's the idea behind this book, *By Heart*, a collection of more than 100 recipes near and dear to my heart. I've spent years developing, tasting, and testing these special recipes, and now that this book is in your hands, I hope they'll become treasured favorites that you'll cherish forever.

But just how we got here is a bit of a story to be told: I grew up in a family of people who instilled a love of food in me at a young age. This love grew and flourished as I got older, which eventually led me to move to the East Coast to attend culinary school. I then spent a handful of years working in restaurants, where I experienced many moments of restaurant industry–related burnout.

To combat that burnout and establish a bit of a creative outlet, I started making cooking videos and posting them on social media. And to my surprise, people watched them. Now, here we are, and I couldn't be more grateful.

I grew up in the Chicago suburbs, so I'm a Midwesterner at heart. The classic Midwestern sense of hospitality—like a good ol' potluck dinner shared among friends—is in my bones. I'm also half Sicilian, so I have a deep appreciation for food and sharing it with the ones I love. I fell in love with cooking and eating early on, probably without even noticing it. As a child, I spent every Sunday with my family at my grandma Tina's house, creating memories over big bowls of penne rigate smothered in gravy (tomato sauce—if you know, you know) and loud conversation. I remember being enamored as she effortlessly prepared a huge pot of gravy amid utter family chaos. She was always calm and collected, the only person who could bring us all together for a moment of peace over some pasta. It was her superpower. Looking back now, these memories shaped my love of food and ignited

my passion for bringing that same joy to people. I've included a whole chapter of recipes inspired by Tina (starting on page 187), as it seems absolutely fitting.

When I was about 12 years old, I became dead set on going to culinary school and becoming a chef. Around this time, I was enthralled with cable cooking shows, as many people were in the early 2000s. I watched one episode of Rachael Ray making citrus-glazed salmon with an iceberg salad, and I was hooked. From that moment, I never wavered in my career choice. I was really lucky to know exactly what I wanted to do at a young age. There was one hiccup, though, that no one really saw coming.

I have a very focused—one could say almost *obsessive*—personality. When I was growing up, this quality always helped me thrive. I was obsessive in every aspect of my life, from getting straight As to strictly following rules to a tee. People would often describe me as a "perfectionist," but it was never in a negative way. Until it was. In my senior year of high school, as I was preparing to move to New York to attend the Culinary Institute of America, my obsessiveness began to manifest in a new way. I started to become extremely ritualistic with certain cleanliness routines, and I was quickly diagnosed with obsessive-

compulsive disorder (OCD). My rituals started with telling myself I had to be really careful when washing my hands, to make sure they were "absolutely" clean. Soon, it snowballed into four-hour shower routines, refusing to touch certain things, and quarantining my brother to the basement because I deemed him too "dirty" to be around. If others around me didn't adapt to my cleaning practices, I would shun them. I went from zero to one hundred very quickly, leaving a mess for me and my family to clean up. Everything culminated when, one day, I locked myself in a bathroom with no intent of ever coming out. In that moment, I was perfectly content with doing nothing else in my life but living in a bathroom to stay "clean forever." After the police finally knocked down the bathroom barricade I had created, my parents hit me with an ultimatum: Get treatment, or consider your dreams of a culinary career out the window. There was no way I could head off to culinary school in that state.

This wasn't my finest moment, but it's an important part of my journey. In the end, it comes back to my love of food and how it saved me. Thankfully, as quickly as I fell into that dark hole, I was able to get out via a treatment program, with the hope of fulfilling my culinary dreams

helping propel me through. This is not to say or imply that this process was easy or that I am totally freed and cured of OCD, but I have been able to get a much better handle on it, so it isn't totally debilitating to my everyday life.

In some ways, I think my obsessive tendencies and attention to detail have actually helped me flourish in the culinary world. When I was working in restaurants, the fast-paced environment was a great place for me to focus all of my nervous energy. Not to mention that cleanliness, diligence, and organization were not only suggested in restaurants; they were strictly enforced on a day-to-day basis. It was perfect for me. Even now, although my job involves cooking at home, I am able to channel a lot of that same energy and need for consistency into writing precise and organized recipes and creating content. Cooking in general has been a great way to harness a lot of my mental struggle and put it toward something productive. I still may be very particular about the way a dish is made, but you won't find me stuck at the bathroom sink, rewashing my hands for hours on end. And to me, that's a win.

I ended up loving culinary school, and I really thrived there. Knowing that I had chosen the right path was such a validating feeling—and so freeing! It was the first time I felt like I was surrounded by like-minded people with similar goals. My partner, Chuck, was one of them. I met him in school, and we've been together ever since. He is the calmest, most patient person I have ever met, and we lift each other up in our own ways. After culinary school, we went on to work in almost all the same restaurants, often cooking on the line together and even on the same station. Some of my best memories we have together are from our

time cooking on the line. Being in such a high-pressure situation with your partner can end in many different ways, but for us, it almost always ended in laughs. And of course, a few accidental burns here and there. We are just two people who love cooking and eating together. Nowadays, we have another member of our team: our dog, Gus. Although he can't quite cook with us, he sure does enjoy watching us. Gus loves to be in the kitchen just as much as we do, even if it's just for the smells and the occasional cheese snacks.

After culinary school, I worked in restaurants for about seven years. As much as I cherish that experience and everything I learned inside and outside the kitchen, there were multiple times I quit jobs due to burnout. The hours were long and demanding. The pay was low and unmotivating. The kitchens were hot and windowless. The off days were short and inconsistent. No matter how much I loved cooking at a particular restaurant, all of these things would end up weighing on me until I inevitably quit. I always ended up crawling back into another kitchen job, just to find myself in exactly the same spot after a while. This never-ending loop is common in restaurant work and something that I just accepted would be part of my experience, too. I was fully convinced I would continue the typical trajectory— go to culinary school and then struggle in restaurants trying to prove myself over and over again—until hopefully one day, Chuck and I could save enough money to open a small restaurant. There really wasn't any other path I saw as possible for us.

But something else happened entirely. In March 2020, the pandemic shook up all of my plans and goals. I was in between restaurant jobs, living in Jersey City, New Jersey, with hopes of working in a New York City restaurant. That didn't end up panning out, so I started working any odd job I could think of. I tried shopping for Instacart, private chef work, and even a traditional corporate 9-to-5 job that really sucked the life out of me. I needed a creative outlet.

One day in 2021, I convinced myself that if I started to post on social media, I could manifest that small restaurant Chuck and I had always pictured as our end goal. That, coupled with the dream to have a work-from-home job so I could be with Gus as much as possible, pushed me to start sharing on social media. Funnily enough, the first videos I made were actually not cooking-related at all. I started with coffee videos that featured just my hands. This seemed more feasible and less overwhelming than making cooking videos. I had worked as a barista, in the mornings before my afternoon line-cook shifts, so it felt fitting.

Soon, I got used to making and posting short-form videos, and I even gained a small following. But my page really began to flourish when I finally mustered up the confidence to post about what I love most: cooking. My first cooking video that really took off was a basic vodka pasta recipe that I almost thought wasn't worth posting. But people really seemed to love it! The rest is history. Although it hasn't resulted in a restaurant (yet!), posting videos on social media changed my life and gave me opportunities I never could have dreamed of. It is truly an honor that I get a chance to share food from my heart and life with so many people.

That brings us back to the book in your hands. I wanted to write a cookbook with recipes from all aspects of my life: recipes inspired by my childhood, restaurant jobs, and everything in between. Everything in this book is truly from my heart, and I hope it becomes a staple in your kitchen, bringing you back time and time again until you know these recipes by heart. When you cook from this book, I hope you feel the joy and serenity that cooking brings me. These recipes are more than just words on a page: They're words from my heart.

Keeping a Calm Kitchen

The kitchen is where I have always found calm and serenity, and nothing makes me happier than sharing that sense of calm with others. With that in mind, I've written the recipes in this book to help guide you through a streamlined cooking process. I've listed most of the ingredients with their basic prep work included; the idea is that you can have everything out and essentially prepped before you start cooking, especially if it's your first time making the recipe. This is called *mise en place*, and it's one of the first things I was taught in culinary school. "Proper prior planning prevents piss-poor performance" was another phrase chefs often screamed, but I find that a bit harsh. We're cooking at home—it's really not that serious! In the end, it all essentially means the same thing: Set yourself up for success, ease, and clarity. I also always suggest doing a quick cleanup after all the prep work is done so you aren't left with a tornado to clean up later. It really makes cooking so much more enjoyable. Clear counter, clear mind.

Chefs and seasoned cooks make cooking look so *easy* because they know exactly what's coming next at all points of the cooking process. That's why I always recommend reading a recipe all the way through before trying it for the first time. There is nothing more anxiety-inducing than blindly going into something you have never done before. I've set up this book to avoid that at all costs. That being said, after you've cooked a recipe multiple times, it will start to become second nature. You will begin to know it *by heart*, and it will feel freeing—as cooking should be. You'll start to notice certain points in the recipe when there's downtime to prep some of the ingredients to come, so you no longer need to have *every single thing* prepped and measured in advance. As you become more comfortable, your mise en place setup can become more flexible, too. You may realize you like a bit more heat, vinegar, or salt in certain recipes, and you should feel empowered to make those changes. This is the point when the recipe really becomes something that's cooked from your heart.

All that being said, when it comes to these recipes, there are certain things that are very important to follow closely. I have included metric and imperial measurements throughout, not only to be as inclusive as possible but also to be precise as possible where it really matters. All of my recipes for baked goods and breads have the metric measurements listed first because I highly recommend using those precise measures. Baking is a science that I don't like to mess with, and using metric measurements produces the best final product. At the end of the day, imperial measurements are just not as precise as baking needs to be. Not to mention how much time you'll save when you don't have to clean a bunch of measuring cups! A kitchen scale is important for this; you'll find more about my favorite one on page 20.

This is a bit of a sneaky book: There are quite a few recipes within recipes, which makes room for fun mixing and matching. Use the sauce from the Spanish Zucchini Tortilla (page 110) on the BL Double T (page 255) in place of the toum for something a bit less garlicky and a touch more spiced. Sprinkle the rye crunchies from the Radicchio and Apple Salad with Rye Crunchies (page 76) onto your morning scrambled eggs for a nice textural component. Use the peach vinaigrette from the Charred Sweet Potatoes with Chunky Peach Vinaigrette (page 114) to bring simple grilled chicken thighs to a new, summery level.

Pair any of the breads with any of the fun butters to complete a meal. Serve a few of the fun, pickle-y condiment items together for an exciting aperitivo hour—alongside some fresh sourdough, of course—or easily match them with recipes from other chapters. Use the Spicy Chicken-Salt Sesame Crackers (page 67) as dippers for the Smoky Caramelized Shallot Dip with Sun-Dried Tomatoes (page 57), or top a sheet-pan pizza (see page 174) with the Chicago-Style Fennel Giardiniera (page 46). The options are seriously endless! Do what your heart desires—that's what it's all about. If you're looking for a good place to start brainstorming recipe pairings, check out my menus on pages 32 and 33.

I've added another touch of hidden treasure in this book: I'm a learn-on-the-job kinda gal—I need to physically do something to learn it—so my recipes use basic cooking techniques without explicitly calling them out. The idea is that the repetition of common methods throughout the book will inherently teach you how to do them without boring you. I find that too much technical jargon takes away from the heart and soul of cooking, so you'll learn how to blanch vegetables by actually doing it, not by reading a "This Is How You Blanch" section. There's a certain calmness in feeling confident in the kitchen that comes with understanding basic techniques. Throughout these recipes, you will learn to pickle, roast, and season, among so many other techniques that you can carry with you beyond this book. I hope that the recipes here inspire you to utilize the methods in your own way to elevate your day-to-day cooking. Because when it comes down to it, the best food is cooked from the heart.

Equipment Essentials

Here, we'll dive into my tool kit and utensil bin, and I'll take you through all of my kitchen equipment standbys. From knives to storage solutions, this section will set you up for cooking success!

Stay Sharp

When it comes to an everyday, all-purpose knife, I personally love a 6-inch (15 cm) utility or chef's knife (sometimes also called a petty knife). It's smaller than a standard chef's knife, so I find it easier to maneuver, and it's useful for many tasks other than just chopping. I can just as easily use it to carve a chicken as I can to dice an onion. The only other knife I find myself reaching for day in and day out is a large serrated knife for cutting tomatoes, sandwiches, and sourdough. I love a Japanese mandoline for precise, thin slicing, especially the Benriner brand. Both a standard box grater and a microplane are nice to have for any and all grating.

Pans: Keep 'Em Stainless (Mostly)

As a very general rule of thumb, oven-safe pans are best, and stainless steel is always my go-to. Stainless steel should be the assumed pan preference for all the recipes in this book, unless otherwise specified. A good set of stainless-steel pans—at least one large pot, a sauce pot, and a few sauté pans in various sizes—and a large cast-iron skillet are all you really need to cook almost anything, and these pans will last a lifetime. Add in a trusty Dutch oven for bread baking and braising and a carbon-steel frying pan for a much lighter, cast iron–comparable pan, and you're *really* set. If you're looking to expand your standard stainless-steel set even further, I highly recommend a 3-quart (2.8 L) saucier. It's the pan I use when I refer to a "medium pot." It's perfect for sauces, of course, but I especially love it for tossing pastas and making smaller-batch soups and broths.

Tray It Up

Rimmed sheet pans are great for so many tasks other than just baking and roasting. They are perfect landing zones, great for breading stations, and ideal for overall kitchen organization. I like to have both the standard "half" (18×13 inches/46×33 cm) and "quarter" (13×9 inches/33×23 cm) sizes to cover all my sheet-pan needs, along with their respective nesting wire racks. In my recipes, "large sheet pan" refers to half sheet pans, and "small sheet pan" refers to quarter sheet pans. (I also tend to use *sheet tray* and *sheet pan* interchangeably. Same thing!)

Baking Pans: Metal, Glass, or Ceramic?

The recipes in this book use standard baking pans, so there's nothing too wild to call out here. I tend to prefer metal pans for baked goods like cakes, rolls, and breads, while glass or ceramic pans are perfectly fine for casserole-style dishes. Metal conducts more heat, making it ideal for achieving professional bakery–style brown edges and crusts in your at-home baked goods. Metal baking pans also tend to have sharper, less-rounded edges than glass or ceramic pans, which I think yield more elegant and professional bakes.

Build Your Utensil Set

When I worked as a cook in restaurants, it was expected that you would bring in your own set of utensils to use for prep and cooking on the line. These items were your own responsibility, and, depending on who you worked with, things could become quite territorial. There wasn't a ton of room for utensils, so you had to be smart with what you brought. That bit of restaurant culture has really helped me determine which small cooking utensils I find essential for day-to-day cooking. I store my most-used utensils in a bain-marie, a tall cylindrical container commonly used in restaurants to hold sauces and personal utensils. These things are always in my bain:

- At least one wooden spoon
- Cake testers
- Fish spatula
- Kitchen scissors
- Kitchen tweezers of various sizes (I find these are sleeker and easier to maneuver than clunky tongs.)
- Metal spoons of various sizes (These are great for basting, stirring, tasting, serving, and more.)
- Pastry brush
- Rubber spatulas, large and small
- Small offset spatula
- Spider and/or slotted spoon
- Whisk
- Y vegetable peeler

Blend, Blend, Blend

Vitamix is my number one. There really isn't any other blender quite like it, and it's an investment that will last you a lifetime. For the smoothest versions of anything blended, the Vitamix blender reigns supreme. Handheld stick blenders are also nice to have for things that don't need to be ultra smooth; they're convenient and result in fewer dishes to clean.

Strain Away

I use fine-mesh strainers for almost every sauce or liquid. My favorite is the chinois. It's conical in shape and has the finest of mesh for the smoothest of sauces. Although it's very nice (and reminiscent of my restaurant days), any fine-mesh strainer you can get your hands on is perfectly suitable for home cooking. I also like to have a standard colander for less-finicky straining, such as draining boiling water from cooking pasta or potatoes and washing fruits and vegetables.

Accuracy Tools: Sometimes Precise Is Nice

I don't like to make my cooking seem super technical, but there are a few tools that I find very helpful when accuracy is needed. An instant-read thermometer is helpful for cooking large proteins, deep-frying, or working with cooked sugar. I always suggest buying a cheap oven thermometer because oven temperatures can be wildly inaccurate. An oven thermometer gives a much more accurate read of your oven temperature than your actual oven does. And I highly recommend a digital kitchen scale (my favorite is from the brand Escali). Most of my recipes for baked goods are written in grams because weight measurements produce much more reliable results than volume measurements when it comes to baking. The weight of 1 cup of flour, for example, can be vastly different depending on how it's measured. Not to mention all the dishes you won't have to clean when you measure ingredients with a scale: no messy measuring cups scattered about!

Sourdough Starter Pack

Although not essential, a batten, lame, and bench scraper make the sourdough process a bit more streamlined. A kitchen towel–lined bowl and a sharp knife can make fine substitutes for the batten and lame, but a bench scraper is always great to have, and not only for sourdough. It's perfect for maneuvering and portioning doughs and is also great for swiftly transferring prepped vegetables from board to bowl or pan.

Pizza and Pasta Extras

We're making some fresh pasta and pizza in this book, both of which are made easier with certain tools. A pizza stone and LloydPans pizza pans ensure the crispiest pizza crust, and a pasta machine and fluted pasta wheel help produce the most beautiful fresh pastas. Although these are nice to have, you can still make very delicious versions of these recipes without the specialty items, which I explain in their respective recipes.

Kitchen Towels: A Line Cook's Treasure

Known in professional kitchens as a "side towel," the humble kitchen towel is useful for so much more than drying dishes or your hands. It is such a staple piece of equipment in professional kitchens that as a line cook, the way you take care of your side towels is often considered a reflection of the type of cook you are. Are your towels clean or messy? Wet or dry? Folded or strewn about the kitchen? It's all analyzed. And if you lose track of your towels during your shift, you can be sure that the next cook will scoop them up. Although I'm no longer working on the line, I still use kitchen towels in many of the same ways at home. They are great makeshift trivets, oven mitts, and drying racks. You will never go back to old, bulky, hard-to-clean oven mitts once you swap in a good kitchen towel. Just make sure they are *completely dry* before using them to transfer hot items because water conducts heat.

Mixers: When by Hand Just Won't Cut It

For the most part, an electric hand mixer is the only mixer you need to successfully make the recipes in this book, and many of the dessert and pastry recipes actually can be made fully by hand. The only exceptions are a few of the bread recipes, like the Spiced Date and Pecan Sticky Buns (page 232) and the Oniony Poppy Seed Dinner Rolls (page 230), which I always suggest making in a stand mixer. These recipes require a hefty bit of "kneading" in the stand mixer with the dough hook. Although I don't recommend it, they technically can be done by hand if you're feeling truly passionate.

Storage: Quart It Up

A brief note on general food storage: I opt for plastic quart, pint, and cup containers for storing almost everything. Restaurants use them to organize food prep, and for good reason. They stack easily in your fridge, which optimizes space and gives the fridge a sense of order and flow. Just like I did when I was working in restaurants, I always label the containers with the name of the food and the date it was made using good ol' painter's tape and a Sharpie. This makes for top-tier organization and gives you peace of mind—no more rummaging through the fridge wondering what exactly something is or when it was made. It's all spelled out for you in a nice, orderly fashion. Love it.

Packing Your Pantry for Success

This is less of an exact, itemized pantry list and more of a pantry mindset. These are ingredients I like to have around for general day-to-day cooking and specifically for the recipes in this book.

Salt and Pepper

Let's start with the absolute basics: salt and pepper. My everyday, go-to, all-purpose salt is always kosher salt: Diamond Crystal kosher salt, specifically. It has an ideal sprinkling texture that just *feels* right when you sift it through your fingers. The crystals aren't too big or too small, and you can physically see them when you sprinkle the salt on food, which is so helpful for even seasoning. It also dissolves easily into anything, hot or cold. My love for the stuff runs deep, so every recipe in this book was developed using Diamond Crystal kosher salt. This is super important to note because substituting in other salts for specific salt measurements in the recipes will not yield the same results. Just grab a big box of the stuff; it will last you a long time. I also always have a nice flaky salt on hand for finishing and sprinkling on top of dishes. Maldon is probably the most common and easy-to-find brand, but there are so many amazing finishing salts you can try out. Jacobsen flake salt also holds a special place in my heart because I fell in love with it while working in restaurants. You may find it at certain specialty food shops but it's also easily found online.

When it comes to black pepper, I of course recommend freshly ground, but I like to take this one step further and toast the peppercorns before adding them to my grinder. Toasting peppercorns intensifies their flavor and gives them the treatment they deserve. If you use as much black pepper as I do, you will run through it before it sits long enough to lose that toasty flavor. I simply toast the peppercorns on a small baking sheet at 300°F (150°C) for 30 minutes or until toasty and very fragrant, let them cool, and add them to my grinder. I know it's a few extra steps, but trust me, you'll never go back.

Vinegars

I love to collect vinegars of all kinds, and I call for a handful of different ones throughout this book. Although my vinegar collection is a fun hobby, it is definitely not necessary for you to have a bunch of different vinegars to cook these recipes successfully. I tend to use a lot of red wine vinegar, so that is always a staple in my pantry. "Lighter," more "neutral" vinegars, such as rice vinegar, white wine vinegar, and apple cider vinegar, can be used interchangeably in most recipes, so feel free to swap as desired. I call for celery vinegar specifically a few times in this book because I love it so much and truly believe it's worth seeking out. I use the brand TART, and I always find myself reaching for it. But like I said, you can always swap for something you already have on hand!

Oils

I keep things pretty basic here. I use olive oil for most of my cooking, unless I'm deep-frying. I like to have two kinds of olive oil on hand: one for general cooking and one for cold or raw preparations and drizzling on top of dishes to finish. There's so much information out there on which olive oil is best to use for different applications, but to keep it simple, here's the general rule I go by: If it's sold in a big jug (usually labeled just "olive oil"), it's good for cooking, and if it's sold in a cute, smaller bottle (usually labeled "extra virgin"), it's nice for finishing. This is a very general rule, but it's a good baseline. For deep-frying and exceptionally high-heat cooking, I often opt for canola oil, but grapeseed, vegetable, and sunflower are also great options.

Sweet Stuff

My go-to sweeteners for cooking are honey and maple syrup. Here and there, I'll call for granulated sugar in savory recipes, but I mainly reserve it for baking and desserts. When it comes to brown sugar, I always go for dark—give me all that deep, molasses-y flavor!

Light brown sugar seems pointless to me in comparison. I also always have demerara sugar stocked for sprinkling on top of crusts or scones for that signature bakery-style sugary crunch.

Spices and Herbs

In this book, you will see a lot of smoked paprika, red pepper flakes, dried bay leaves, and fennel seeds. If you are convinced you hate fennel seed, try it once more in one of these recipes! I truly adore it and am actively trying to convert the naysayers. Although mushroom powder technically isn't a spice, I always have some in my spice cabinet. It adds so much umami flavor to whatever you sprinkle it on. You can buy mushroom powder at many stores, but it's so easy to make yourself. All you have to do is blitz some dried mushrooms (I like porcini, shiitakes, or a combo) into a powder in a spice grinder or blender. I'm also a big fan of toasting and grinding your own whole spices, like fennel seeds and coriander. I like to do this as needed to ensure my spices taste fresh and vibrant, so toasting instructions pop up frequently in the recipes throughout the book. A coffee grinder (dedicated to spices, not coffee), a mortar and pestle, or even a blender will work for grinding whole spices after toasting.

Oregano is the only dried herb I keep around; I actually prefer the dried version over the fresh. The floral, woodsy notes of fresh oregano are a bit overpowering to me. Other than that, I'm team fresh herb all the way. I classify most fresh herbs into two categories, tender or hearty, referring to the toughness of their leaves and stems. When I call for fresh herbs of the tender, leafy variety, such as dill, parsley, and cilantro, I always mean the leaves and tender stems. For heartier-stemmed herbs, such as rosemary, thyme, tarragon, mint, and basil, I use just the leaves; I remove the stem either before chopping or after cooking.

One last little note: When it comes to vanilla, I always call for vanilla bean paste (and a whole bean here and there) because I think it brings sweets to the next level, but subbing with an equal amount of pure vanilla extract is always just fine. I recommended using 1 tablespoon of paste or extract if substituting for a whole bean.

Nuts and Seeds

Pepitas, sesame seeds, sunflower seeds, pistachios, pine nuts, almonds, and pecans are the major players in this book. Just like whole spices, nuts and seeds are best toasted as you use them, although I do call for raw nuts in a few instances, mainly when they are being blended into a sauce or dip for creaminess. Store shelled nuts and seeds at room temperature, but if you don't find yourself running through your stash very quickly, I recommend freezing them to maintain their freshness and quality for much longer. I currently have some in my freezer that are still fresh and ready to go from eight months ago!

Flours

There are quite a few bread, pastry, and pasta recipes in this book, so it's nice to have a few "specialty" flours on hand alongside the old standby, all-purpose flour. Semolina flour is great for things like fresh pasta, cake flour is perfect for cake (obviously), bread flour and whole-wheat flours are good for sourdough, and rye flour is nice for a few fun special occasions, like battering a delicious fish fry. Choosing the right flour for the job is essential, so I don't suggest subbing in different flours for specific ones called for in a recipe.

Standby Starches

A few simple notes here. I always have white jasmine rice on hand. It's my go-to for the rice cooker, and a simple side of fresh steamed rice completes almost any meal. When it comes to dry pasta, I think it's great to have one variety of short-cut pasta and one type of long pasta in your pantry so you can choose the appropriate option for whatever sauce you're making.

Spicy Add-Ins

If you're familiar with my recipes, you know how much I love jarred, chopped Calabrian chiles in oil for their kick of fermented heat. I always have a jar or two in my pantry, along with a couple other spicy go-tos. Chili crisp, pepperoncini, pickled cherry peppers, and a vinegary hot sauce (I love Crystal) are great to have around for simple yet dynamic ways to add heat to your cooking.

Canned and Tinned Things

I love anchovies. I have a stock of tins in my pantry at all times. I don't love anchovy paste, so I always suggest using the tinned whole fillets. If I don't use a whole tin in a recipe or snack, I transfer any remaining fillets (with their oil) to a small, airtight container and store them in the fridge. They will last for at least a month refrigerated. When it comes to other canned items, I always have a can or two of beans, some artichoke hearts, and of course my most-used tomato products: Whole canned San Marzano tomatoes, tomato paste, and passata.

Leaveners

For baked goods and other leavened things, we have our usual suspects here—baking powder and baking soda—but I want to talk mainly about dry yeast, which is used a few times in this book. I always call for instant yeast because I find it to be easier to use and more reliable than active dry. With instant yeast, no activation is needed, so you can just add it right in with the dry ingredients. Nice and simple. My favorite brand is Saf-instant, which is often sold in larger quantities. I transfer it to an airtight container and keep it in the freezer. It lasts essentially forever in there.

Mustards

Just popping in here to express my love of mustard. Even the smallest spoonful can make such an impact. I mainly reach for Dijon because it can be used in many different applications, and I always have both the creamy and whole-grain varieties available. Sometimes the whole-grain just looks cuter in certain things. Don't ask me why; I don't make the rules.

In Brine

I'm a big olive and caper lover. They bring a lovely, salty punch that can easily elevate a dish. It's also nice to add the brine to recipes for a unique salinity. A splash of olive or caper brine in a vinaigrette or sauce can really bring it to a new level. I add a bit of olive brine to my A Very Olive-y Focaccia (page 226) to really drive home the olive flavor throughout the dough. Castelvetrano and Niçoise olives are two versatile varieties I always have in my pantry.

Pecorino

You will notice quite a bit of pecorino Romano cheese called for in this book. I grew up eating pecorino, not Parmesan, and my love for this cheese is one that I can't quite shake. I find it to be more flavorful and just better than Parmesan in most cases. Of course, feel free to substitute with Parmesan if that's where your heart lies. When I call for finely grated pecorino cheese to be stirred or mixed into a recipe, I am always referring to cheese that is freshly and finely grated on a box grater or pulsed in a food processor to a fine texture similar to that achieved by box grating. For finely grated garnishing pecorino, I like to use a microplane for a fluffy, snow-like texture.

A Beginner's Guide to Farmers Markets:
For Fun and Function

Sometimes you head to the farmers market solely for leisure. You grab a coffee and a pastry and meander among the beautiful produce without much intent. You take a few pictures of tomatoes and buy a bag of cherries. It's nice. Sometimes you head there with a strict plan of action, ready to attack, without stopping to smell the roses. Each approach has its time and place, but this is my streamlined guide to hopefully help you accomplish both: a peaceful and calm farmers market stroll that also leaves you prepared for a week of fun, seasonal cooking. If you're intimidated by the farmers market and have yet to go to one, this should be quite helpful! I like to think of it simply in three stages: how to prepare beforehand, how to shop while at the market, and how to organize everything when you get home. So let's get into it.

Before Heading Out

No need to stress out too much here. Going to the farmers market should feel fun and freeing. These few simple steps will help you organize your trip so you don't end up in a fever dream state and go home with five varieties of radishes and one artisan kombucha. (Although if you are planning a solo radish taste test, that does sound quite nice.) I like to be mindful of what is in season before heading out and make a general list of items to pick up accordingly. If there's an in-season item you maybe haven't cooked before but are excited to try, it's great to pick out a recipe that uses that ingredient before you head out. That way, you can add any other ingredients needed for that recipe to your market list as well. I find that when I don't have an established plan for a seasonal item, my excitement can quickly deteriorate, just like a squishy head of kohlrabi shriveling up at the bottom of a produce bin. Sad! When making your list, it's also very important to take a quick look in your refrigerator. Note how much space you actually have to store new produce and what you already have on hand. Many times I have returned home from the market with

what seems like an entire bushel of kale and nowhere to store it. As much as a list is important for a successful trip, I also would say you should leave a little wiggle room for a few extra items that may catch your eye. Everything doesn't have to be super planned out; it's about having a balance between knowing exactly what you need and leaving space for some fun spontaneous picks. Not every farmers market trip needs to end with a huge haul of everything the market has to offer. To me, a more conscious approach leads to less waste while also keeping you coming back to the market more frequently than just one random weekend per season.

At the Market

Once you've made it to the market—list and cortado in hand, tote on shoulder—it's time for the real fun. I always start off by walking through the whole market to get a feel for everything. This is a great way to check if there are any new vendors and just get a general lay of the land, especially if it's your first time there. Not to mention how lovely it is to saunter joyfully through the market without attacking your list right away. When you become a regular at certain stands, it's almost inevitable that you become friends with the farmer, which has so many perks even beyond a lovely human connection. In my experience, the farmer will often give you tips on how to cook things if you are unsure, share intel on upcoming produce, and sometimes even offer a deal or two. What's more fun than a deal on local strawberries? Another thing to keep in mind as you shop is the shelf life of certain products. Leafy greens, ripe tomatoes, mushrooms, and delicate fruit will really only hold up for about a week, while root vegetables can last two or maybe even three weeks. Having a rough idea of a fruit or vegetable's shelf life is essential for determining how much to buy.

I usually keep to my list, leaving room for a few other items that catch my eye, but there are also some staples

that I always get when they're available. I love to stock up on farmers market honey because it's most likely local and super delicious. If I don't feel like baking that week, I love to buy a couple loaves of bread because most markets have a local bakery stand with some lovely options. I always stock up on herbs because they tend to be sold in much bigger bunches than the sad small plastic containers offered at the grocery store. I also find that they stay fresh much longer. Of course, every market is different, so look around, take it all in, and enjoy the stands available. Maybe even grab a bit of local cheese!

Unpacking Your Haul

The overarching theme here is actually *using* what you buy at the market, and that starts with unpacking and storing your haul. The last thing you want to do is let all that fresh, gorgeous produce go to waste. I don't suggest washing everything right when you get home: I would actually suggest the opposite! Once you introduce moisture to your produce, it rapidly speeds up the spoiling process. I prefer to wash things as I need them, with a couple exceptions: I often give beets, turnips, carrots, and other root vegetables a good scrub before storing so I don't get dirt all over the refrigerator. If they have any leafy tops, I cut those off and store them separately because I find myself more likely to use them this way; they are super easy to throw into a sauce, salad, or smoothie. Removing the leafy tops is also better for the shelf life of the roots because when attached, the leaves drain the root of moisture and end up drying up the root much more quickly. My other exception is fresh herbs. They tend to be quite sandy straight from the market, so I wash them right away. Just be sure to fully dry them before storing. My favorite way to store fresh herbs is by lightly rolling each bunch in a paper towel and placing all the herb bundles in an airtight container or sealable bag. It keeps them organized, fresh, and moisture free.

Even with the best planning, you may find yourself with bits and pieces of produce that are on their last leg by the end of the week, but fear not! There are so many ways to use them or preserve them. If I find myself with a bunch of herbs and greens, I love making the Herb-Drawer Clean-Out Green Sauce (page 54) or the Anything Pesto (page 49). Use any berries that are on their way out in the (Almost) Any-Berry, Any-Herb Jam (page 50), or freeze

them for later use. When it comes to heartier veggies, pickling is always a great option to preserve them, and the pickling liquid from either the Pink Pickles (page 37) or the Turmeric Pickled Onions (page 41) is great poured over so many different vegetables! Creativity is key in preventing food waste. When all else fails, I just cut up each of the random vegetables I have, toss them with olive oil and any seasoning I feel like, and roast them together. Add a fried egg on top and some steamed rice on the side, and you have a great fridge clean-out meal—especially if you have any of that green sauce on hand to drizzle all over.

Hopefully this guide gives you a bit of insight into how I like to navigate the farmers market and, especially, more confidence going into one if you are new to it! Another great option to seek out local produce is a CSA box. CSA stands for "community-supported agriculture." You sign up for a box (often a weekly subscription) to help support a farmer through an entire growing season. These boxes tend to include a combination of a bunch of in-season (and sometimes less conventional) produce and are a great way to support local farms and try new things! The "Vegetables: From Everyday to CSA" chapter, starting on page 95, has a bunch of fun recipes that use different seasonal vegetables and is a great resource to put some of your farmers market or CSA finds to good use. As is the entire book, for that matter!

Menus

There are endless recipe pairings to be made from this book to form a beautiful menu, but I thought it would be nice to include a few of my favorites to get the creativity flowing. From a perfect Friday night dinner (yay FND!) to a meal centered around focaccia, there's a lot of fun to be had with the recipes in this book, and these menus are just a start.

A Focaccia Gathering

Focaccia is one of my favorite breads of all time, and to me it deserves to be treated as the main event every now and then. All the recipes in this menu pair perfectly with the focaccia while still letting it shine.

- A Very Olive-y Focaccia (page 226)
- Caponata with Dried Cherries and Green Olives (page 96)
- Roasted Garlic Sunflower Seed Dip (page 58)
- Spicy Green Marinated Mushrooms (page 42)
- Pickled Shrimp (page 38)
- Antipasto Salad with Pecorino-Pepperoncini Dressing (page 79)

Pack It Up for the Beach

You won't leave the beach hangry if you pack this beautiful, easy-to-transport spread.

- Maple Cheddar Snack Mix (page 64)
- Mushy Pea Pasta Salad (page 80)
- Mean, Green Turkey Sandwich (page 256)
- Malted Milk Butter Cookies (page 262)

First-Time Dinner Party Host

These are all elegant yet simple recipes to impress anyone you have over. No fussy cooking methods, and a lot of it can be prepared ahead, which we love.

- Radicchio and Apple Salad with Rye Crunchies (page 76)
- Pot Roast au Poivre with Charred Onions (page 168)
- Mustardy Herb-Buttered Potatoes (page 117)
- Figgy Tapioca Pudding (page 277)

It's Tomato Season, So That's All I'm Eating

Have a tomato party; it's fun!

- Tomato and Anchovy Salad with Stracciatella (page 71)
- Butter Bean, Sungold, and Smashed Cucumber Salad (page 75)
- Grated Tomato Linguine (page 135)
- A Loaf of Sourdough Bread (page 218)

An Ideal Friday Night Dinner

There is something about a meal of pasta and salad that screams end-of-week comfort to me. That, along with a simple sweet treat to really celebrate, makes this meal something you'll look forward to all week.

- Little Gem Salad with Garlicky White Bean Spread (page 83)
- Mortadella "Nduja" Lumache with Pistachios (page 128)
- Vanilla Bean and Brown Butter Chocolate-Chunk Cookie Bars (page 266)

Meat and Potatoes: A Midwestern Delight

This is a stick-to-your-ribs kinda meal. Utterly decadent, satisfying, and an ode to my Midwestern upbringing.

- Oniony Poppy Seed Dinner Rolls (page 230)
- Steak Night Dinner: Anchovy-Basted Rib Eye with Dilly Creamed Spinach (page 164)
- Chicken Fat Mashed Potatoes (page 118)
- Blueberry Pretzel Galette with Cream Cheese Whip (page 272)

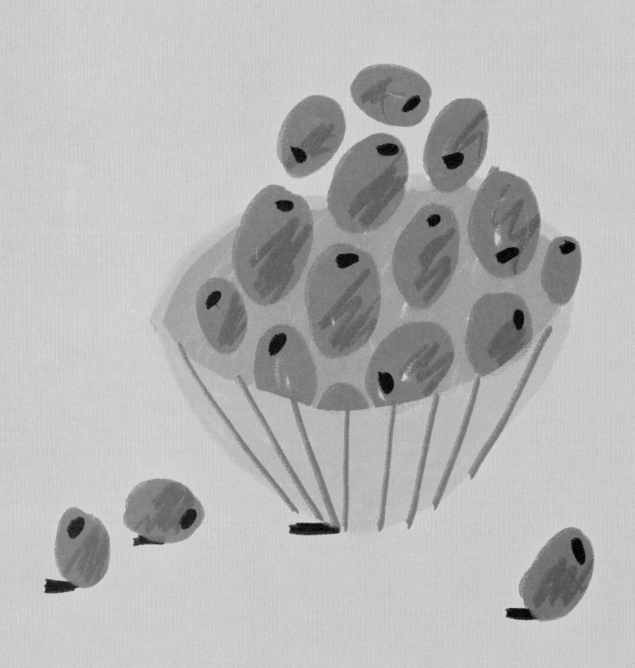

Pickles, Condiments, and Dips

In this chapter, we have a bunch of versatile little items to mix and match and fill your fridge. Choose any pickle, condiment, or dip from this section to serve with some fresh bread for a delightful appetizer spread, or get creative and pair them with other recipes in the book. The options are endless! Many of the recipes here will last quite a while in your fridge, keeping you stocked up on fun add-ins and spreads to elevate any of your meals.

Pink Pickles

MAKES ABOUT 2 QUARTS (2 L)

1 small head cauliflower (about 2 pounds/907 g), leaves removed, cored, and cut into bite-size florets

1 medium beet (about 6 ounces/170 g), scrubbed and sliced into paper-thin rounds on a mandoline

1 small red onion (about 5 ounces/142 g), thinly sliced on a mandoline

3 inches (8 cm) ginger, peeled and thinly sliced on a mandoline

2 tablespoons pink peppercorns, crushed

1 tablespoon black peppercorns

1 teaspoon coriander seeds

2¼ cups (540 ml) unseasoned rice vinegar

1 cup (240 ml) water

½ cup (168 g) honey

3 tablespoons kosher salt

2 dried bay leaves

Pickling cauliflower, beets, and red onion all together makes the most beautifully pink jar of pickles—a Barbie pickle! The cauliflower turns vibrant pink from the beets and onions, and the vegetables pair so well with the fruity pink peppercorns in the brine. I love these for a pop of color and vinegary-ness on a charcuterie or cheese board, tossed in any big leafy salad, or eaten on the side of a big ol' sandwich. These pretty pink pickles instantly make any meal more fun. Be sure to wear gloves when handling the beets if you don't want pink-stained hands!

1. Place the cauliflower, beet, onion, and ginger in a large bowl, and toss to combine.

2. Evenly divide the vegetables into two 1-quart (1 L) mason jars or similar airtight containers, pressing down as needed to fit snugly.

3. Heat the pink peppercorns, black peppercorns, and coriander seeds in a small saucepan over medium-low heat. Toast until fragrant, 3 to 5 minutes.

4. Add the vinegar, water, honey, salt, and bay leaves, and increase the heat to medium. Heat just until the salt dissolves, about 5 minutes. The liquid doesn't have to come to a full boil.

5. Pour the warm liquid evenly over the veggies in the jars, leaving about ½ inch (1 cm) headspace between the veggies and the lid. Let cool to room temperature and then cover and place in the refrigerator for at least 24 hours. (After 24 hours, the pickles will be delicious and ready to eat, but the cauliflower won't be fully pink yet. After 2 or 3 days, the color will have fully developed.)

6. Serve, or store in the refrigerator for up to 2 months.

Pickled Shrimp

SERVES 4 TO 6

2 teaspoons kosher salt, plus more for poaching the shrimp

1 pound (454 g) jumbo shrimp (16/20), peeled and deveined (tails left on)

2 celery stalks, thinly sliced on a bias

1 large shallot, thinly sliced

½ cup (120 ml) extra virgin olive oil

½ cup (120 ml) white wine vinegar

Zest and juice of 1 lemon

2 teaspoons chopped jarred Calabrian chiles in oil

½ teaspoon fennel seeds, toasted and slightly crushed (see Tip)

Freshly cracked black pepper

3 tablespoons capers, drained

¼ cup (10 g) chopped fresh parsley

2 tablespoons thinly sliced fresh chives

Celery leaves, for garnish

Pickled shrimp is a popular appetizer in the South, and this is a fun, Italian-inspired take on the recipe. Think Italian seafood salad with Italian salsa verde flavors all mashed up into a pickle-y, punchy shrimp dish. This is a great dinner party appetizer because the whole dish is essentially made ahead. Serve as is or with some saltines for a fun, crunchy bite. I also love this over some steamed white rice for a lovely light lunch or quick dinner.

1. Bring a large pot of water to a boil over high heat. Season with a big pinch of salt. Prepare a large ice bath and set aside.

2. Drop the shrimp in the boiling water, and stir to ensure the shrimp are submerged. Turn off the heat, and cover with a lid until the shrimp are cooked through, pink, and barely starting to curl, 3 to 4 minutes. (This time will vary depending on the size of your shrimp. Feel free to uncover the pot to take a peek! If you are unsure, you can remove one shrimp and cut a small bit off the top to be sure it is opaque all the way through.)

3. Immediately transfer the shrimp to the ice bath to cool completely. Drain and pat dry with a paper towel. Add to a large bowl along with the celery and shallot.

4. Add the olive oil, vinegar, lemon zest, lemon juice, chiles, 2 teaspoons salt, fennel seeds, and a generous amount of pepper. Toss to coat.

5. Transfer the mixture to an airtight container (ideally something shallow so the dressing covers the shrimp), place in the refrigerator, and let the shrimp sit overnight or up to 2 days. (I find the sweet spot to be around the 24-hour mark.) The olive oil may solidify slightly in the refrigerator but will return to normal after sitting at room temperature for a few minutes.

6. When you're ready to serve, toss the shrimp with the capers, parsley, and chives. If there is too much accumulated liquid, feel free to drain off some of the marinade before tossing. (I like a generous amount!) Garnish with celery leaves, and serve.

TIP I toast my spices in a small, dry sauté pan over medium-low heat until fragrant, 2 to 3 minutes.

Turmeric Pickled Onions

1 large sweet onion, sliced about ¼ inch (6 mm) thick

1 tablespoon black peppercorns

1 teaspoon yellow mustard seeds

1½ cups (360 ml) apple cider vinegar

3 tablespoons granulated sugar

1 tablespoon kosher salt

1 teaspoon ground turmeric

1 Thai chile (also known as bird's eye chile), halved

These vibrant yellow onions are inspired by bread-and-butter pickles, a slightly sweet pickle with turmeric and mustard seeds. They are the perfect "everything pickle." Similar to pickled red onions, they can be added to anything, and they instantly make a dish more fun and tasty. I love them in a salad, on avocado toast, alongside any grilled item, or even mixed into an egg salad or rémoulade. They are an exciting and colorful onion to add to your pickle rotation.

1. Place the onion in a 1-quart (1 L) mason jar or similar airtight container.

2. Heat the peppercorns and mustard seeds in a small saucepan over medium-low heat. Toast until fragrant, 3 to 5 minutes.

3. Add the vinegar, sugar, salt, turmeric, and chile to the pan, and increase the heat to medium. Heat just until the sugar and salt dissolve, about 5 minutes. The liquid doesn't have to come to a full boil.

4. Pour the warm liquid over the onions in the jar, packing them down so they are just about covered by the brine. The more they sit, the more they will settle into the brine. Let cool to room temperature and then cover and place in the refrigerator for at least 12 hours.

5. Serve, or store in the refrigerator for up to 2 months.

Spicy Green Marinated Mushrooms

MAKES ABOUT 1 QUART (1 L)

6 tablespoons plus ½ cup (120 ml) olive oil, divided

2 pounds (907 g) cremini (also known as baby bella) mushrooms, cleaned, stems trimmed, and halved or quartered if larger than 1 inch (2.5 cm) (see Tip)

2 teaspoons kosher salt, plus more to taste

Freshly cracked black pepper, to taste

1½ ounces (43 g) fresh dill fronds and tender stems (from about ¼ large bunch)

1½ ounces (43 g) fresh parsley leaves and tender stems (from about 1 large bunch)

1 ounce (28 g) fresh basil leaves (from about ½ large bunch)

Zest of 2 lemons

Juice of 1 lemon

2 tablespoons honey

1 teaspoon dried oregano

4 oil-packed anchovy fillets

2 serrano peppers, roughly chopped (seeded and deveined if you're timid with spice)

1 garlic clove, finely grated

These might not technically be a pickle, condiment, or dip, but I'm including them in this chapter because to me, they serve the same function. I love having them as an appetizer with sourdough bread (see page 218) or just as a fun thing to nosh on before a meal. The luscious green sauce the mushrooms are tossed in is like a dip in itself, and the acidity from the lemon juice gives them a pickle-y vibe. They make a lovely addition to a veggie sandwich. Eat them on the side of your eggs in the morning with some rice or toast, and you'll have a beautiful breakfast. I find these are best served at room temperature.

1. Coat a large skillet with 3 tablespoons olive oil, and heat over high heat until the oil is very hot and has just started to smoke.

2. Add half of the mushrooms, cap side down and in an even layer, and let them cook, without stirring, until deeply seared, about 5 minutes.

3. Flip and char the second side, about 2 minutes more. Season with a hefty pinch of salt and a few grinds of pepper. Transfer to a sheet tray or large plate, and repeat with another 3 tablespoons oil and the remaining mushrooms. Let cool completely to room temperature.

4. While the mushrooms cool, bring a small pot of water to a boil over high heat. Prepare a large ice bath.

5. Add the dill, parsley, and basil to the boiling water, and blanch for 30 seconds.

6. Immediately transfer to the ice bath to shock and cool. Squeeze out all excess moisture from the herbs.

7. Roughly chop the herbs and then transfer to a blender along with the remaining ½ cup (120 ml) oil, lemon zest, lemon juice, honey, 2 teaspoons salt, oregano, anchovies, serranos, and garlic. Blend until smooth.

8. Transfer the mushrooms to a medium bowl, add the green sauce, and toss to coat.

9. Serve right away (they are so perfectly yummy as is), or transfer to an airtight container to marinate in the refrigerator for a few hours or overnight.

10. Store in the refrigerator for up to 3 days. The mushrooms won't be as green after marinating in the refrigerator for some time, but they will be extra delicious.

TIP I like to clean mushrooms by simply wiping off any dirt with a wet towel.

Marinated Havarti and Green Olives

SERVES 6

½ cup (120 ml) olive oil

5 garlic cloves, finely chopped

Kosher salt, to taste

1 teaspoon urfa biber chile (see Note)

1 dried bay leaf

Zest of 1 lemon

Zest of ½ orange

½ pound (227 g) Havarti, cut into irregular ½-inch (1 cm) pieces

4 ounces (about 1 heaping cup/113 g) whole pitted Castelvetrano olives

3 tablespoons chopped fresh dill

Fresh lemon juice, to taste

This tasty nosh is a great alternative to a big, intricate cheese plate and brings cheese and olives together with a flavorful olive oil marinade. Endless cheese options will work for this—feta, bocconcini, aged white cheddar, and Comté, just to name a few. Be sure to pick something "sturdy" enough to hold up to the marinade. I love Havarti in this for its signature creaminess and classic pairing with dill. Serve with some fresh sourdough (see A Loaf of Sourdough Bread; page 218) or crackers (like the Spicy Chicken-Salt Sesame Crackers; page 67).

1. Heat the olive oil and garlic in a small sauté pan over medium-low heat. Fry the garlic, stirring often, until lightly golden brown and crispy, 4 to 6 minutes. The garlic won't seem very crisp at this point, but it will crisp up when fully cooled.

2. Carefully pour the garlic through a fine-mesh strainer into a small heatproof bowl to strain the oil. Transfer the garlic to a paper towel to drain, and sprinkle with a touch of salt. Set aside.

3. Add the chile, bay leaf, lemon zest, and orange zest to the hot oil. Stir and let the flavors infuse using the residual heat. Let the infused oil cool to room temperature, about 30 minutes.

4. Combine the Havarti and olives in a medium bowl. Pour in the oil, and let marinate at room temperature for at least 30 minutes or up to 2 hours. (If making ahead, store the marinated Havarti and olives in an airtight container in the refrigerator for up to 2 days. The oil may solidify slightly in the refrigerator but will return to normal after sitting at room temperature for a few minutes. Store the garlic in a separate airtight container at room temperature, with a bit of paper towel at the bottom to absorb any oil, for up to 2 days.)

5. When ready to serve, add the dill and lemon juice, and toss. Serve topped with the reserved fried garlic.

NOTE Urfa biber is a Turkish chile with a slightly spicy, smoky, and almost-cured flavor profile. It's easily found online, but you can also substitute with red pepper flakes to taste or equal amounts of Espelette or Aleppo pepper.

Chicago-Style Fennel Giardiniera

MAKES ABOUT 1 QUART (1 L)

10 serrano peppers (about 6 ounces/170 g), stemmed and sliced

4 Fresno peppers (about 3 ounces/85 g), stemmed and small diced

1 medium carrot (about 4 ounces/113 g), peeled and small diced

1 celery stalk (about 2 ounces/57 g), small diced

1 medium fennel bulb (about 10 ounces/283 g), cored and small diced

4 garlic cloves, minced

3 tablespoons kosher salt

3 tablespoons granulated sugar

1 dried bay leaf

1 cup (240 ml) unseasoned rice vinegar

¾ cup (180 ml) olive oil

1 teaspoon dried oregano

½ teaspoon freshly cracked black pepper

Before moving to the East Coast, I thought all giardiniera was the same oily, spicy, tangy chopped vegetable mix that I grew up eating in Chicago. I was sadly mistaken when the only giardiniera I could find here was a much less-chopped, less-spicy, oil-free, pickled version. Although good in its own right, that giardiniera is far from the beloved Chicago condiment. This recipe substitutes the classic cauliflower with fennel for a slightly different—but still nostalgic—giardiniera, perfect for serving with the Chicago-Style Braised Italian Beef Sandwiches (page 207) or on anything your spicy heart desires.

1. Toss the serranos, Fresnos, carrot, celery, fennel, garlic, salt, and sugar in a medium bowl.

2. Add enough cold water just to cover the veggies. Cover and place in the refrigerator for 12 to 24 hours.

3. Strain the vegetables into a fine-mesh strainer or colander, discarding the brine. Rinse the vegetables under cold water. Transfer to a 1-quart (1 L) mason jar or similar airtight container. Nestle in the bay leaf.

4. Whisk the vinegar, olive oil, oregano, and pepper in a small bowl until combined.

5. Pour the dressing over the veggies, packing them down so they are covered by the dressing and there's about ½ inch (1 cm) headspace between the veggies and the lid.

6. Cover and place in the refrigerator for at least 2 days. The longer it sits, the better it will get.

7. Store in the refrigerator for up to 2 months (see Note).

NOTE The oil may solidify slightly in the refrigerator but will return to normal after sitting at room temperature for a few minutes or when added on top of other warm foods. As you use the giardiniera, be sure the veggies stay submerged in the dressing by replenishing the oil as needed.

Anything Pesto

MAKES ABOUT 1 CUP (240 G)

3 ounces (about 4 heaping cups/85 g) fresh leafy herbs and/or greens, such as basil, parsley, mint, dill, chives, spinach, destemmed kale, or arugula (just one or any combo you'd like)

½ cup plus 2 tablespoons (150 ml) olive oil, plus more as needed

2 tablespoons pine nuts, toasted (see Tip 1)

Zest of 1 lemon

1 garlic clove, peeled and smashed

⅓ cup (35 g) freshly grated pecorino Romano

Kosher salt and freshly cracked black pepper, to taste

*Blanching isn't a traditional step in making pesto, but I do find it essential for making the brightest, most vibrantly green pesto that will **stay** green. I wrote this recipe to be super versatile, so you can use it as a base to make any kind of pesto your heart desires. Even if I'm going for a simple basil pesto, I love throwing in any random kale or spinach that I may have—not only for color but also as a way to use up random last bits of greens before they go bad. Some of my favorite combos are basil and chive, dill and kale, and arugula and mint. The tender stems of the leafy herbs are always welcome, of course—just be sure to remove any fibrous, thick stems from greens like kale or herbs like basil. I love playing with fun herb-green combos in pesto, but when it comes to the nuts, I will always be a pine nut gal.*

1. Bring a large pot of water to a boil over high heat. Prepare a large ice bath.

2. Add the herbs and/or greens to the boiling water, and blanch for 30 seconds. Using a slotted spoon, immediately transfer the herbs to the ice bath to shock.

3. Squeeze out all the excess moisture from the herbs, and roughly chop. Transfer to a high-powered blender or food processor along with the olive oil, pine nuts, lemon zest, and garlic. Blend until fairly smooth, adding more oil, 1 tablespoon at a time, if needed.

4. Transfer the pesto to a bowl, and fold in the pecorino Romano. Season with salt and pepper.

5. Serve, or store in an airtight container in the refrigerator for up to 5 days (see Tip 2).

TIPS

1. Toast the pine nuts on a sheet tray in the oven at 350°F (180°C) for 3 to 5 minutes, until aromatic and golden.

2. My mom used to make big batches of pesto and freeze it in ice cube trays, which is a really great way to always have fresh pesto on hand! After freezing, transfer the cubes to a large, airtight, freezer-safe container. They will keep for up to 6 months.

(Almost) Any-Berry, Any-Herb Jam

MAKES ABOUT 2½ CUPS (845 G)

2 pounds (907 g) fresh or frozen berries, such as blueberries, raspberries, blackberries, or quartered strawberries

2 cups (400 g) granulated sugar

2 tablespoons chopped hearty herbs, such as rosemary, thyme, tarragon, or sage (see Note)

1 lemon, halved and juiced (halves reserved)

½ teaspoon kosher salt

Homemade jams are such a fun medium for creative flavor combinations. Adding a subtle but interesting secondary flavor to a jam can easily take it from good to great. This recipe was created to be flexible and versatile. Choose a seasonal berry and hearty herb, and relish in jam success! The lemon adds more natural pectin, resulting in a thicker, "jammier" jam. Any flavor combination of this jam is delightful on some ricotta toast.

1. Add the berries, sugar, herbs, lemon juice, lemon halves, and salt to a large bowl, and toss to combine. Cover and refrigerate overnight (at least 8 and up to 24 hours) to let the berries macerate and the flavors infuse.

2. The next day, transfer the mixture, lemon halves and all, to a medium pot over medium heat. Cook, stirring, while also mashing up the berries with a wooden spoon, until the mixture comes to a soft boil, about 8 minutes.

3. Reduce the heat to medium-low, and continue to cook and stir occasionally, until the berries are broken down, the mixture is thick, and the temperature reads 220°F (104°C) on an instant-read thermometer, 35 to 45 minutes. You can also check the jam for doneness by placing a small amount on a freezer-cold plate and running your finger through it. If the jam holds the part and looks a bit wrinkled on the surface, it should be good to go! Skim off any foam from the top of the jam that may form during the cooking process.

4. Remove the pot from the heat, and let the jam cool to room temperature. Remove and discard the lemon halves.

5. Serve, or store in an airtight container in the refrigerator for up to 3 months.

NOTE Some of my favorite fruit-and-herb pairings to use in this recipe are blackberry-rosemary, blueberry-sage, raspberry-tarragon, and strawberry-thyme. Fresh or dried bay leaves would be great with any berry, too. Just add one to the mixture before macerating overnight and then remove it with the lemon halves in step 4.

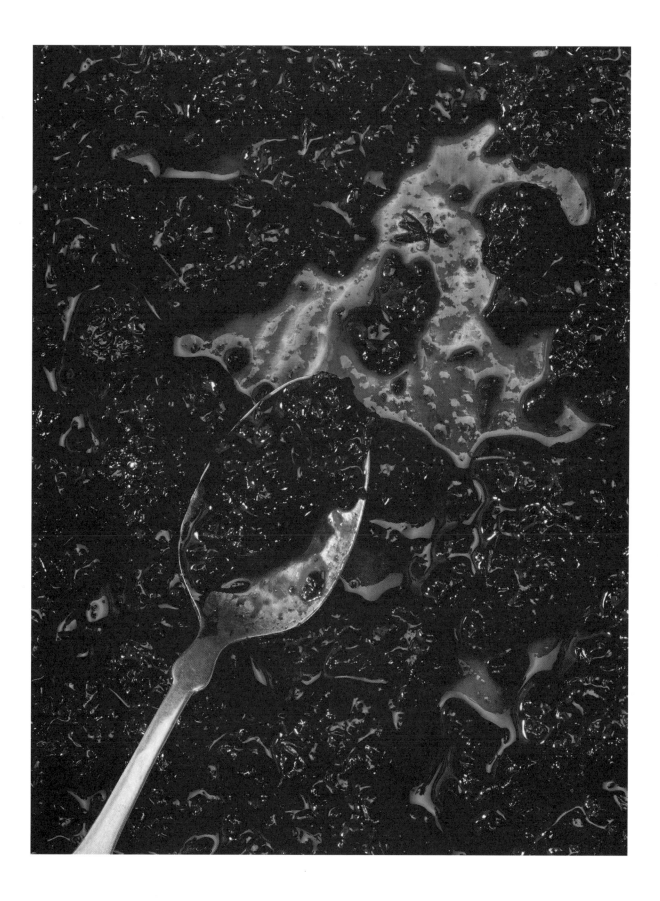

Hot Cherry Pepper Jam

MAKES ABOUT 1½ CUPS (350 G)

One 24-ounce (680 g) jar sliced pickled hot cherry peppers, drained

4 Fresno peppers, stemmed and roughly chopped

3 inches (8 cm) ginger, peeled and finely grated

1 cup (200 g) granulated sugar

½ cup (120 ml) white wine vinegar

½ teaspoon kosher salt

If you're a hot honey lover like me (who isn't, really!?), this is another great condiment to add to your repertoire. It's a fun little jam to have in your fridge that's quick to make and can be used in so many ways. Use it to make a quick appetizer (see Note) or elevate an everyday sandwich. Stir some into a bowl of white beans to liven them up a bit, or use it as a base for a vinaigrette. The options are endless. I like using pickled hot cherry peppers as opposed to fresh because they are easily available all year round, and I love the extra acidic zip they bring to the jam.

1. Add the cherry and Fresno peppers to a food processor, and pulse until finely chopped.

2. Transfer the peppers to a small saucepan along with the ginger, sugar, vinegar, and salt. Cook over medium heat, stirring occasionally, until slightly thick and jammy, 15 to 20 minutes.

3. Let cool slightly and then transfer to an airtight container.

4. Serve, or store in the refrigerator for up to 3 months.

NOTE I love topping ricotta with dollops of this jam, some olive oil, herbs, salt, and pepper for a great quick dip for focaccia! It's also divine on top of pizza, spread on a sub (with mortadella!), or even blended until smooth and mixed with some melted butter for a great wing sauce.

Herb-Drawer Clean-Out Green Sauce

MAKES ABOUT 1 SCANT CUP
(345 G)

Kosher salt and freshly cracked black
    pepper, to taste

3 ounces (about 4 heaping cups/85 g) any
    tender, leafy herbs you have on hand, such
    as basil, chives, cilantro, dill, mint, or
    parsley

3 ounces (about 4 heaping cups/85 g) baby
    spinach or kale

1/3 cup (50 g) pepitas, toasted (see Tip)

2 scallions, roots trimmed and roughly
    chopped

1 serrano pepper, stemmed and roughly
    chopped

1/2 cup (120 ml) olive oil

1/4 cup (60 ml) cold water, plus more as
    needed

1 tablespoon unseasoned rice vinegar

2 teaspoons honey

This is my go-to, good-on-anything green sauce that's designed to use up any random herbs or greens you have in your fridge before they go bad. No more slimy greens buried at the bottom of your vegetable drawer! A lot of the recipes in this book call for fresh herbs, so I wanted to provide a simple recipe to make use of any herbs you may not totally use up in another recipe. Drizzle this sauce on salads, breakfast tacos, or grain bowls, or eat it with any roasted proteins (it's great with a simple roasted chicken) or veggies. It's also amazing on scrambled eggs in the morning!

1. Bring a small pot of water to a boil over high heat. Season with a generous amount of salt. Prepare a large ice bath.

2. Add the herbs and spinach to the boiling water, and blanch for 30 seconds. Using a slotted spoon, immediately transfer the greens to the ice bath to shock.

3. Squeeze out all the excess moisture from the herbs and spinach, roughly chop, and add to a blender.

4. Add the pepitas, scallions, serrano, olive oil, water, vinegar, and honey to the blender, and blend until very smooth. Add more water if needed to reach a drizzle-able consistency. Season with salt and pepper.

5. Serve, or store in an airtight container in the refrigerator for up to 4 days.

TIP Toast the pepitas in a small saucepan over medium heat, tossing frequently, until fragrant and golden in spots, 3 to 5 minutes.

Smoky Caramelized Shallot Dip
with Sun-Dried Tomatoes

MAKES ABOUT 2 CUPS (488 G)

2 tablespoons olive oil

1 tablespoon unsalted butter

10 medium shallots (about 1 pound/454 g), diced

Kosher salt and freshly cracked black pepper, to taste

¼ cup (40 g) chopped olive oil–packed sun-dried tomatoes

1 teaspoon sweet smoked paprika

¾ cup (180 g) labne or sour cream

¼ cup (60 g) Kewpie mayonnaise, or any mayo you have on hand

1 tablespoon Dijon mustard

1 teaspoon Worcestershire sauce

For Serving

Thinly sliced fresh chives

Wavy potato chips, bagel chips, crackers, and/or any raw veggies you'd like

I definitely got my love of dips from my mom and from growing up in the Midwest (where everything is either a dip or a casserole!). My mom had two go-to dips: French onion for game days and sun-dried tomato during the holidays. They both hold a special place in my heart, so this dip is an ode to Cindy and those nostalgic dip memories. It's a fun mash-up of the two, with shallots for extra-yummy, sweet, caramelized flavor and some paprika for a bit of a smokiness. Long live Midwestern dip culture!

1. Heat the olive oil and butter in a large skillet over medium heat until the butter is melted, 2 minutes. Add the shallots, and season with a small pinch of salt.

2. Reduce the heat to medium-low, and cook, stirring often, until deeply caramelized, 40 to 45 minutes. As the shallots cook, a fond (brown sticky stuff) will start to form on the bottom of the pan. I like to add small splashes of water during the cooking process when this happens and then scrape up the fond from the pan into the shallots.

3. Add the sun-dried tomatoes and paprika. Cook just to toast the paprika slightly and incorporate the sun-dried tomatoes, about 2 minutes more. Remove from the heat, and let cool to room temperature.

4. Mix the labne, mayonnaise, mustard, Worcestershire sauce, and shallots in a medium bowl. Season with salt and pepper. Cover and place in the refrigerator for at least 1 hour for flavors to meld.

5. Top the dip with chives, and serve with your desired vehicles for dipping.

6. Store any leftovers in an airtight container in the refrigerator for up to 4 days.

Roasted Garlic Sunflower Seed Dip

MAKES ABOUT 1½ CUPS (386 G)

Dip

⅔ cup (95 g) raw sunflower seeds

3 heads garlic, tops trimmed to expose the cloves

½ cup (120 ml) olive oil, plus more for drizzling

2 tablespoons lemon zest (from about 2 lemons)

5 tablespoons lemon juice (from about 2 lemons)

5 tablespoons cold water

1 tablespoon honey or agave

Kosher salt and freshly cracked black pepper, to taste

Topping

¼ cup (60 ml) olive oil

5 large garlic cloves, peeled and thinly sliced on a mandoline

Kosher salt, to taste

1 teaspoon sweet smoked paprika

Torn fresh dill, for serving

A dairy-less dip! Soaked sunflower seeds blend into the creamiest, smoothest dip, with a texture similar to a hummus but without the chickpeas or tahini. Substitute agave for the honey, and it's vegan. This garlicky dip pairs great with crudités or the Sourdough Discard Flatbread (page 223). I also use it as a base for a fun green spread on the Mean, Green Turkey Sandwich (page 256).

1. **Make the dip:** Preheat the oven to 425°F (220°C) with a rack positioned in the center.

2. Place the sunflower seeds in a small bowl, and cover with about ½ inch (1 cm) of boiling water. Set aside to soak.

3. Place each head of garlic on a small sheet of foil, drizzle with olive oil, and wrap tightly. Place on a sheet tray, and roast for 35 to 45 minutes, until very soft and lightly golden. Unwrap the garlic, and let cool until it's easy to handle, about 15 minutes.

4. Drain and discard the soaking liquid from the sunflower seeds, and transfer the seeds to a high-powered blender.

5. Squeeze in the cooled garlic cloves (discarding the skins). Add ½ cup (120 ml) olive oil, lemon zest, lemon juice, water, honey, a generous pinch of salt, and a few cracks of pepper. Blend on high until very smooth. Blend, blend, blend! Season with more salt and pepper. Set aside.

6. **Make the topping:** Heat ¼ cup (60 ml) olive oil and the sliced garlic in a small sauté pan over medium-low heat. Fry the garlic, stirring often, until lightly golden brown, 3 to 5 minutes. The garlic won't seem very crisp at this point, but it will crisp up when fully cooled.

7. Using a slotted spoon, carefully transfer the garlic to a paper towel to drain. Sprinkle with a pinch of salt.

8. Add the paprika to the garlic oil (off the heat), and let it toast in the residual heat in the pan.

9. Serve the dip drizzled with some paprika oil (reserving the rest for another use), fried garlic, and fresh dill and alongside your desired dippers (see headnote).

10. Store any leftover dip and paprika oil in separate airtight containers in the refrigerator for up to 3 days. Store the fried garlic in an airtight container at room temperature for with a bit of paper towel at the bottom to absorb any oil for up to 2 days.

Cold Crab Dip

with Buttery Poppy Seed Saltines

MAKES ABOUT 3 CUPS (750 G) DIP
AND 48 CRACKERS

Dip

⅔ cup (140 g) labne or sour cream

⅓ cup (70 g) Kewpie mayonnaise, or any mayo you have on hand

2 tablespoons whole-grain mustard

1 large shallot, minced

¼ cup (10 g) chopped fresh dill

¼ cup (10 g) chopped fresh parsley

Zest and juice of 1 lemon

1 pound (454 g) lump crab, drained and picked through for shells (I prefer jumbo lump)

Kosher salt and freshly cracked black pepper, to taste

Saltines

48 saltine crackers (about 1¼ sleeves)

½ cup (1 stick/113 g) unsalted butter, melted

1½ teaspoons poppy seeds

Freshly cracked black pepper, to taste

For Serving

1 large celery stalk, thinly sliced on a heavy bias

2 teaspoons chopped jarred Calabrian chiles in oil, or to taste

Celery leaves, for garnish

Seafood dips may just be my favorite of all the dip categories. Whether they're hot, cold, or smoked, they forever exceed all my appetizer dreams. And it's always a good party if a seafood dip makes its way into the appetizer spread. This one features crab, but the crab can be substituted with hot smoked trout or hot smoked salmon. The celery that is often added to these dips tends to be my favorite part, so I pulled that out of the dip itself to feature as a crisp and crunchy topping. The celery is just as much of a star here as the crab! And although I love the poppy seeds on these saltines, feel free to get creative with toppings: Furikake or sesame seeds would be delightful, too. If you aren't feeling the cracker vibe, this dip and celery combo also makes a delicious topping on a slice of sourdough toast (see page 218). This recipe can also easily be halved for a smaller crowd.

1. Preheat the oven to 400°F (200°C) with a rack positioned in the center. Line a sheet tray with parchment paper.

2. **Make the dip:** Add the labne, mayonnaise, mustard, shallot, dill, parsley, lemon zest, and lemon juice to a medium bowl, and stir to combine.

3. Gently fold in the crab without breaking up the meat too much. Season with a touch of salt (be careful because the crab has natural salinity) and a good amount of pepper. Place in the refrigerator to chill while you prepare the saltines.

4. **Make the saltines:** Spread out the saltines evenly on the sheet tray. Brush the melted butter over the saltines, generously coating the top of each cracker. Sprinkle with the poppy seeds and pepper.

5. Bake for 10 to 12 minutes, until golden and crispy. Let cool completely, about 15 minutes.

6. Mix the celery and chiles in a small bowl.

7. Serve the cold dip topped with the spicy celery and celery leaves, with the saltines on the side for dipping.

Three Crunchy Snacks

In more instances than not, I find myself reaching for a crunchy nosh. I find a certain comfort in knowing I have a good snack on hand at all times. These are three of my favorites.

Maple Cheddar Snack Mix

MAKES ABOUT
3 QUARTS (3 L)

5 cups (175 g) corn Chex cereal

2 cups (120 g) Cheez-Its

1 cup (125 g) roasted unsalted cashews, or any nut you'd like

1 cup (60 g) oyster crackers

1 cup (50 g) mini pretzels

1 cup (90 g) sesame sticks

¼ cup (35 g) sesame seeds

½ cup (1 stick/113g) unsalted butter

½ cup (110 g) packed dark brown sugar

½ cup (120 ml) pure maple syrup

2 teaspoons soy sauce

½ teaspoon sweet smoked paprika

¼ teaspoon cayenne

¼ teaspoon kosher salt

¼ cup (28 g) cheddar cheese powder, plus more to taste (see Tip)

This flavor combo might seem odd at first, unless you've had the pleasure (or curse—because it's much too addicting) of trying Chicago mix popcorn: cheddar and caramel popcorn mixed together for the most craveable savory, sweet, and cheesy combo. It's yet another example of cheese being combined with just about anything in the Midwest (Shout out Garrett Popcorn!). Here, I coat a bunch of crunchy stuff in a caramelly maple glaze and toss it in tons of cheddar cheese powder for that classic Chicago taste in a fun and crunchy snack mix.

1. Preheat the oven 275°F (135°C) with racks positioned in the upper and lower thirds. Line two sheet trays with parchment paper.

2. Toss the Chex, Cheez-Its, cashews, oyster crackers, pretzels, sesame sticks, and sesame seeds in a large bowl.

3. Heat the butter, brown sugar, and maple syrup in a small saucepan over medium heat. Cook, stirring occasionally, until the butter and sugar have melted and the mixture is bubbling, 4 or 5 minutes.

4. Remove from the heat, and stir in the soy sauce, paprika, cayenne, and salt.

5. Pour the maple mixture over the crunchies, and toss to evenly coat. Evenly divide the mixture between the sheet trays, and spread out into even layers.

6. Bake for 40 to 45 minutes, tossing every 10 to 15 minutes, until the mixture is deeply golden and glossy, rotating the sheet pans between the racks halfway through the baking time. The mixture might seem slightly sticky, but it will crisp as it cools.

7. Let cool for 10 minutes, tossing occasionally so the mixture doesn't clump together.

8. Evenly sprinkle the cheese powder over each tray, and toss to coat.

9. Serve right away, or store in an airtight container at room temperature for up to 2 weeks for future snacking.

TIP Cheddar cheese powder is easy to find online. Anthony's brand is my fave! You can substitute the cheese powder with ¼ cup (20 g) nutritional yeast for a more readily available cheese powder–like swap!

Porcini Herb Snacking Peanuts
with Fried Garlic

MAKES ABOUT 2¼ CUPS (385 G)

3 tablespoons olive oil

6 large garlic cloves, peeled and thinly sliced on a mandoline

2 cups (300 g) roasted, unsalted Spanish red-skinned peanuts

1 tablespoon porcini mushroom powder (see Tip)

1 tablespoon chopped fresh thyme leaves

2 teaspoons chopped fresh rosemary leaves

1½ teaspoons kosher salt

1 teaspoon granulated sugar

1 teaspoon freshly cracked black pepper

When I visited Chuck's family in the Philippines, there were never-ending snacks around at all times. From chicharrones to fresh fruit to small, sweet treats, there was always something to munch on. It was just lovely. One of my favorite snacks we enjoyed on repeat was adobong mani, or fried garlic peanuts. It's the perfect combination of salty, roasted peanuts and thin, crunchy-fried garlic. This recipe is heavily inspired by that snack, with the addition of some hearty aromatic herbs and mushroom powder. These peanuts pack an incredible umami punch that will have you hooked. I love using skin-on peanuts here for the bit of extra texture and flavor they impart, but roasted, unsalted peanuts will work just as well.

1. Preheat the oven to 300°F (150°C). Line a sheet tray with parchment paper.

2. Heat the olive oil and garlic in a small sauté pan over medium-low heat. Fry the garlic, stirring often, until lightly golden brown, 3 to 5 minutes. The garlic won't seem very crisp at this point, but it will crisp up when fully cooled.

3. Using a slotted spoon, carefully transfer the garlic to a paper towel–lined plate to drain. Remove the oil from the heat, and set aside.

4. Add the peanuts, reserved garlic oil, mushroom powder, thyme, rosemary, salt, sugar, and pepper to a large bowl. Toss to coat the peanuts in the oil and spices and then transfer them to the sheet tray.

5. Bake for 30 to 35 minutes, until the peanuts smell toasty and are slightly browner, tossing halfway through the baking time.

6. Let the peanuts cool to room temperature, about 30 minutes, and then stir in the reserved fried garlic and toss on the sheet pan.

7. Serve, or store in an airtight container at room temperature for up to 3 days.

TIP You can make the porcini mushroom powder by grinding about ¼ ounce (7 g) of dried porcini mushrooms in a spice grinder or blender until powdery.

Spicy Chicken-Salt Sesame Crackers

SERVES 4 TO 6

Cracker Dough

1¼ cups (163 g) all-purpose flour

¼ cup (45 g) semolina flour, plus more for dusting

1 teaspoon instant yeast (I like Saf-instant brand)

½ teaspoon kosher salt

1 egg, beaten

3 tablespoons warm water

Olive oil

Sesame seeds, for sprinkling

Chicken Salt

1½ teaspoons chicken bouillon powder

1½ teaspoons nutritional yeast

¾ teaspoon sweet smoked paprika

½ teaspoon garlic powder

½ teaspoon onion powder

½ teaspoon freshly cracked black pepper

¼ teaspoon cayenne

¼ teaspoon celery seeds

These thin and crispy crackers taste like what you'd get if you transformed a pack of instant ramen into a cracker, all thanks to chicken salt, a quintessentially Australian seasoning. Chicken salt is often sprinkled on fries and found in Australian cracker brands. These spicy homemade crackers are great to have around for everyday snacking. They are baked in large sheets and then cracked into pieces after cooling. Feel free to break them as big or as small as you'd like—the irregularity adds to their charm! They make a lovely addition to a cheese board or are great paired with a fun dip like the Smoky Caramelized Shallot Dip with Sun-Dried Tomatoes (page 57) or the Roasted Garlic Sunflower Seed Dip (page 58).

1. **Make the dough:** Whisk the all-purpose flour, semolina flour, yeast, and salt in a medium bowl. Add the egg and water, and mix with your hands to form a shaggy dough. Turn out the dough onto a clean work surface, and knead to form a stiff, cohesive dough, about 3 minutes.

2. Place the dough back into the bowl, and cover with plastic wrap or a kitchen towel. Let rest for 1 hour at room temperature. The dough will rise very slightly.

3. **Meanwhile, make the chicken salt:** Whisk the chicken bouillon powder, nutritional yeast, paprika, garlic powder, onion powder, pepper, cayenne, and celery seeds in a small bowl.

4. Preheat the oven to 350°F (180°C) with a rack positioned in the center. Line a sheet tray with parchment paper.

5. Working with half of the dough at a time (and keeping the other half covered), roll the dough through each setting on a pasta machine until it's about ⅛ inch (3 mm) thick, dusting with semolina as needed. This should be the fourth or fifth setting on your pasta machine. Alternatively, lightly dust a clean work surface and rolling pin with semolina flour, and roll out the dough to a rough rectangle, about ⅛ inch (3 mm) thick. Trim any uneven edges if desired. These are a rustic cracker, but sometimes it's still nice to trim!

6. Drizzle the lined sheet tray with olive oil, and place the cracker on the tray, trimming as needed to fit. Brush the cracker all over with more oil to coat evenly.

7. Generously sprinkle the cracker with sesame seeds and about half of the chicken salt, and prick the cracker all over with a fork. Place another sheet of parchment on top of the cracker, and top with another sheet tray.

8. Bake for 20 minutes. Remove the top sheet tray and parchment, and bake for an additional 8 to 10 minutes, until the cracker is crisp and golden. Transfer the cracker to a wire rack to cool to room temperature.

9. Repeat the rolling and baking process with the second half of the dough (see Tip).

10. After both the crackers are baked and cooled, break them into irregular pieces of your desired size. Serve, or store in an airtight container at room temperature for up to 3 days.

TIP If you have four same-size sheet trays, feel free to roll out all the dough and bake both crackers at once, with the oven racks in the upper and lower thirds.

Salads
Some Light, Some Hearty

Salads can—and should—be so much more than sadly dressed
lettuce in a bowl. From pasta to iceberg to shaved radishes,
almost anything can be a salad. This chapter features a broad
spectrum of delicious salad varieties.

Tomato and Anchovy Salad
with Stracciatella

SERVES 4 TO 6

2 pounds (about 3 large/907 g) heirloom tomatoes, sliced into ½ inch (1 cm) thick rounds

Flake salt, to taste

10 to 15 oil-packed anchovy fillets

8 ounces (227 g) stracciatella or torn burrata

Extra virgin olive oil, for drizzling

Freshly cracked black pepper, to taste

Thinly sliced fresh chives, to taste

This platter salad is a celebration of my two favorite things: tomatoes and anchovies! It's a simple peak-summer salad that can be thrown together in no time to round out any meal. For this beautiful, simple dish, in-season tomatoes and high-quality tinned anchovies are essential. It's also fun to choose a few different colors of tomatoes to make it even more stunningly summer.

1. Arrange the sliced tomatoes on a large platter. Season delicately with flake salt. (Be careful because the anchovies are salty!)

2. Drape the anchovy fillets over the tomatoes. Add bits of stracciatella all over the tomatoes and anchovies.

3. Drizzle everything with olive oil, and top with a bunch of pepper. Garnish with chives, and serve.

Shaved Radish and Persimmon Salad
with Ricotta Salata

SERVES 4

2 firm but ripe fuyu persimmons (see Note), cut into slices ⅛ inch (3 mm) thick on a mandoline

1 medium watermelon radish, cut into slices ⅛ inch (3 mm) thick on a mandoline

3 ounces (85 g) ricotta salata

1 Meyer lemon

Extra virgin olive oil, for drizzling

Flake salt and freshly cracked black pepper, to taste

Aleppo pepper, to taste

This stunningly vibrant platter salad is great for fall. Platter salads are so magical because they are arranged in a way that makes for optimal dressing and seasoning disbursement. Drizzle the olive oil right across the platter, and each bit of salad will have the perfect amount. Same with the lemon zest and juice, salt, and pepper. Be sure to use fuyu persimmons for this. You want the persimmons to be crisp and firm, and the hachiya variety is meant to be eaten very soft. Any radish will work if you can't find watermelon radish, as will regular lemon instead of the Meyer. Serve this salad with a roast chicken (see page 160) for a gorgeous and simple fall meal.

1. Arrange the persimmons and radishes on a medium platter. I like to alternate them and fill the whole platter.

2. Using a vegetable peeler, shave the ricotta salata all over the persimmons and radishes.

3. Zest the lemon over the salad and then halve the lemon and squeeze the juice from half over the top. Save the other half for another use, or add more lemon juice, if desired.

4. Drizzle with olive oil. Season with salt, black pepper, and Aleppo pepper, and serve.

NOTE The skin on a fuyu persimmon is edible, and I like to keep it on. If you don't love the texture of the skin, feel free to peel the persimmons prior to slicing.

Butter Bean, Sungold, and Smashed Cucumber Salad

SERVES 4

6 ounces (170 g) sungold tomatoes, halved

2 mini seedless cucumbers, smashed and cut into irregular ½-inch (1 cm) chunks

3 tablespoons celery vinegar or red wine vinegar

Kosher salt and freshly cracked black pepper, to taste

One 15.5-ounce (439 g) can butter beans, drained and rinsed

⅓ cup (80 ml) extra virgin olive oil, plus more for serving

2 scallions, thinly sliced

1 red finger chile (or a Fresno chile for a bit less heat!), thinly sliced

¼ cup (8 g) loosely packed torn fresh basil leaves

When sungold tomato season rolls around, I find myself tossing them in just about any dish I can. They truly are the jewels of summer! Marinating the sungolds and smashed cucumbers slightly ahead of time gives them a chance to release a bit of their juices, making a lovely, flavorful base for the salad. I find the easiest way to smash the cucumbers is by placing my knife flat on top of the cucumber and smashing down with my palm, as you would crush a garlic clove. I call for celery vinegar here (TART Vinegar makes one) because I find it adds such a special touch to this salad. However, red wine vinegar is lovely, too, and a more readily available swap. There will be quite a bit of delicious liquid that forms at the bottom of the bowl as the salad sits, perfect for dipping into with a chunk of focaccia (see page 226).

1. Toss the tomatoes, cucumbers, vinegar, salt, and pepper in a medium bowl. Let marinate at room temperature for 15 minutes.

2. Add the beans, olive oil, scallions, chile, and basil (see Note), and toss to combine. Season with more salt and pepper.

3. Serve, topped with more olive oil and pepper.

NOTE This can be made up to 1 hour ahead and stored in the refrigerator before adding the basil. Add the basil right before serving.

Radicchio and Apple Salad
with Rye Crunchies

SERVES 4 TO 6

Rye Crunchies

2 thick slices caraway rye bread
(6 ounces/170 g), torn into
chunks

1 teaspoon coriander seeds

1 teaspoon fennel seeds

¼ cup (35 g) raw pepitas

3 tablespoons olive oil

2 tablespoons maple syrup

1 tablespoon sesame seeds

2 tablespoons raw sunflower
seeds

Kosher salt and freshly cracked
black pepper, to taste

Dressing

2 tablespoons maple syrup

2 tablespoons sherry vinegar

1 tablespoon Dijon mustard

1 small shallot, minced

¼ cup (60 ml) extra virgin
olive oil

Kosher salt and freshly cracked
black pepper, to taste

Salad

1 medium head radicchio (about
12 ounces/340 g), cut into
quarters, cored, and leaves
separated

1 large Granny Smith apple,
thinly sliced

¼ cup (10 g) chopped fresh dill,
plus more for garnish

Give me a crisp and crunchy salad of bitter greens, and I'm a happy gal! Radicchio and apples can be found almost all year round, so this is a great salad for those dreary months of the year when there's seemingly no fun produce in sight. Feel free to substitute the rye with sourdough if that's more your vibe, but I must say, the rye in this is really quite special! I like to keep this salad completely vegan, but it's also great topped with a soft crumbly cheese like chèvre or Gorgonzola.

1. Preheat the oven to 425°F (220°C). Line a sheet tray with parchment paper.

2. **Make the rye crunchies:** Add the bread, coriander seeds, and fennel seeds to a food processor, and pulse until the bread is the size of large (panko-like) crumbs.

3. Transfer the crumbs to a medium bowl. Add the pepitas, olive oil, maple syrup, sesame seeds, and sunflower seeds, and toss to coat. Season with a couple pinches of salt and a few grinds of pepper.

4. Transfer to the sheet tray, spread into an even layer, and bake for 12 to 15 minutes, tossing halfway through the baking time, until golden brown. Let cool completely. (The crunchies will crisp up as they cool.)

5. **Prepare the dressing:** Whisk the maple syrup, vinegar, mustard, and shallot in a small bowl. Slowly stream in the oil, and whisk until emulsified. Season with salt and pepper.

6. **Make the salad:** Place the radicchio, apple, and dill in a large bowl. Toss with the dressing, and season with more salt and pepper.

7. Serve the salad piled high on a platter, topped with as much of the rye crunchies as desired and more dill. Save any remaining rye crunchies for future salad topping in an airtight container at room temperature for up to 1 week.

Antipasto Salad
with Pecorino-Pepperoncini Dressing

SERVES 6

Salad

2 romaine hearts, chopped into bite-size pieces (about 6 cups/325 g)

1 medium fennel bulb, halved and thinly sliced on a mandoline

½ medium red onion, thinly sliced on a mandoline

4 large radishes, thinly sliced on a mandoline

3 mini seedless cucumbers, sliced into rounds

Dressing

½ cup (120 ml) extra virgin olive oil

⅓ cup (35 g) finely grated pecorino Romano

¼ cup (60 ml) pepperoncini brine

2 tablespoons honey

1 tablespoon mayonnaise

1 tablespoon Dijon mustard

1 tablespoon red wine vinegar

1 teaspoon dried oregano

½ teaspoon kosher salt

¼ teaspoon freshly cracked black pepper

Toppings

6 Campari tomatoes, cut into quarters

½ cup (110 g) sliced roasted red peppers

½ cup (90 g) jarred quartered marinated artichokes in oil

½ cup (75 g) halved and pitted mixed olives of choice

3 ounces (85 g) thinly sliced prosciutto

3 ounces (85 g) sliced mild provolone, chopped into bite-size pieces

2 ounces (57 g) hot or sweet soppressata, chopped into bite-size pieces

¼ cup (40 g) sliced pepperoncini

¼ cup (8 g) loosely packed torn fresh basil leaves

I truly fell in love with antipasto salads after moving to New Jersey. Every pizza spot seems to have its own version, and the variety has opened my eyes to how great this salad can be. This is a cumulation of all the different ones I've tried, with all of my favorite parts of each put into one salad. I find the best way to serve any antipasto salad is to toss the lettuce and smaller cut veggies with the dressing and then top the salad with the meats, cheeses, and other fun toppings. This way, none of the heavier ingredients sink to the bottom and you have not only a beautiful salad but a properly dressed one as well. I have given the specific amounts that I like for all the toppings here, but feel free to add more or less of any of them depending on your preference.

1. **Make the salad:** Place the romaine, fennel, and onion in an ice bath. Let sit for 5 minutes to crisp the lettuce and fennel and remove the onion's astringency.

2. Remove the vegetables from the ice bath and dry in a salad spinner, or lay out on a kitchen towel to dry completely. You don't want a watery salad! Transfer to a large bowl along with the radishes and cucumbers. Set aside.

3. **Prepare the dressing:** Add the olive oil, pecorino Romano, pepperoncini brine, honey, mayonnaise, mustard, vinegar, oregano, salt, and pepper to a jar, and shake until combined. Alternatively, whisk the ingredients in a small bowl.

4. Add about half of the dressing to the lettuce mix, and toss to coat. Add more dressing as desired, and season with salt and pepper if needed. Transfer the salad to a large serving platter.

5. **Add the toppings:** Top the salad with the tomatoes, peppers, artichokes, olives, prosciutto, provolone, soppressata, sliced pepperoncini, and basil. Serve any remaining dressing on the side for extra topping.

Mushy Pea Pasta Salad

SERVES 8

8 ounces (about 1 cup/227 g) frozen peas, thawed

½ cup (120 ml) extra virgin olive oil

Kosher salt and freshly cracked black pepper, to taste

8 ounces (227 g) lumachine pasta or your desired small shape, cooked according to the package directions until al dente and cooled

4 ounces (113 g) feta, small diced

3 ounces (about ¾ cup/85 g) whole pitted Castelvetrano olives, thinly sliced

½ large fennel bulb, cored and thinly sliced on a mandoline

½ small red onion, thinly sliced on a mandoline and rinsed (see Tip 1)

¼ cup (10 g) chopped fresh dill

¼ cup (10 g) chopped fresh parsley

¼ cup (8 g) chopped fresh mint leaves

Zest and juice of 1 lemon

I couldn't write a whole chapter on salads without including one of the best iterations of a salad: the pasta salad. When it comes to a good pasta salad, I'm a firm believer that it's all about ratios. You can put almost anything in and it's gonna be good, but the best pasta salads, in my opinion, have a 1:1 ratio of salad ingredients to pasta. I want as many fun add-ins as pasta—it should quite literally be pasta and a salad. This one is half peas and half pasta, which, if you know how much I love peas, makes a lot of sense. The peas are pulsed a few times in a food processor to give them a "mushy" texture, similar to the classic English side dish, so they can coat the pasta completely. So fun!

1. Add the peas, olive oil, salt, and pepper to a food processor, and pulse a few times until the peas become a chunky mash.

2. Add the pasta, feta, olives, fennel, onion, dill, parsley, mint, and mashed peas to a large bowl (see Tip 2). Add the lemon zest and lemon juice, and toss to combine.

3. Season with more salt and pepper, and serve.

TIPS

1. I like to rinse raw onions in cold water to help crisp them and remove a bit of the pungent, raw-onion astringency. I place the onions in a fine-mesh strainer and run them under cold water for about 30 seconds and then dry them completely. You can also let the onions soak in a bowl of ice water for about 5 minutes for the same results.

2. This can be made—reserving the fresh herbs and lemon—and stored in the fridge up to a day ahead. Right before serving, add the herbs, lemon zest, and lemon juice. Season with more salt, pepper, and olive oil, if needed.

Little Gem Salad
with Garlicky White Bean Spread

SERVES 4

Bean Spread

One 15.5-ounce (439 g) can cannellini beans (or any can of white beans you have), drained and rinsed

4 oil-packed anchovy fillets

Zest and juice of 1 lemon

½ cup (120 ml) extra virgin olive oil

1 small garlic clove, finely grated

Kosher salt and freshly cracked black pepper, to taste

Salad

3 or 4 heads little gem lettuce (about 1 pound/454 g), cored and leaves separated

⅓ cup (9 g) loosely packed fresh whole cilantro leaves

⅓ cup (9 g) loosely packed fresh whole parsley leaves

¼ cup (7 g) loosely packed torn fresh dill

¼ cup (7 g) loosely packed fresh whole mint leaves

2 tablespoons thinly sliced fresh chives, plus more for topping

Extra virgin olive oil, to taste

Fresh lemon juice, to taste

Kosher salt and freshly cracked black pepper, to taste

Finely grated Parmesan, to taste

This salad might look somewhat unassuming at first glance, but it's full of little surprises that make it exciting and seriously craveable. Adding a hidden spread at the bottom of a big, leafy salad makes this such a fun eating adventure. I love eating this with my hands and dragging the lettuce leaves through the Caesar salad–inspired bean spread. When it comes to dressing, I keep it very simple with just a light touch of lemon and olive oil. Add a fried egg on top for the perfect little lunch with some sourdough (see page 218) on the side. If you can't find little gem, feel free to use 1 large head of romaine and tear the leaves into large, irregular pieces.

1. **Make the bean spread:** Add the beans, anchovies, lemon zest, lemon juice, olive oil, and garlic to a blender, and blend on high until very smooth. Season with salt and pepper.

2. **Make the salad:** Place the little gem leaves in a large ice bath. Let sit for a few minutes to crisp the lettuce. Remove from the ice bath and dry in a salad spinner, or lay out on a kitchen towel to dry completely. You don't want a watery salad!

3. Add the little gem, cilantro, parsley, dill, mint, and chives to a large bowl.

4. Dress the salad to taste with olive oil, lemon juice, salt, and pepper. I like to have a deft hand with the lemon here.

5. Spread the white bean puree on the bottom of a large platter, and mound the little gem high on top.

6. Top generously with Parmesan and more chives, and serve.

Wedge Salad
with Creamy Chili Crisp Dressing

SERVES 6

Dressing

½ cup (120 g) labne or sour cream

¼ cup (60 ml) buttermilk

¼ cup (7 g) loosely packed fresh dill, roughly chopped

3 tablespoons thinly sliced fresh chives

2 tablespoons mayonnaise

1 tablespoon chili crisp

1 teaspoon Dijon mustard

Zest of 1 lemon

Juice of ½ lemon

Kosher salt and freshly cracked black pepper, to taste

Topping

½ cup (120 ml) canola oil

5 large garlic cloves, thinly sliced on a mandoline

3 large shallots, thinly sliced into rings on a mandoline

Kosher salt, to taste

Salad

1 large head iceberg lettuce, cut into small wedges, core removed, and some leaves separated

Fresh cilantro leaves, to taste

Torn fresh dill, to taste

Torn fresh mint leaves, to taste

I love a good wedge salad. There's nothing quite as satisfying as a cold, crisp hunk of iceberg paired with a creamy dressing and a crunchy topping. When it comes to lettuce, the watery crispness of iceberg is unmatched. I also love a dark, hearty green, but there's definitely a time and place for iceberg, and I simply will not tolerate any more iceberg slander. This wedge is void of a lot of the traditional toppings, like bacon and blue cheese, which are replaced with a bunch of fresh herbs, a little spice, and fried garlic and shallots for crunchy umami. The leftover oil from frying the garlic and shallots is super flavorful, so be sure to save it in an airtight container in the fridge for future roasting, sautéing, or vinaigrette-making. I make the creamy dressing first so the flavors have time to meld a bit while I prep the rest of the salad.

1. **Prepare the dressing:** Mix the labne, buttermilk, dill, chives, mayonnaise, chili crisp, mustard, lemon zest, and lemon juice in a small bowl. Season with salt and pepper. Place in the refrigerator until ready to use.

2. **Make the topping** (see Tip)**:** Heat the canola oil and sliced garlic in a small sauté pan over medium-low heat. Fry the garlic, stirring often, until lightly golden brown, 3 to 5 minutes. The garlic won't seem very crisp at this point, but it will crisp up when fully cooled.

3. Using use a slotted spoon or skimmer, carefully transfer the garlic to a paper towel–lined plate or small sheet pan to drain. Sprinkle with a touch of salt.

4. Add the shallots to the same hot oil over medium-low heat, and cook, stirring frequently, until pale golden, 8 to 10 minutes. When the shallots are one shade lighter than golden brown, use the slotted spoon or skimmer to transfer them to a paper towel–lined plate or small sheet pan to drain. They will crisp up more as they cool. Sprinkle with a touch of salt.

5. **Make the salad:** Arrange the iceberg wedges on a platter. Spoon the dressing all over, and top with cilantro, dill, and mint. Finish with the crispy garlic and shallots, and serve.

TIP The crispy garlic and shallots can be made 1 day ahead, fully cooled, and stored in an airtight container at room temperature.

Smoked Trout Niçoise

SERVES 3 TO 4 AS A MAIN

Salad

8 ounces (227 g) baby red potatoes, scrubbed clean

Kosher salt, to taste

6 ounces (170 g) green beans, trimmed

3 eggs, at room temperature

5 ounces (142 g) green leaf lettuce, torn into large pieces

6 ounces (170 g) tinned smoked trout (see Note), skin removed, if needed, and flaked

6 ounces (170 g) cherry tomatoes, halved

½ small red onion, thinly sliced and rinsed (see Tip 1 on page 80)

½ cup (75 g) pitted and halved Niçoise or kalamata olives

Thinly sliced fresh chives, to taste

Dressing

4 oil-packed anchovy fillets, finely chopped

3 tablespoons celery vinegar or red wine vinegar

2 tablespoons finely chopped fresh parsley

1 tablespoon capers, drained and chopped

1 tablespoon Dijon mustard

½ cup (120 ml) extra virgin olive oil

Kosher salt and freshly cracked black pepper, to taste

A dish from the south of France, the Niçoise salad is a meal salad. It's not a dainty little side dish; it's a full commitment. It's the salad that really has it all, and I love it for that. While it traditionally has anchovies and/or tuna as the fish component, I love adding smoked trout or really any smoked tinned fish, for that matter. Smoked mackerel, salmon, or whitefish would also be great in this! Finely chopping the anchovies and adding them into the dressing makes for an even distribution of salty fish flavor over the entire salad. I love serving this salad with a crusty baguette on the side for a complete meal.

1. **Make the salad:** Add the potatoes to a medium pot, and cover with water. Bring to a boil over high heat. Generously salt the water, reduce the heat to medium, and simmer until the potatoes are just fork-tender, 13 to 15 minutes. Try not to overcook them so they aren't mushy in the salad.

2. Remove the potatoes from the water using a slotted spoon, and transfer to a colander to drain and cool completely. Keep the water in the pot, and increase the heat to high to bring the water back to a boil.

3. Prepare an ice bath.

4. Add the green beans to the boiling water, and cook until tender but not mushy, 4 to 6 minutes.

5. Immediately transfer the beans to the ice bath to shock. Drain (reserving the ice water), and cut into 1-inch (2.5 cm) pieces.

6. Carefully add the eggs to the same boiling water. (Add more water to the pot if needed to cover the eggs, and bring back to a boil.) Boil for 7 minutes for medium-ish, jammy eggs or up to 10 minutes for hard-boiled eggs. Immediately transfer to the ice bath (adding more fresh ice if needed).

7. Peel the eggs over the ice bath while still warm (it's much easier to peel eggs when they're warm) and then place them back into the ice bath to chill completely. Cut into quarters.

8. Cut the potatoes into halves or quarters to make bite-size pieces.

9. **Prepare the dressing:** Add the anchovies, vinegar, parsley, capers, and mustard to a small bowl, and whisk until combined. Slowly whisk in the olive oil until emulsified. Season with salt and pepper.

10. To assemble the salad, add the lettuce to a large bowl and lightly dress with a few spoonfuls of the dressing. Gently toss to coat and then arrange the lettuce on the bottom of a large platter.

11. Top with the potatoes, green beans, eggs, trout, tomatoes, onion, and olives. I like to keep all the toppings in sections, but top as you wish!

12. Spoon more dressing over the toppings and then top with chives and more pepper. Serve any remaining dressing on the side for extra topping.

NOTE I love the tinned smoked trout from Fishwife or Trader Joe's.

A Quick Broth Intermission

So many of the recipes in the book feature broths and stocks in their ingredient lists, so I had to include my preferred methods to make the major three: chicken, beef, and vegetable. Stocks and broths really are the heart of a lot of cooking; they provide such an incredible depth of flavor, and it's so easy to make your own!

Beef Stock

MAKES 4 TO 5 QUARTS
(4 TO 5 L)

8 to 10 pounds (3.5 kg to 4.5 kg) beef bones

6 quarts (5.7 L) water

3 celery stalks, roughly chopped

2 heads garlic, halved crosswise (skins and all)

2 yellow onions, quartered (skins and all)

1 bunch fresh parsley, roughly chopped (stems and all)

1 small bunch fresh thyme

2 dried bay leaves

1 dried guajillo chile

1 tablespoon black peppercorns

From beef stock to bone broth to sipping broth, there are so many names for essentially the same thing. At its core, beef stock is simply beef bones that have slowly simmered in water with some aromatics to make a flavorful liquid. This stock is obviously great in so many recipes, but it's also great on its own, served in a nice mug for sipping. Ask your butcher for beef bones with marrow for the tastiest stock. This has quite a lengthy simmer time, so I often roast the bones a day ahead (and deglaze the pan) to get a head start on things. Store the bones in the refrigerator along with the deglazing liquid, and continue with the recipe the next day.

1. Preheat the oven to 450°F (230°C).

2. Place the bones on two sheet trays, and roast for 45 to 60 minutes, until deeply golden brown.

3. Transfer the bones to a 12-quart (11 L) stock pot (see Note).

4. While the sheet pans are still hot, carefully pour off any rendered fat. (Strain and cool the fat for future cooking!) Add a good splash of water to deglaze the pans, and scrape up any brown bits. Pour that liquid into the pot along with the 6 quarts (5.7 L) water.

5. Bring to a boil over high heat. Reduce the heat to low, and simmer, uncovered, for 8 to 12 hours, skimming off any scum that accumulates on the top of the stock. Add more water if needed to keep the bones submerged throughout the entire cooking process.

6. Add the celery, garlic, onions, parsley, thyme, bay leaves, chile, and peppercorns, and simmer for 1 hour more.

7. Prepare a large ice bath.

8. Remove and discard the large bones and pieces of vegetables. Strain the stock through a fine-mesh strainer (line the strainer with cheesecloth or a coffee filter for the clearest stock) into another large pot or container. Place the container of stock over the ice bath to cool quickly to room temperature.

9. Ladle the cooled stock into quart (1 L) containers, and place in the refrigerator to chill completely.

10. Store the stock in the refrigerator for up to 3 days or in the freezer for up to 4 months.

NOTE If you don't have a 12-quart (11 L) stock pot, you can split the recipe in half and use two smaller pots.

Chicken Broth

MAKES 3 TO 4 QUARTS
(3 TO 4 L)

6 pounds (2.7 kg) chicken wings

1 pound (454 g) chicken feet

5 quarts (4.8 L) water

3 celery stalks, roughly chopped

2 yellow onions, quartered
(skins and all)

2 heads garlic, halved crosswise
(skins and all)

1 small fennel, bulb quartered
and stems and fronds roughly
chopped

1 bunch fresh parsley, roughly
chopped (stems and all)

4 dried shiitake mushrooms

2 dried bay leaves

1 dried guajillo chile

1 tablespoon black peppercorns

There's such power in having your own homemade chicken broth on hand. It's so satisfying to grab some out of your refrigerator or freezer to use in a quick soup, sauce, or braise. It just feels right, ya know? This recipe is considered a broth, not a stock, because it uses both meat and bones. (A stock uses just bones.) In practice, that's just a technicality, so this can be used interchangeably in recipes that call for broth or stock. This broth has a gloriously gelatinous texture, so if you're using it in a recipe that calls for a specific measurement, heat it up slightly to easily pour and measure. You can substitute more chicken wings for the chicken feet, but the feet play a key role in achieving the Jell-O-y texture.

1. Add the chicken wings, chicken feet, and water to a 12-quart (11 L) stock pot (see Note on page 90). Bring to a boil over high heat. Reduce the heat to low, and simmer, uncovered, for 2 hours, skimming off any scum that accumulates on the top of the broth. Try not to remove too much of the liquid itself as you skim. Add more water if needed to keep the chicken submerged throughout the cooking process.

2. Add the celery, onions, garlic, fennel, parsley, mushrooms, bay leaves, chile, and peppercorns, and continue to barely simmer for 2 more hours.

3. Prepare a large ice bath.

4. Remove and discard the larger pieces of chicken and vegetables. Strain the broth through a fine-mesh strainer (line the strainer with cheesecloth or a coffee filter for the clearest broth) into another large pot or container. Place the container of broth over the ice bath to cool quickly to room temperature.

5. Ladle the cooled broth into quart (1 L) containers, and place in the refrigerator to chill completely.

6. Store the broth in the refrigerator for up to 3 days or in the freezer for up to 4 months.

Vegetable Stock

MAKES 3 TO 4 QUARTS
(3 TO 4 L)

5 quarts (4.8 L) water

3 small leeks, roots trimmed, cleaned, and roughly chopped

3 celery stalks, roughly chopped

2 parsnips, roughly chopped

2 heads garlic, halved crosswise (skins and all)

1 bunch fresh parsley, roughly chopped (stems and all)

1 small fennel, bulb quartered and stems and fronds roughly chopped

4 dried shiitake mushrooms

2 dried bay leaves

One 5 × 3-inch (13 × 8 cm) piece of kombu

1 dried guajillo chile

1 tablespoon black peppercorns

Vegetable stocks can sometimes end up tasting like mirepoix water, which is fine and suffices, I suppose, but it also can be kind of lackluster. I wanted to make a vegetable stock that shines in its own right and adds just as much of a flavor boost to recipes as a meat-based stock. The addition of dried mushrooms and kombu provides an extra level of plant-based umami. The beauty of this vegetable stock is that it needs only 1 hour of simmering for maximum flavor extraction, so even if you are short on time, you can still whip up a lovely stock!

1. Add the water, leeks, celery, parsnips, garlic, parsley, fennel, mushrooms, bay leaves, kombu, chile, and peppercorns to an 8-quart (7.6 L) stock pot. Bring to a boil over high heat. Reduce the heat to low, and simmer, uncovered, for 1 hour.

2. Prepare a large ice bath.

3. Strain the stock through a fine-mesh strainer (line the strainer with cheesecloth or a coffee filter for the clearest stock) into another large pot or container. Place the container of stock over the ice bath to cool quickly to room temperature. Discard the vegetables.

4. Ladle the cooled stock into quart (1 L) containers, and place in the refrigerator to chill completely.

5. Store the stock in the refrigerator for up to 3 days or in the freezer for up to 4 months.

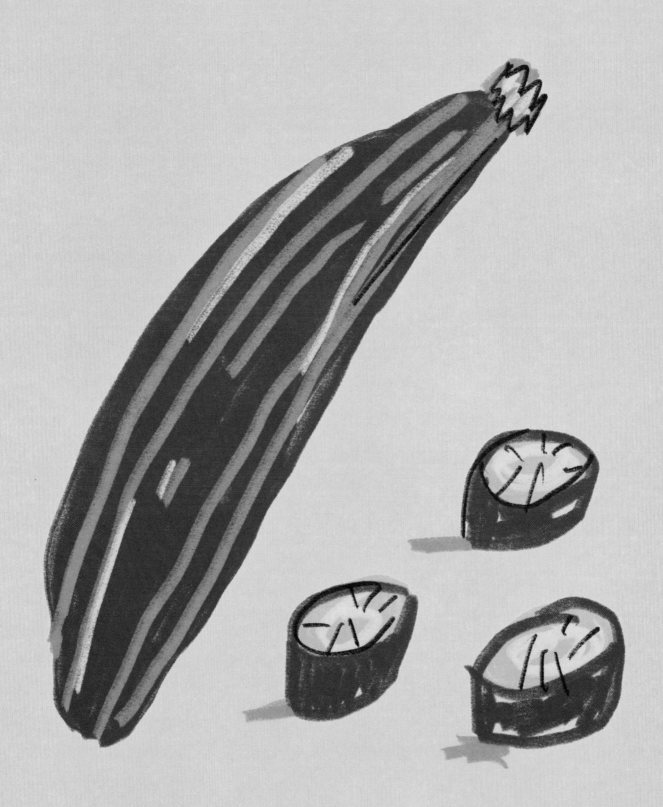

Vegetables

From Everyday to CSA

This is a fun little section to try out a new vegetable or cooking method. It's a celebration of all things vegetables, with exciting recipes for both lesser-utilized veggies and old standbys. Turn to this chapter for inspiration to help use up your CSA box or farmers market haul. These recipes lean cozy and comforting, which I find to be a nice complement to the more salad-y, vegetable-forward recipes in the book.

Caponata
with Dried Cherries and Green Olives

SERVES 6

1 medium eggplant (1 to 1¼ pounds/454 to 567 g), cut into ½-inch (1 cm) cubes

¼ cup (60 ml) olive oil, plus more for coating the pan

Kosher salt and freshly cracked black pepper, to taste

5 garlic cloves, minced

3 large shallots, diced

1 medium fennel bulb, cored and diced

1 medium red bell pepper, ribs and seeds removed, and diced

2 tablespoons tomato paste

One 14.5-ounce (411 g) can diced tomatoes

2 teaspoons chopped jarred Calabrian chiles in oil, plus more to taste

⅓ cup (50 g) chopped pitted Castelvetrano olives

¼ cup (35 g) dried cherries, roughly chopped

2 tablespoons pine nuts, toasted (see Tip 1 on page 49)

1 tablespoon honey

1 teaspoon red wine vinegar, plus more to taste

3 tablespoons finely chopped fresh parsley

In my half-Sicilian family, caponata would often be a part of our appetizer spread at big family gatherings. If you ever find yourself with a bunch of eggplant, caponata is a great way to use it and is a super-versatile item to have in your fridge. I like it best served at room temperature. It's great on top of ricotta toast, alongside your fried eggs in the morning, or as a base for a delicious veggie sandwich. You will normally see celery in caponata, but I love subbing in fennel because it goes so well with eggplant. Give me any opportunity to use fennel, and I'm gonna take it!

1. Preheat the oven to 400°F (200°C). Line a sheet tray with parchment paper.

2. Place the eggplant on the sheet tray, and drizzle with ¼ cup (60 ml) olive oil. Season with salt and pepper, and toss to coat. Spread out the eggplant in an even layer on the sheet tray.

3. Roast for 25 to 30 minutes, tossing halfway through the cooking time, until soft and golden.

4. Meanwhile, coat the bottom of a large sauté pan with olive oil, and heat over medium heat. When hot, add the garlic, shallots, and fennel, and season with salt and pepper. Cook, stirring occasionally, until soft, 10 to 12 minutes.

5. Toss in the bell pepper, and cook until it starts to soften, 3 or 4 minutes. Add the tomato paste, and cook until darkened, 2 or 3 minutes.

6. Stir in the diced tomatoes, chiles, and roasted eggplant. Reduce the heat to low, and cook until everything melds and stews together, 10 to 12 minutes.

7. Turn off the heat and stir in the olives, cherries, pine nuts, honey, and vinegar. Season with salt and pepper, and add more chiles and vinegar to taste if desired.

8. Let cool to room temperature and then stir in the parsley.

9. Serve, or store in an airtight container in the refrigerator for up to 5 days.

Fried Squash Blossom "Mozzarella Sticks"

SERVES 6

Tomato Sauce

3 tablespoons olive oil

4 garlic cloves, finely grated

½ teaspoon red pepper flakes

One 24-ounce (680 g) jar passata

Kosher salt and freshly cracked black pepper, to taste

2 Parmesan rinds (about 5 ounces/142 g), optional but encouraged

Squash Blossoms

12 large or 16 small squash blossoms

8 ounces (227 g) low-moisture whole-milk mozzarella, shredded

¾ cup (6 ounces/170 g) whole-milk ricotta

½ teaspoon kosher salt

½ teaspoon freshly cracked black pepper, plus more for serving

Canola oil, for frying

3 eggs

3 tablespoons all-purpose flour

2 cups (180 g) panko breadcrumbs

Freshly grated Parmesan, for serving

Squash blossoms are a true gift of summer. They're only around for a brief moment during the season, so whenever I see them at the market, I scoop them up and make something special. Fried squash blossoms are often filled with creamy cheeses like ricotta, as we are doing here, but in this case, the ricotta is used merely as a binder for the shredded mozzarella. The end result is a mash-up of a classic, creamy, cheese-filled blossom and a stringy, pull-y mozzarella stick. Truly a delight! I have included a simple tomato sauce recipe here for dipping, but warm up your favorite store-bought marinara to make this even quicker and easier if you'd like. The Fried Garlic Pizza Sauce (page 177) would also make a great side dipper if you happen to have it around!

1. **Make the sauce:** Heat the olive oil and garlic in a small saucepan over medium heat. Cook, stirring constantly, until the garlic is lightly golden, 2 or 3 minutes. Add the red pepper flakes and passata, and season with salt and black pepper. Bring to a simmer and then reduce the heat to low.

2. Add the Parmesan rinds, if using, and let the sauce simmer for 45 minutes to 2 hours (depending on how much time you have) to develop the flavor. Remove and discard the Parmesan rinds, and season with more salt and black pepper before serving.

3. **Meanwhile, make the squash blossoms:** Clean each blossom by gingerly tearing off the spiky leaves at the bottom and then snipping off the pistil inside with kitchen shears.

4. Mix the mozzarella, ricotta, salt, and black pepper in a medium bowl.

5. Carefully, without tearing the blossoms, spoon the filling into each blossom, leaving about ½ inch (1 cm) of space at the top. Gently pinch the top of the blossom to enclose the filling and ensure none is exposed.

6. Heat about 1½ inches (4 cm) of canola oil in a large pot over medium heat to 325°F (165°C).

7. While the oil heats, bread the blossoms. Add the eggs and flour to a small, shallow dish and whisk until combined (a few small lumps are okay!). Add the panko to another small, shallow dish.

8. Cover each blossom in the egg mixture and then the panko, being sure to fully coat in each step.

9. Working in batches, gently add the blossoms to the hot oil and fry, flipping them as needed, until golden brown all over, 2 or 3 minutes. Using a slotted spoon, transfer the fried blossoms to a wire rack–lined sheet tray or paper towel–lined plate. Immediately season with a small pinch of salt. Repeat the frying process until all blossoms are fried. This should take 2 or 3 batches, depending on the size of the blossoms.

10. Serve immediately, topped with a generous amount of grated Parmesan and more black pepper and the warm tomato sauce on the side for dipping.

Chunky Kohlrabi Potato Salad

SERVES 4

Salad

1 pound (454 g) baby Yukon
   Gold potatoes

Kosher salt, to taste

1 pound (454 g) kohlrabi, peeled
   and cut into 1-inch (2.5 cm)
   cubes

¼ medium red onion, thinly
   sliced and rinsed (see Tip 1 on
   page 80)

3 tablespoons chopped fresh
   cilantro, plus more torn leaves
   for garnish

2 tablespoons chopped fresh
   dill, plus more torn fronds for
   garnish

2 tablespoons chopped fresh
   mint, plus more torn leaves
   for garnish

Dressing

⅓ cup (80 ml) extra-virgin
   olive oil

3 tablespoons tahini

Zest and juice of 1 lemon

1 tablespoon whole-grain
   mustard

1 tablespoon cold water

1 teaspoon honey

½ inch (1 cm) ginger, peeled
   and finely grated

Kosher salt and freshly cracked
   black pepper, to taste

Toasted sesame seeds, to taste
   (see Tip on page 234)

Believe it or not, I've gotten quite a few requests over the years for kohlrabi recipes. I was first introduced to kohlrabi when my parents signed up for a CSA box, and every week, kohlrabi was included. Every. Single. Week. *I imagine the abundance of requests for recipes using kohlrabi is due to the same phenomenon. (It's simple to grow, so I think that's why so many CSAs include them!) Kohlrabi is great shaved or julienned into a salad, but I feel like cooked kohlrabi recipes are more scarce, so I wanted to have a dedicated cooked kohlrabi recipe in this book. I recommend peeling the kohlrabi with a paring knife, rather than a vegetable peeler, so you can peel off a slightly thicker portion because the outer layer tends to be tough. Be careful when cooking it; it can go from nicely tender to quite mushy in no time.*

1. **Make the salad:** Add the potatoes to a medium pot, cover with water, and set over high heat. Bring to a boil, generously salt the water, and reduce the heat to medium to maintain a simmer. Cook until just fork-tender, 10 to 12 minutes.

2. Use a slotted spoon to transfer the potatoes to a large bowl, and let cool completely. Cut the potatoes in half or quarters to make 1-inch (2.5 cm) pieces.

3. Meanwhile, bring the pot of water back to a boil over high heat, and prepare an ice bath. Add the kohlrabi to the boiling water, and boil until just tender, 8 to 10 minutes. Immediately transfer to the ice bath to shock and cool. Remove the kohlrabi from the ice bath, and set aside.

4. **Prepare the dressing:** Whisk the olive oil, tahini, lemon zest, lemon juice, mustard, water, honey, and ginger in a large bowl until smooth. Season with salt and pepper. If the dressing separates after whisking, add 1 teaspoon cold water at a time and whisk; it will emulsify.

5. Add the potatoes, kohlrabi, onion, cilantro, dill, and mint to the large bowl.

6. Toss to coat everything in the dressing, and season with salt and pepper.

7. Serve, topped with more fresh herbs and sesame seeds.

Celery Root and Potato Pierogi

Celery root is a crazy-looking root vegetable that may seem intimidating; it's almost like something you'd find in outer space. The truth is, it's as easy to cook and as versatile as any other root vegetable. It has a pretty strong celery taste, which I love, but it's also delightful when balanced out with the addition of potato in a dish. These pierogi wrap up that lovely combination into a cute little package of deliciousness.

MAKES ABOUT 30 PIEROGI

Pierogi

1½ cups (195 g) all-purpose flour, plus more for dusting

½ cup (70 g) semolina flour

1 teaspoon kosher salt, plus more to taste

3 tablespoons unsalted butter, at room temperature, cut into pieces

4 egg yolks

⅓ cup (80 g) sour cream

2 tablespoons water

2 small Yukon Gold potatoes, peeled and cut into 1-inch (2.5 cm) chunks (6 ounces/170 g peeled)

1 small celery root, peeled and cut into 1-inch (2.5 cm) chunks (6 ounces/170 g peeled)

3 ounces (85 g) sharp white cheddar, grated

Freshly cracked black pepper, to taste

Dill Sour Cream

1 cup (240 g) sour cream

3 tablespoons finely chopped fresh dill

2 scallions, white and green parts thinly sliced

Zest of 1 lemon

Kosher salt and freshly cracked black pepper, to taste

For Finishing

6 tablespoons unsalted butter

1 large sweet onion, sliced

Kosher salt and freshly cracked black pepper, to taste

Fresh dill, to taste

Lemon zest, to taste

1. **Make the pierogi:** Place the all-purpose flour, semolina flour, and salt in a food processor, and pulse to combine. Add the butter, and pulse until the butter is about the size of small peas. Add the egg yolks, sour cream, and water, and pulse to form a shaggy dough.

2. Transfer the dough to a sheet of plastic wrap, use the wrap to press the dough into a disc ½ inch (1 cm) thick, and wrap completely. Set the dough in the refrigerator to chill for at least 1 hour or up to 24 hours while you prepare the filling.

3. Place the potatoes and celery root in a medium pot, cover with about 2 inches (5 cm) of water, and set over high heat. Bring to a boil, generously salt the water, and reduce the heat to medium. Simmer until tender, 8 to 10 minutes.

4. Drain the vegetables into a colander and then return them to the pot. Mash until mostly smooth; some chunks are fine.

5. Stir in the cheddar, and season with salt and pepper. Set aside to cool completely, or store in an airtight container in the refrigerator for up to 3 days.

6. **Meanwhile, make the dill sour cream:** Mix the sour cream, dill, scallions, and lemon zest in a small bowl. Season with salt and pepper. Place in the refrigerator until ready to serve.

7. Bring a large pot of water to a boil over high heat while you form the pierogi (see Note). Lightly flour a sheet tray. Remove the dough from the refrigerator.

8. On a lightly floured surface, working with half of the dough at a time, roll out the dough into a rough circle about ⅛ inch (3 mm) thick. Flip the dough and add more flour as needed to prevent sticking while rolling.

9. Cut out circles of dough using a 3-inch (8 cm) round biscuit cutter (or similar-sized cup), cutting them as close together as possible to prevent a lot of excess scraps. Form the scraps into a ball, wrap in plastic wrap, and set aside.

10. Fill each circle of dough with about 2 teaspoons of the cooled filling. Fold the dough over the filling into a half-moon shape. Pinch the edges with your fingers to close and then use a fork to crimp the edges to seal. Lightly flour the fork if it gets too sticky. Transfer the pierogi to the sheet tray, and repeat with the remaining dough. If the dough starts to dry out while you crimp, use a little water to wet the edges and continue crimping.

11. Repeat steps 8 through 10 with the remaining half of the dough and filling. If you have any remaining filling, reroll the reserved scrap dough, cut, and form more pierogi.

12. Line another sheet tray with parchment paper. Generously salt the boiling water from step 7, and drop in half of the pierogi. Boil until the pierogi float, 3 or 4 minutes. Transfer to the sheet tray using a slotted spoon, and repeat with the remaining pierogi.

13. **To finish,** heat a large skillet over medium heat. Add 2 tablespoons butter and melt. Add about one-third of the sliced onions, and season with salt. Sauté until the onions start to soften, 1 or 2 minutes. They will continue to brown and cook with the pierogi.

14. Add one-third of the pierogi to the skillet, and sauté until they are golden brown on both sides and the onions are brown, soft, and delicious, 3 to 5 minutes. Transfer to a platter.

15. Repeat steps 13 and 14 in two more batches with the remaining butter, onions, and pierogi. Wipe out the pan between batches if there are any dark or burned bits on the bottom.

16. Serve, garnished with dill, lemon zest, more pepper, and dollops of the dill sour cream.

NOTE Formed and filled raw pierogi can be made ahead and kept frozen for up to 3 months. Fully freeze them in a single layer on a sheet tray first and then transfer them to a ziplock plastic freezer bag. To cook the pierogi from frozen, start at step 12. They may just take a bit longer to boil and float.

Sunchoke Clam Chowder

SERVES 6

5 dozen littleneck clams

¼ cup (40 g) kosher salt, for cleaning the clams, plus more to season the soup

¼ cup (40 g) cornmeal, for cleaning the clams

1 cup (240 ml) dry white wine

8 ounces (227 g) bacon, diced

3 large celery stalks, diced

1 large yellow onion, diced

Freshly cracked black pepper, to taste

2 tablespoons unsalted butter

½ cup (65 g) all-purpose flour

4 cups (940 ml) low-sodium chicken broth, homemade (see page 92) or store-bought

2 dried bay leaves

2 large (about 1 pound/454 g) Yukon Gold potatoes, diced

8 ounces (227 g) sunchokes, peeled and diced

½ cup (120 ml) heavy cream

1 lemon, zested and then cut into wedges for serving

For Serving

Hot sauce

Celery leaves

Thinly sliced fresh chives

Fresh dill

Oyster crackers

NOTE After straining the clam liquid, you may have a touch more or a touch less than 2 cups (480 ml). It will depend on your clams. The goal is to have a total of 6 cups (1.4 L) of liquid for the soup, so if you end up with more or less clam liquid, add as much chicken broth as needed (more or less than the 4 cups/940 ml called for) to yield 6 cups (1.4 L) total.

Sunchokes are like a fun little cross between an artichoke and a potato. They have an artichoke flavor and a potato-like texture when cooked, which makes them the perfect candidate for a fun chowder! The sunchoke flavor in this almost enhances the overall "clammy-ness" of the chowder without having to use an obscene amount of clams, which I think is super cool. I like them peeled for this chowder, but no need to go crazy; some skin is just fine.

1. Place the clams in a large bowl. Rinse and scrub off any visible dirt or grit. Cover with cold water, and add ¼ cup (40 g) salt and ¼ cup (40 g) cornmeal. Let sit for 30 minutes to purge the clams of their sand. Lift the clams out of the water and transfer to a colander. (If there is still sand remaining in the water, change out the water and repeat the purging-and-soaking process until no sand remains.) Rinse off any remaining cornmeal, and discard any cracked or chipped clams along with any open ones that don't close with a gentle nudge.

2. Add half of the clams to a large pot along with the wine. Bring to a boil over medium-high heat, cover, and reduce the heat to medium-low. Steam the clams until they open, 6 or 7 minutes. Discard any clams that do not open. Transfer the clams to a large bowl using a slotted spoon. Add the remaining clams to the same cooking liquid, and repeat the steaming process.

3. Strain the clam cooking liquid through a fine-mesh strainer into a large bowl. You should have about 2 cups (480 ml) of liquid (see Note). Rinse and dry the pot.

4. Return the pot to medium heat, add the bacon, and cook, stirring often, until crispy, 6 to 8 minutes.

5. Add the celery and onion, and season with salt and pepper. Cook, stirring occasionally, until the veggies soften, 6 to 8 minutes.

6. Add the butter and melt. Sprinkle in the flour, and stir until the veggies are coated in a thick paste.

7. Pour in the reserved clam liquid and chicken broth, and whisk to incorporate, scraping the bottom of the pot to release any brown bits. Toss in the bay leaves. Bring to a boil, scraping the bottom of the pot to prevent scorching, and reduce the heat to a low simmer.

8. Stir in the potatoes and sunchokes. The soup will start to thicken. Simmer over low heat, uncovered and stirring often, until the potatoes and sunchokes are soft, 25 to 35 minutes.

9. Meanwhile, remove the clam meat from the steamed clams and roughly chop.

10. When the soup has thickened, remove the bay leaves. Stir in the cream and chopped clam meat. Simmer just 1 or 2 minutes longer to heat the cream and clams. Season with salt and pepper (I like a good amount of pepper in this!), and stir in the lemon zest.

11. Serve, garnished with hot sauce, celery leaves, chives, dill, and oyster crackers and with lemon wedges on the side for squeezing.

Charred Cumin Beets

SERVES 4 AS A SIDE

1¼ pounds (567 g) medium red beets (about 6), scrubbed clean

Olive oil, for coating and charring the beets

Kosher salt and freshly cracked black pepper, to taste

1 tablespoon chili crisp (see Tip)

1 tablespoon Chinese black vinegar

1 teaspoon granulated sugar

1 tablespoon unsalted butter

1 teaspoon cumin seeds, crushed in a mortar and pestle (or with the bottom of a pan)

½ cup (20 g) loosely packed, roughly chopped cilantro (a combo of leaves and stems)

¼ small red onion, thinly sliced on a mandoline and rinsed (see Tip 1 on page 80)

These beets take their inspiration from one of my favorite Chinese dishes: cumin lamb. Although it is originally from the Xinjiang region of China, I had it for the first time at a Sichuan restaurant in Jersey City. It was so delicious that it became a staple part of our order whenever we'd visit. Earthy, charred beets are so delicious with similar seasonings and are a fun vegetable take on the dish. If your beets come with the greens attached, remove them for this recipe—but save them for tossing into salads, soups, and more!

1. Preheat the oven to 400°F (200°C).

2. Add the beets to a medium bowl, drizzle with the olive oil and a big pinch of salt, and toss to coat. Wrap the beets tightly in a foil packet, sealing the sides very well to ensure no steam releases during roasting. Place on a sheet tray.

3. Roast for 50 to 60 minutes, until the beets are tender. You can check them for doneness by piercing through the foil with a paring knife; if it slides in easily, they are done.

4. Meanwhile, mix the chili crisp, vinegar, and sugar in a small bowl. Set aside.

5. When the beets are tender, carefully open the foil packet to release the steam. Rub off the skin with a paper towel. (You can let the beets cool a bit if needed.) Cut the beets in half.

6. Coat a large cast-iron skillet with olive oil, and heat over medium-high heat until almost smoking.

7. Add the beets, cut side down, and cook until charred, 3 or 4 minutes. Flip over the beets, and char for another 1 or 2 minutes.

8. Turn off the heat, and add the butter and cumin seeds. Let the butter melt and the cumin seeds toast in the residual heat, and baste the beets in the cumin butter to coat, about 1 minute. Season with salt and pepper.

9. Transfer the beets and buttery pan bits to a serving platter, and spoon over the reserved chili crisp mixture. Top with cilantro and red onions, and serve.

TIP Be sure to mix the chili crisp well before measuring so you get an even ratio of chiles to oil. Using some chili crisp oil is essential in this recipe.

Spanish Zucchini Tortilla

SERVES 4 TO 6

Red Pepper Almond Sauce

¾ cup (95 g) blanched slivered almonds

½ cup (114 g) roughly chopped roasted red peppers

¼ cup (60 ml) olive oil

2 garlic cloves, smashed

Juice of 1 lemon

½ teaspoon sweet smoked paprika

¼ teaspoon cayenne
Kosher salt and freshly cracked black pepper, to taste

Tortilla

½ cup (120 ml) olive oil

1 large zucchini (about 12 ounces/340 g), sliced into rounds ⅛ inch (3 mm) thick on a mandoline

1 teaspoon kosher salt, plus more to taste

1 large Yukon Gold potato (about 8 ounces/227 g), sliced into rounds ⅛ inch (3 mm) thick on a mandoline

1 small white onion, sliced into rounds ⅛ inch (3 mm) thick on a mandoline

Freshly cracked black pepper, to taste

8 eggs

Whenever I cook with zucchini, I always think back to my mom's garden in the summertime and the endless amount of zucchini she would grow. Zucchini would make a sneaky appearance in almost everything we ate in late summer. My mom was always searching for new ways to use it all, and this recipe is for anyone else who may find themselves in a similar zucchini predicament. A traditional Spanish tortilla uses just eggs, potatoes, and onions, but I find the addition of sliced zucchini to be quite nice! The tortilla is particularly good dipped in a creamy almond sauce that pulls inspiration from two Spanish classics, ajo blanco and romesco. I like to eat it at room temperature, so I make the sauce after the tortilla is completely cooked, to give it time to cool. I also like to use a well-seasoned carbon-steel pan here, but for first-time makers of this recipe, I recommend an oven-safe nonstick pan for the least possible risk of stickage.

1. **Prepare the almonds for the sauce:** Place the almonds in a small bowl, and cover with 2 inches (5 cm) of boiling water. Soak for 1 hour at room temperature and then strain, reserving ¼ cup (60 ml) of the soaking liquid.

2. Meanwhile, preheat the oven to 350°F (180°C) with a rack positioned in the center.

3. **Make the tortilla:** Heat the olive oil in a 10-inch (25 cm) well-seasoned carbon-steel or oven-safe nonstick skillet over medium-high heat. Add the zucchini in two batches, and fry, stirring often, until golden, 6 to 8 minutes. (Doing this in batches is essential to get nicely golden zucchini.) Transfer to a paper towel, sprinkle with a little salt, and repeat with the remaining zucchini.

4. Add the potato and onion to the skillet in an even layer, and season with a touch of salt and pepper. Reduce the heat to medium-low, cover, and cook, uncovering the pan to stir occasionally, until the potatoes are just fork-tender (not overly soft), 8 to 12 minutes. The goal is to cook the potatoes through, not to brown them, so adjust the heat as needed.

5. Meanwhile, whisk together the eggs and 1 teaspoon salt in a large bowl until homogeneous.

6. When the potatoes and onions are cooked, drain them from the oil using a slotted spoon and add them to the eggs along with the fried zucchini. Stir to combine.

7. Increase the heat to medium, and heat the oil left in the pan. When hot, add the egg mixture, and cook, stirring as you would for scrambled eggs, until the eggs are somewhat cooked but still quite soft and runny, 1 or 2 minutes. Turn off the heat, and flatten the egg mixture into an even layer.

8. Transfer to the oven, and bake for 10 to 15 minutes, until just set.

9. Run a spatula around the sides of the tortilla to loosen, and shake the pan to ensure the eggs are fully released from the pan. Invert onto a plate. The tortilla should be golden. Set aside.

10. **Make the sauce:** Place the almonds, reserved almond soaking liquid, peppers, olive oil, garlic, lemon juice, paprika, and cayenne in a high-powered blender, and blend on high until very smooth. Season with salt and pepper.

11. Cut the tortilla into wedges, and serve with the sauce on the side.

Steamed Kabocha Squash
with Herby Marcona Almond Topping

SERVES 4 TO 6

Steamed Squash

1 small kabocha squash (about 2 pounds/907 g), skin on, seeded, and cut into wedges 1½ inches (4 cm) thick (see Tip)

1 tablespoon olive oil

Kosher salt and freshly cracked black pepper, to taste

Topping

½ cup (75 g) roasted and salted Marcona almonds, finely chopped

¼ cup (15 g) finely chopped fresh parsley

3 tablespoons extra virgin olive oil

1 or 2 tablespoons maple syrup, or to taste

1 tablespoon apple cider vinegar

1 teaspoon chopped jarred Calabrian chiles in oil, plus more to taste

Kosher salt and freshly cracked black pepper, to taste

Thinly sliced fresh chives, to taste

The go-to cooking preparation for squash is often roasting, but this recipe showcases the delight that is steamed squash. Steaming squash really locks in and intensifies its inherent sweetness without overpowering its delicate flavor. It also yields the most satisfyingly silky yet dense texture. This recipe can be made with any edible skinned squash such as delicata, red kuri, or acorn. The almond topping makes it elegant enough for a holiday spread while still being simple and quick enough for an everyday dinner. Feel free to sub in your favorite roasted nut, but I do feel like the Marconas make this quite special.

1. **Make the squash:** Set up a steamer over medium heat.
2. While the steamer heats, add the squash and olive oil to a medium bowl, and toss to coat. Season with salt and pepper.
3. When the water in the steamer comes to a low boil, add the squash and cook, covered, until just fork-tender, 10 to 12 minutes.
4. **Meanwhile, make the topping:** Combine the almonds, parsley, extra virgin olive oil, syrup, vinegar, and chiles in a small bowl. Season with salt and pepper.
5. Transfer the steamed squash to a platter. Sprinkle the almond topping all over, followed by the chives, and serve.

TIP For easier cutting, microwave the whole squash for about 45 seconds and then cut it. This will soften the squash ever so slightly.

Charred Sweet Potatoes
with Chunky Peach Vinaigrette

SERVES 6

1½ pounds (680 g) mini sweet potatoes, scrubbed clean

¼ cup (60 ml) olive oil, plus more for coating the potatoes and skillet

Kosher salt and freshly cracked black pepper, to taste

1 large ripe yellow peach, pitted and roughly chopped

1 to 2 tablespoons maple syrup, or to taste (depending on peach sweetness)

2 tablespoons unseasoned rice vinegar

1 teaspoon urfa biber chile (see Note on page 45)

2 tablespoons unsalted butter

¼ cup (5 g) fresh mint leaves

Flake salt, to taste, optional

I love a good sweet potato all year round. I find them equally as enjoyable in summertime as I do on the Thanksgiving table. This recipe highlights the seasonal versatility of sweet potatoes, pairing them with a rustic peach vinaigrette. It's a fun side dish for a barbecue or any summer meal. Substitute a very ripe hachiya persimmon for the peach for an equally delicious fall variation. A ripe hachiya persimmon is extremely soft to the touch and almost squishy. Simply cut the hachiya in half and use a spoon to scoop the flesh out of the skin. Roughly chop the flesh, and proceed with the recipe.

1. Preheat the oven to 400°F (200°C).

2. Rub the sweet potatoes with a little olive oil, and season all over with salt.

3. Wrap the potatoes all together in one tight foil packet, sealing the sides very well to ensure no steam releases. Place on a sheet tray.

4. Bake for 35 to 50 minutes, until the potatoes are tender. You can check them for doneness by simply piercing through the foil with a paring knife or cake tester. If they aren't done, it's okay to continue roasting them with the pierced foil.

5. Meanwhile, add the peach and syrup to a medium bowl. Mash the peach with a fork to break it up slightly. Whisk in the vinegar, ¼ cup (60 ml) olive oil, and chile, and season with salt and pepper.

6. When the potatoes are tender, carefully open the foil packet to release the steam. Halve the potatoes lengthwise. (You can let them cool off a bit if needed.)

7. Heat a 12-inch (30 cm) cast-iron skillet over medium-high heat. Coat the bottom of the pan with olive oil. Add the sweet potatoes, cut side down, and cook until they release from the pan and are nicely golden and charred, 5 to 7 minutes. Season with salt and pepper. Transfer the potatoes to a serving platter.

8. Add the butter to the pan and melt and then reduce the heat to medium-low. Add the mint, and cook until the mint is crispy and the butter starts to brown, about 1 minute. Remove from the heat. Use a slotted spoon to remove the mint to a paper towel–lined plate. (It will crisp slightly as it cools.)

9. Pour the brown butter over the potatoes and then top with a few spoonfuls of the reserved peach dressing. Garnish with the fried mint and a sprinkle of flake salt, if using, and serve with extra dressing on the side.

Mustardy Herb-Buttered Potatoes

SERVES 4

2 pounds (907 g) fingerling potatoes

Kosher salt and freshly cracked black pepper, to taste

¼ cup (57 g) unsalted butter

1 tablespoon whole-grain mustard

2 teaspoons Dijon mustard

2 teaspoons honey

3 tablespoons chopped fresh dill

2 tablespoons thinly sliced fresh chives

2 tablespoons finely chopped fresh parsley

This is a simple potato side dish that goes with just about any protein. It's great served with the Roast Chicken with Red Wine Vinegar and Honey (page 160), the Pot Roast au Poivre with Charred Onions (page 168), or the Steak Night Dinner: Anchovy-Basted Rib Eye with Dilly Creamed Spinach (page 164). It's just an all-around good go-to potato recipe to have in your back pocket. Feel free to substitute any waxy baby potato of choice for the fingerlings. I love serving these right out of the same pot I make them in!

1. Place the potatoes in a large pot, cover with water, and bring to a boil over high heat. Generously salt the water, reduce the heat to medium to maintain a simmer, and cook until the potatoes are just cooked through and fork-tender, 12 to 15 minutes. (Maintaining a simmer instead of a rapid boil ensures even cooking.)

2. Drain the potatoes into a colander, and set aside.

3. Dry the pot, set over low heat, and add the butter to melt. Add both mustards and the honey, and stir until smooth.

4. Remove from the heat, and add the potatoes, dill, chives, and parsley. Gently toss to coat the potatoes.

5. Season with salt and pepper, and serve.

Chicken Fat Mashed Potatoes

Skin from 4 bone-in, skin-on chicken thighs (see Tip)

¼ cup (60 ml) water

Kosher salt and freshly cracked black pepper, to taste

3 pounds (1.3 kg) russet potatoes (about 4), scrubbed, peeled, and cut into 2-inch (5 cm) chunks

5 garlic cloves, peeled

¾ cup (180 ml) heavy cream

½ cup (120 ml) whole milk

¼ cup (57 g) unsalted butter, cubed

Thinly sliced fresh chives, to taste

Chicken fat and potatoes are a match made in culinary heaven—they're just meant to be together, simple as that. This is not your average, everyday mashed potato. These are rich and decadent, perfect for a holiday or special occasion. I call for chicken skin from chicken thighs here because I find them to be the easiest to render, but if you happen to have other random skins saved from another preparation, feel free to use them here. Of course, save the chicken thighs themselves for another recipe, like Chicken Broth (page 92) or Tina's Chicken Bake (page 208), which can also be made with skinless chicken thighs. If you have any leftover chicken fat, store it in an airtight container in the fridge for up to 2 weeks for future cooking!

1. Arrange the chicken skins in a single layer in a medium nonstick pan. (It's okay if the skins are crowded in the pan; they will shrink as they cook.) Add the water, set over medium-low heat, and cook, flipping occasionally, until the chicken skins are rendered and crispy and the water has evaporated, 30 to 35 minutes.

2. Transfer the skins to a wire rack or paper towel–lined plate, and season with salt. Let cool completely.

3. Strain the rendered chicken fat left in the pan through a fine-mesh strainer into a bowl, and set aside.

4. Preheat the oven to 325°F (165°C). Line a sheet tray with parchment paper.

5. Place the potatoes and garlic in a medium pot, cover with water, set over high heat, and bring to a boil. Generously salt the water, reduce the heat to medium, and simmer until the potatoes and garlic are very tender, 14 to 16 minutes.

6. Meanwhile, combine the cream, milk, and butter in a small saucepan over low heat to melt the butter and keep warm while you finish the potatoes.

7. When the potatoes and garlic are tender, drain them into a colander and then transfer them to the sheet tray. Hang onto the pot; you'll use it again later.

8. Bake the potatoes and garlic until they've dried out and the potatoes have a chalky white appearance on the outside, 6 to 8 minutes. This drying-out step makes for the fluffiest mash!

9. Return the potatoes and garlic to the pot they were boiled in. Mash the potatoes using a potato masher. Alternatively, for extra-smooth mash, spoon the potatoes and garlic from the sheet pan into a ricer, working in batches as needed, and press through the ricer into the pot.

10. Add the warm butter-cream mixture and 2 or 3 tablespoons of the reserved chicken fat (depending on your preference and how much fat you have), and mix well. Season with salt and pepper.

11. Break the reserved chicken skins into shards.

12. Serve the mash, topped with the crispy skins, chives, and more pepper.

TIP To remove the chicken skin from the thigh, simply tear the skin from the meat. It should come off relatively easily.

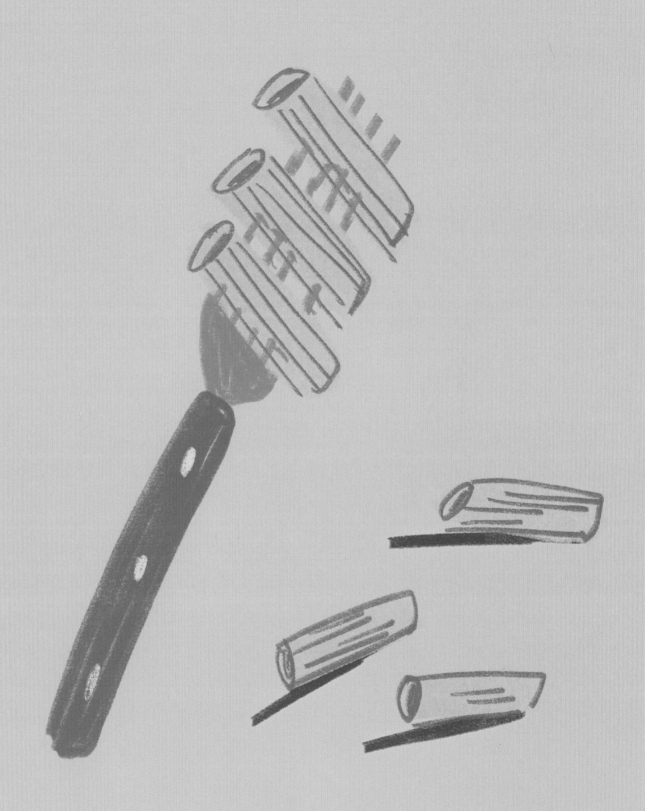

Seasonal Pastas

There's a pasta for every emotion, occasion, and season. It's never an inappropriate time for pasta! This chapter is a mash-up of seasonal pasta dishes (shout out farmers market finds!) and ones that are perfect year-round.

Goat Cheese Sfoglia Lorda
in Mushroom Broth

Sfoglia lorda, these little, rustic, ravioli-like pasta pillows, are fairly simple to put together as far as filled pasta shapes go. When I first made this broth, I planned to serve fresh tortellini with it, but this shape brings a similar vibe with a bit more ease. This pasta also creates very few scraps, so there's no rolling and rerolling of the dough, which I love. **Sfoglia lorda** *means "dirty pasta," referring to a couple things: One is the layer of cheese that is spread so thinly over the sheet of pasta that it just barely "dirties" it. The other refers to the broth it's served in, as the pasta is usually cooked directly in it, "dirtying" the broth with starch and the occasional pasta that pops open. I like to boil the pasta separately to keep the flavors of the broth and pasta separate. Be sure the goat cheese is very soft before making the cheese filling, or you will end up with a clumpy mess that will be hard to spread.*

SERVES 4 TO 6

Pasta Dough

100 grams (¾ cup) all-purpose flour

100 grams (½ cup plus 3 tablespoons) semolina flour, plus more for dusting

6 egg yolks

1 egg

Mushroom Broth

Olive oil, for searing

3 large shallots, halved

1 head garlic, halved

6 cups (1.4 L) chicken broth, homemade (page 92) or store-bought

9 dried porcini mushrooms (½ ounce/14 g)

3 dried shiitake mushrooms (0.2 ounces/5 g)

1 dried bay leaf

1 tablespoon black peppercorns

1 small bunch fresh thyme (tied with butcher's twine if you have it)

Kosher salt, to taste

Cheese Filling

4 ounces (113 g) mild chèvre, at room temperature

4 ounces (113 g) whole-milk ricotta

½ cup (55 g) grated pecorino Romano, plus more for serving

Kosher salt, to taste

Extra virgin olive oil, for serving

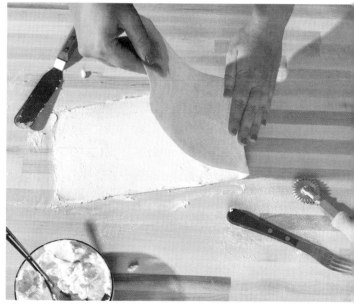

1. **Make the dough:** Add the all-purpose flour and semolina flour to a large bowl, and whisk to combine. Make a large well in the flour, and add the egg yolks and egg. Using a fork, whisk the eggs in the center of the well until beaten. Slowly beat small amounts of the flour into the eggs until the mixture becomes stiff enough to mix with your hands and then continue to mix with your hands until mostly combined.

2. Turn out the dough onto a clean work surface, and knead to form a cohesive ball of dough, 1 or 2 minutes. Wrap the dough in plastic wrap, and let it rest for at least 1 hour at room temperature. (The dough can be made a day ahead, wrapped in plastic wrap, and stored in the refrigerator.)

3. **Meanwhile, make the broth:** Heat a medium pot over medium heat. When hot, add a small bit of olive oil along with the shallots and garlic, cut side down, and sear until deeply golden and charred, 4 or 5 minutes.

4. Add the chicken broth, porcinis, shiitakes, bay leaf, peppercorns, and thyme, and bring to a boil. Reduce the heat to low, and simmer, uncovered, for 45 minutes. Strain the broth through a fine-mesh strainer and then return it to the pot. Season with salt to taste. Keep warm over very low heat. (The broth also can be made up to 2 days ahead, cooled, and stored in the refrigerator.)

5. **Meanwhile, make the cheese filling:** Add the chèvre to a medium bowl, and beat with a rubber spatula until smooth. Add the ricotta and pecorino Romano, and stir until combined. Season with salt.

6. Bring a large pot of water to a boil over high heat.

7. Lightly dust a clean work surface with semolina. Set up a pasta machine. Dust a large sheet tray with semolina and set aside.

8. Working with one quarter of the dough at a time, run the pasta through the pasta machine until it's a touch thinner than ⅟₁₆ inch (1.5 mm). This should be the second- or third-to-last setting on your pasta machine.

9. Fold the long sheet of pasta in half three times. Starting with the raw, rough end, run it through the pasta machine again until it's a touch thinner than ⅟₁₆ inch (1.5 mm).

10. Fold the sheet in half like a book to make a slight crease. This will indicate how far you should spread out the cheese mixture. Open up the sheet again.

11. Spread about 2 ounces (57 g) of the cheese mixture evenly over half of the sheet of pasta in a very thin layer, edge to edge. Fold the bare side of the pasta sheet over to cover the cheese. Gently press to adhere.

12. Using a fluted pasta cutter (see Tip), trim the top, the bottom, and the one unfolded edge to seal. Prick the pasta all over with a fork.

13. Cut the pasta into roughly 1½-inch (4 cm) squares. The squares don't have to be perfect! Use a bench scraper to carefully transfer the squares to the semolina-dusted sheet tray. Cover with a clean kitchen towel while you repeat steps 8 to 13 to form the remaining pasta.

14. Generously season the boiling water from step 6 with salt. Reduce the heat to medium-low to maintain a gentle, bare simmer. (Boiling water will cause this pasta to open!)

15. Carefully drop about a third of the pasta into the water, and simmer until the pasta floats and the dough is cooked, 2 or 3 minutes. Remove the pasta from the water with a slotted spoon, and place in a colander over a large bowl. Drizzle with olive oil, and toss very gently to coat. Repeat with the remaining pasta in two more batches.

16. Divide the pasta among serving bowls, and pour the hot mushroom broth over the pasta. Top with pecorino Romano and extra virgin olive oil, and serve.

TIP In a pinch, you can use a pizza wheel instead of a fluted pasta cutter to cut and seal the pasta, but it won't be as well sealed.

Stew-y Green Bean and Bacon Pasta

SERVES 4

Olive oil, for frying

4 ounces (113 g) thick-cut bacon, cut into lardons

8 ounces (227 g) green beans, trimmed and cut into 1-inch (2.5 cm) pieces

1 large shallot, thinly sliced

3 garlic cloves, thinly sliced

1 tablespoon tomato paste

½ cup (120 ml) dry white wine

8 ounces (227 g) cherry tomatoes, halved

Crushed red pepper flakes, to taste

Kosher salt and freshly cracked black pepper, to taste

8 ounces (227 g) dry casarecce pasta, or any short-cut pasta you'd like

⅓ cup (35 g) finely grated pecorino Romano

Extra virgin olive oil, for drizzling

Toasted panko breadcrumbs, to taste (see Tip)

Torn fresh basil leaves, to taste

Lemon zest, to taste

Admittedly, I often think of green beans as sort of a boring vegetable. Sure, they're good, but I wouldn't say they are the most inspiring green vegetable out there. That being said, there's one green bean dish that always sticks with me and is something I often crave. My grandma Tina would cook bacon until crispy, add some tomato sauce, and stew down the green beans in the beautiful saucy mixture. I wouldn't usually endorse an almost-mushy green bean, but here it not only works, it's essential. I take her classic dish, toss it with some pasta, and add a little bit of breadcrumbs on top for crunch. I like cutting the green beans about the same size as the casarecce pasta, so I get perfectly balanced bites.

1. Bring a large pot of water to a boil over high heat.

2. Add a small drizzle of olive oil to a large skillet, add the bacon, and cook over medium heat, stirring often, until rendered and crisp, 5 to 8 minutes. Transfer to a paper towel to drain.

3. Add the green beans and shallot to the skillet with the bacon drippings. Sauté until the shallots are translucent and the beans are starting to soften, 4 or 5 minutes.

4. Add the garlic, and cook for another 1 or 2 minutes. Stir in the tomato paste, and cook until browned, 1 minute more.

5. Stir in the white wine, and cook until reduced by half, scraping up all the brown bits from the bottom of the pan, 1 or 2 minutes.

6. Toss in the cherry tomatoes and red pepper flakes, and season with salt and black pepper. Reduce the heat to medium-low, and cook until the tomatoes burst and the green beans are very tender, 8 to 10 minutes.

7. Meanwhile, heavily salt the boiling water from step 1, and drop in the pasta. Cook according to the package directions until al dente.

8. Drain the pasta, reserving at least 2 mugsful of pasta water, and add the pasta to the skillet with the tomatoes and green beans. Toss in the reserved bacon. Add a splash of pasta water and the pecorino Romano, and toss to combine. Add more pasta water as needed to create a nice, saucy consistency. Season with more salt and black pepper.

9. Serve, topped with a drizzle of extra virgin olive oil and the breadcrumbs, basil, and lemon zest.

TIP To toast the panko breadcrumbs, heat 2 tablespoons unsalted butter in a medium sauté pan over medium heat. Melt the butter and add ½ cup (50 g) panko. Toast, stirring frequently, until deep golden brown, 3 to 5 minutes. Season with salt and pepper.

Mortadella "Nduja" Lumache
with Pistachios

SERVES 4 TO 6

"Nduja"

4 ounces (113 g) thinly sliced mortadella (with or without pistachio), roughly chopped

3 ounces (85 g) thinly sliced prosciutto, roughly chopped

3 tablespoons chopped jarred Calabrian chiles in oil

2 tablespoons olive oil

1 teaspoon red wine vinegar

1 teaspoon sweet smoked paprika

2 garlic cloves, smashed

Pasta

2 tablespoons unsalted butter

2 large shallots, minced

3 ounces (85 g) tomato paste

½ cup (120 ml) dry white wine

¾ cup (180 ml) heavy cream

Kosher salt and freshly cracked black pepper, to taste

1 pound (454 g) dry lumache

½ cup (55 g) finely grated pecorino Romano

⅓ cup (45 g) roasted salted pistachios, roughly chopped

Torn fresh basil leaves, to taste

Nduja is one of those ingredients that you can count on to make a dish taste special with minimal effort. It's a lovely, sausage-like mash of cured pork and Calabrian chiles that has a spreadable texture. Nduja's one setback is it tends to be difficult to find. In this recipe, I made my own quick spicy pork spread inspired by nduja, and although it's heavily nontraditional, it still captures the essence. The combination of mortadella and prosciutto makes for a fatty and luscious "nduja" that packs quite a punch in this pasta alla vodka–inspired sauce. Feel free to add another tablespoon of Calabrian chiles to the nduja if you like things really spicy. If you can't find lumache, any short tubular pasta shape, such as rigatoni, penne, or ziti, will work great here.

1. Bring a large pot of water to a boil over high heat.

2. **Meanwhile, make the "nduja":** Add the mortadella, prosciutto, chiles, olive oil, vinegar, paprika, and garlic to a food processor. Process until the mixture is paste-like, with no big chunks of meat remaining. Set aside.

3. **Make the pasta:** Melt the butter in another large pot over medium heat. Add the shallots, and cook until translucent, 2 or 3 minutes.

4. Add the "nduja," and cook, stirring occasionally, until the fat starts to separate out and the mixture browns slightly, 3 or 4 minutes.

5. Stir in the tomato paste, and cook, stirring, until darkened, 1 or 2 minutes. Pour in the wine, and cook, scraping up any brown bits from the bottom of the pan, 1 minute.

6. Reduce the heat to low, stir in the cream, and very gently simmer the sauce while the pasta boils.

7. Generously season the boiling water from step 1 with salt. Drop in the lumache, and cook according to the package directions until al dente.

8. Drain the pasta, reserving at least 2 mugsful of pasta water, and add it to the pot with the sauce. Reduce the heat to low. Add a splash of pasta water and the pecorino Romano, and toss to combine, adding more splashes of pasta water as needed, until the sauce coats the pasta nicely and everything is nice and saucy, 1 or 2 minutes.

9. Top with pistachios, torn basil, more pecorino Romano, and a bit of pepper, and serve.

Spinach and Artichoke Ziti

SERVES 4 TO 6

One 14-ounce (397 g) can quartered artichoke hearts, drained and patted dry

2 large shallots, halved

1 head garlic, top trimmed to expose the cloves

⅓ cup (80 ml) olive oil, plus more for drizzling

Kosher salt and freshly cracked black pepper, to taste

5 ounces (142 g) baby spinach

¼ cup (60 ml) cold water

1 pound (454 g) dry ziti

½ cup (55 g) finely grated pecorino Romano, plus more for serving

Extra virgin olive oil, for drizzling

Toasted panko breadcrumbs, to taste (see Tip on page 127)

Lemon zest, to taste

As I mentioned earlier, I hold dip culture very near and dear to my Midwestern heart. This pasta was inspired by the tried-and-true spinach and artichoke dip, but I didn't want it to feel just like boiled pasta tossed with a creamy dip. I set out to make something less cloying, with a sense of freshness, all while staying true to that classic taste. It wouldn't feel right if this cookbook didn't include a bright-green-sauced pasta, ya know?

1. Preheat the oven to 425°F (220°C).

2. Place the artichokes, shallots, and garlic in a small baking dish. Drizzle with a little olive oil, season with salt and pepper, and toss to coat. Arrange the garlic heads cut side down.

3. Roast for 35 to 45 minutes, tossing occasionally, until the artichokes are golden and the shallots and garlic are soft. Let cool enough to handle and then squeeze out the garlic from the bulb.

4. Bring a large pot of water to a boil over high heat. Prepare a large ice bath.

5. Add the spinach to the boiling water to blanch for 30 seconds. Immediately transfer the spinach with a slotted spoon to the ice bath to shock and cool. Squeeze out all the excess water from the spinach, and roughly chop. Set aside.

6. Reduce the heat to low, and keep the pot covered for boiling the pasta later.

7. Add the artichokes, shallots, garlic, ⅓ cup (80 ml) olive oil, and cold water to a blender. Blend (vented, in case the ingredients are very warm) on high until very smooth. Add the spinach, and blend again until very smooth and creamy. Season with salt and pepper.

8. Increase the heat under the pot of water to high, and bring back to a boil. Heavily season with salt. Add the ziti, and cook according to the package directions until al dente. Drain the pasta, reserving at least 2 mugsful of pasta water.

9. Return the pasta to the pot, and set over low heat. Add the artichoke sauce, a couple of splashes of pasta water, and the pecorino Romano, and toss to combine.

10. Add more splashes of pasta water as needed to thin the sauce so it coats the pasta evenly without being too thick. (You're looking for an elegantly coated pasta, not a gloppy one!) Season with more salt and pepper.

11. Serve, topped with a drizzle of extra virgin olive oil, more pecorino Romano, panko, and lemon zest.

Spicy Carrot Rigatoni

SERVES 4 TO 6

Pasta

1 pound (454 g) carrots (6 to 8 medium) with tops, peeled and cut into 1-inch (2.5 cm) pieces, green tops reserved (see Topping)

4 garlic cloves

½ cup (55 g) grated pecorino Romano, plus more for serving

½ cup (120 ml) olive oil

¼ cup (60 ml) water

1 tablespoon chopped jarred Calabrian chiles in oil

1 tablespoon pine nuts, toasted (see Tip 1 on page 49)

Kosher salt and freshly cracked black pepper, to taste

1 pound (454 g) dry rigatoni

Topping

¼ cup (20 g) finely chopped reserved carrot tops (see Pasta)

¼ cup (15 g) finely chopped fresh parsley

¼ cup (60 ml) olive oil

Zest of 1 lemon

Juice of ½ lemon

Kosher salt and freshly cracked black pepper, to taste

Ricotta cheese, for topping, optional

Classic spicy vodka rigatoni is such a glorious sight, beautifully orangey-red and glossy. That iconic look and luxurious texture sparked the idea for this dish. This pasta highlights the humble carrot by making it the star of the show and the base for a creamy, spicy, orange sauce. I like buying carrots with the tops attached for this to make a lovely herby topping to balance the richness of the pasta, but if you can't find them, this dish is still a stunner. Simply top with more pecorino Romano, black pepper, and olive oil to really lean into the vodka pasta vibe!

1. **Make the pasta:** Set up a steamer over medium heat, and bring the water to a low boil.

2. Add the carrots and garlic, cover, and cook until very tender, 12 to 15 minutes.

3. Transfer to a blender along with the pecorino Romano, olive oil, water, chiles, and pine nuts, and blend (vented, to account for the hot carrots) on high until very, very smooth and creamy. Season with salt and pepper. Set aside.

4. Bring a large pot of water to a boil over high heat.

5. **Meanwhile, make the topping:** Mix the carrot tops, parsley, olive oil, lemon zest, lemon juice, salt, and pepper in a small bowl. Set aside.

6. Heavily salt the boiling water from step 4, and drop in the rigatoni. Cook according to the package directions until al dente.

7. Drain the pasta, reserving at least 2 mugsful of pasta water. Return the pasta to the pot, and set over low heat.

8. Add the carrot sauce and a couple splashes of pasta water, and toss to combine. Add as much pasta water as needed to thin out the sauce so it coats the pasta evenly without being too thick. (You are looking for an elegantly coated pasta, not a gloppy one! I like a very saucy vibe here.) Season with more salt and pepper, if needed.

9. Serve the pasta, drizzled with the herby topping, a dollop of ricotta, if using, pepper, and more grated pecorino Romano.

Grated Tomato Linguine

SERVES 4 TO 6

3½ pounds (1.5 kg) beefsteak or heirloom tomatoes

¼ cup (60 ml) olive oil, plus more for serving

6 garlic cloves, minced

3 oil-packed anchovy fillets

Kosher salt and freshly cracked black pepper, to taste

1 pound (454 g) dry linguine

½ cup (55 g) finely grated pecorino Romano

1 cup (15 g) torn fresh basil leaves, plus more for serving

4 ounces (113 g) burrata, at room temperature, optional

Embarrassingly enough, there was a time in my life when I thought I hated fresh tomatoes. Wild, I know. It turns out, I'd just never had a good, ripe, in-season tomato. That being said, this pasta is designed to be made in the summertime when tomatoes are at their peak deliciousness. Basic tomatoes just won't do this justice! Grating the tomatoes is a really easy way to break them down into a pulpy sauce with minimal skin.

1. Grate the tomatoes on the large holes of a box grater into a large bowl, discarding the skin when you get down to the end.

2. Place the olive oil, garlic, and anchovies in a large pot. Set over medium heat, and cook, stirring, until the anchovies melt into the oil and the garlic is slightly golden, 2 or 3 minutes.

3. Add the grated tomatoes, and season with a small pinch of salt and a few grinds of pepper.

4. Reduce the heat to medium-low, and cook, uncovered and stirring occasionally, until the tomatoes cook down and the sauce thickens, 45 to 55 minutes. Season with a small pinch of salt and a few grinds of pepper.

5. When the tomato sauce is close to being finished, bring a large pot of water to a boil over high heat. Generously season with salt.

6. Drop in the linguine, and cook according to the package directions until it's about 1 minute under al dente. Drain the pasta, reserving 1 mugful of pasta water.

7. Add the pasta to the pot with the tomato sauce, toss to coat, and reduce the heat to low.

8. Add the pecorino Romano, and toss again. Add a small splash of pasta water if needed to create a nice cohesive sauce that coats the pasta evenly. (This pasta dish may not need any pasta water, depending on the water content of your tomatoes.) Drizzle in a bit more olive oil, and season with salt and pepper.

9. Turn off the heat, and toss in the basil to wilt slightly.

10. Divide the pasta among serving bowls. Top with more fresh basil, torn burrata, if using, a drizzle of olive oil, and pepper, and serve.

Lamb Stuffed Shells with Smoked Mozzarella

SERVES 6 TO 8

Lamb Ragu

1 small fennel bulb, cored and roughly chopped

1 medium yellow onion, roughly chopped

5 garlic cloves, smashed

Olive oil, for browning

1 pound (454 g) ground lamb (80/20)

Kosher salt and freshly cracked black pepper, to taste

1 tablespoon tomato paste

¼ teaspoon red pepper flakes, plus more to taste

2 dried bay leaves

½ cup (120 ml) dry red wine

One 24-ounce (680 g) jar passata

2 Parmesan rinds (if you have them)

1 small bunch fresh thyme, tied together with butcher's twine

Ricotta Filling

Two 15-ounce (425 g) containers whole-milk ricotta

¾ cup (83 g) freshly grated pecorino Romano

¼ cup (10 g) chopped fresh parsley

Kosher salt and freshly cracked black pepper, to taste

For Assembly

One 12-ounce (340 g) box jumbo shells

12 ounces (340 g) fresh smoked mozzarella, grated

¼ cup (28 g) freshly grated pecorino Romano

½ cup (14 g) fresh mint leaves, torn

½ cup (14 g) fresh parsley leaves

If there's one thing everyone in my family agrees on, it's that Aunt Renne makes the best stuffed shells. They are always expertly filled and topped with the perfect amount of sauce, making a seemingly heavy dish feel delicate and refined. My overwhelming love and appreciation for the dish is all thanks to her, so shout out Aunt Renne. Love ya! I adore using ground lamb in a ragu like this because it lends a very rich, slow-cooked depth of flavor with only about an hour of simmer time. Pair that with the smoked mozzarella and fresh mint, and you're in for the perfect pocket of pasta heaven. I don't add egg to my ricotta filling, as you might see in other recipes, because I feel the filling stays much creamier and more luscious after baking without it. When I originally developed this recipe, I topped this with some mint pesto using the Anything Pesto recipe (page 49), which was amazing but slightly more work. The torn fresh mint in its place here is equally as delightful, but if you are looking for more of a project, I can't recommend the pesto addition enough.

1. **Make the ragu:** Add the fennel, onion, and garlic to a food processor, and pulse to a fine paste.

2. Add a thin coating of olive oil to the bottom of a large pot, and set over medium heat. Add the lamb, in about 2-inch (5 cm) chunks, season with salt and black pepper, and cook, without disturbing or moving the meat, until browned on one side, 5 or 6 minutes. Continue to cook, fully breaking up the meat, until browned, 2 or 3 minutes more.

3. Add the vegetable mixture from the food processor, and season with salt and black pepper. Cook, stirring occasionally and scraping up the fond, until all the liquid in the vegetables cooks out and the mixture becomes dry, 10 to 15 minutes.

4. Add the tomato paste, and cook until slightly darkened in color, another 2 minutes. Stir in the red pepper flakes and bay leaves.

5. Deglaze with the red wine, and cook for 1 minute. (The wine won't really reduce here, but it will be absorbed by the tomato paste.)

6. Stir in the passata, and add the Parmesan rinds, if using, and thyme.

7. Bring the sauce to a simmer, reduce the heat to low, and cover. Cook for 1 hour. Uncover the sauce occasionally and stir to prevent scorching.

8. Remove and discard the bay leaves, thyme, and rinds, and season the sauce with salt and black pepper. Remove from the heat, and set aside while you prep the rest of the dish. (The sauce can be made up to 3 days ahead, cooled, and stored in an airtight container in the refrigerator.)

9. Bring a large pot of water to a boil over high heat.

10. **Meanwhile, make the filling:** Mix the ricotta, pecorino Romano, and parsley in a large bowl. Season with salt and black pepper.

11. Heavily season the boiling water from step 9 with salt. Drop in the jumbo shells, and cook until they just start to soften, about 8 minutes. They will finish cooking in the oven.

12. Drain the shells in a colander, and toss with a drizzle of olive oil to prevent stickage.

13. Preheat the oven to 400°F (200°C) with a rack positioned in the center. Grease a 9×13-inch (23×33 cm) baking dish with a bit of olive oil.

14. Add about one-third of the lamb ragu to cover the bottom of the baking dish.

15. Fill each shell with about 1 heaping tablespoon of the ricotta mixture (see Tip), placing the shells snugly, seam side up, side by side as you fill, overlapping as needed if you have too many for one layer.

16. Top the filled shells with the remaining lamb ragu, and sprinkle the mozzarella and pecorino Romano all over. Cover the dish tightly with foil.

17. Bake for 40 minutes. Remove the foil and broil on high until the cheese is golden brown and bubbly, 2 to 5 minutes.

TIP To fill the shells easily, transfer the ricotta mixture to a pastry bag or ziplock plastic bag with the corner trimmed off and pipe in the filling.

18. Add the mint and parsley to a small bowl. Drizzle with a small touch of olive oil, season with salt and black pepper, and toss to coat. Top the entire dish of shells with the herb mixture, and serve.

Creamy Corn Orzo

SERVES 4

3 tablespoons unsalted butter

2 large shallots, minced

2 garlic cloves, minced

2 ears fresh sweet corn, kernels removed (about 2 cups/365 g kernels)

Kosher salt and freshly cracked black pepper, to taste

8 ounces (227 g/1 cup) dry orzo

3 cups (720 ml) unsalted chicken broth, homemade (see page 92) or store-bought, at room temperature

3 ounces (85 g) mascarpone

⅓ cup (35 g) finely grated pecorino Romano, plus more for serving

Mild chile flakes or powder, to taste (see Note)

Extra virgin olive oil, for drizzling

Cooking orzo in the style of risotto makes for the creamiest texture that pairs so well with sweet corn. Everything is cooked together in one pot, so it also makes things super easy. This dish is like a mix between a creamed corn and a pasta. It's lovely served alongside grilled chicken, steak, or shrimp but is also great as a simple and comforting stand-alone summer meal, maybe with an easy tomato salad, like the Tomato and Anchovy Salad with Stracciatella (page 71). I could even see this being a great addition to a Thanksgiving spread! Feel free to swap in vegetable stock for the chicken broth to make this dish totally vegetarian.

1. Heat the butter in a large pot over medium-low heat until melted. Add the shallots and garlic, and cook until softened, 3 or 4 minutes.

2. Add the corn, and cook until it starts to soften, 2 or 3 minutes. Season lightly with salt and pepper.

3. Add the orzo, and stir to coat it in the butter. Add about 1 cup (240 ml) chicken broth, and cook, stirring frequently while scraping the bottom of the pan, until most of the liquid is absorbed, about 5 minutes.

4. Add another 1 cup (240 ml) broth, and continue to cook, stirring frequently while scraping the bottom, until most of the liquid is absorbed, about 5 minutes.

5. Repeat with the last 1 cup (240 ml) broth, and cook until the orzo is al dente, most of the broth has been absorbed, and the mixture has a loose, stew-y risotto texture, 15 to 20 minutes. Maintain a simmer (not a full boil) throughout this process so the pasta cooks gently and the liquid doesn't all cook off before the pasta is able to absorb it and cook through.

6. Reduce the heat to low, and stir in the mascarpone and pecorino Romano. Season with salt and pepper.

7. Garnish with more pecorino Romano, a pinch of chile flakes, and a drizzle of extra virgin olive oil, and serve.

NOTE I like using the Guntur Sannam Chilli from Diaspora Co. for my garnishing chile, but Aleppo or Espelette would also be great!

Pasta alla Norcina
with Roasted Squash

SERVES 4 TO 6

1 small butternut squash (about 24 ounces/680 g), peeled and cut into ½-inch (1 cm) cubes

Olive oil, for drizzling

Kosher salt and freshly cracked black pepper, to taste

1 pound (454 g) hot Italian sausage (4 or 5 links), casing removed if needed

3 garlic cloves, thinly sliced

2 large shallots, minced

¼ teaspoon freshly grated nutmeg, plus more for topping

¾ cup (180 ml) dry white wine

1 cup (240 ml) heavy cream

1 pound (454 g) dry mezze rigatoni

½ cup (55 g) freshly grated pecorino Romano, plus more for serving

This creamy pasta originates from the Umbria region of Italy and usually uses a sausage seasoned with nutmeg. This flavor profile feels very cozy and autumnal to me, so I love adding a bit of roasted squash to really drive home that vibe. I also like using spicy Italian sausage for the contrasting kick to the squash, but feel free to substitute with mild Italian sausage. I'm using butternut in this recipe, but any hearty squash, such as kabocha, red kuri, or acorn, would be great, too.

1. Preheat the oven to 425°F (220°C). Line a sheet tray with parchment paper.

2. Place the squash in a medium bowl. Drizzle liberally with olive oil, season with salt and pepper, and toss to coat. Spread out on the sheet tray.

3. Roast the squash, tossing halfway through the cooking time, until tender and caramelized but not mushy, 30 to 35 minutes.

4. Bring a large pot of water to a boil over high heat.

5. Meanwhile, heat another large pot over medium-high heat. Coat the bottom of the pan with a thin layer of olive oil. Add the sausage, and cook, breaking up the meat into bite-size chunks, until browned, 6 to 8 minutes. (The sausage won't be fully cooked.)

6. Reduce the heat to medium, and add the garlic, shallots, and nutmeg. Cook, stirring occasionally, until the shallots are translucent and the garlic is soft, 3 or 4 minutes.

7. Deglaze the pan with the wine, and scrape up any brown bits from the bottom of the pan. Cook until the wine is reduced by half, 1 or 2 minutes.

8. Add the cream, bring to a simmer, and reduce the heat to very low to keep the sauce warm while the pasta cooks, about 10 minutes.

9. Generously salt the boiling water from step 4, and drop in the mezze rigatoni. Cook according to the package directions until al dente. Drain the pasta, reserving at least 2 mugsful of pasta water, and add it to the pot with the sausage.

10. Add a splash of pasta water and pecorino Romano to the pot, and toss to combine. Cook, adding splashes of pasta water as needed, until the sauce coats the pasta nicely, 1 or 2 minutes.

11. Turn off the heat, and gently stir in the squash. Season with salt and pepper.

12. Serve, topped with more pecorino Romano and a small grating of fresh nutmeg.

Ditalini and Peas in Parmesan Broth

SERVES 4 TO 6

Parmesan Broth

4 ounces (113 g) bacon (about 3 thick slices), chopped

1 medium fennel bulb, roughly chopped (fronds and all)

1 large yellow onion, roughly chopped

5 garlic cloves, smashed

6 cups (1.4 L) unsalted chicken or vegetable broth, homemade (see pages 92 and 93) or store-bought

12 ounces (about 2 cups/340 g) Parmesan rinds

½ bunch (1½ ounces/43 g) fresh parsley

1 tablespoon black peppercorns

2 dried bay leaves

2 dried shiitake mushrooms

¾ cup (80 g) finely grated Parmesan, plus more for serving

Ditalini and Peas

8 ounces (227 g) dry ditalini

8 ounces (227 g) fresh or frozen peas

Extra virgin olive oil, for coating the pasta and peas and to garnish

Zest of 1 lemon

Kosher salt and freshly cracked black pepper, to taste

NOTE Parmesan rinds tend to stick to the bottom of the pan, so stirring the broth every now and then helps mitigate this. Whatever you use to stir the broth will inevitably get some Parmesan stuck to it, which can be a little tricky to clean, but trust me, the broth is very much worth it!

Pasta and peas was one of the staple meals my mom made for us growing up. We probably had it at least once a week. She learned the recipe from my grandma Tina, and it was a simple, inexpensive dish to throw together—just pasta and frozen peas cooked with a bit of chicken broth and aromatics topped with grated Parm. It's such a nostalgic, cozy meal from my childhood, and I often find myself making different versions of it. This one is all about the broth: A creamy, rich, Parmesan-fortified chicken broth brings together all the same flavors in a homey elegance. This recipe calls for a hefty number of Parmesan rinds, which many stores now carry on their own, but you can also just save your own rinds in the freezer. I love adding a runny egg on top for a complete meal with a bit more richness. If you have any extra broth left over, it will separate in the fridge, but if you heat it gently on the stove, it will come right back together. You can even blend it again if you feel like it!

1. **Make the broth:** Place the bacon in a large pot, set over medium heat, and cook, stirring occasionally, until the bacon starts to render and brown, 5 or 6 minutes.

2. Add the fennel, onion, and garlic, and cook, stirring occasionally, until the vegetables start to brown and soften, 5 to 7 minutes.

3. Add the broth, Parmesan rinds, parsley, peppercorns, bay leaves, and mushrooms. Bring to a boil and then reduce the heat to low. Simmer, uncovered and stirring occasionally (see Note), for 1 hour. Be sure to maintain a bare simmer through the cooking so you don't boil away your lovely broth!

4. After the broth has simmered for 1 hour, bring another large pot of water to a boil over high heat.

5. Strain the broth through a fine-mesh strainer into a large bowl. Transfer about one-third of the broth to a blender. Add the grated Parmesan, and carefully (the mixture will be hot), with the blender vented, blend on low until the Parmesan is emulsified into the broth.

6. Stir the blended broth into the rest of the broth, and keep warm, stirring often to keep it emulsified, while you boil the pasta.

7. **Make the ditalini and peas:** Generously salt the boiling water from step 4, and drop in the ditalini. When the pasta is about 4 minutes from being al dente, drop in the fresh peas and cook until both the pasta and peas are cooked. If you're using frozen peas, drop them in just 1 minute shy of the pasta being done.

8. Strain the pasta and peas, and return them to the pot. Toss with olive oil to coat and then stir in the lemon zest and season with salt.

9. Divide the pasta and peas among serving bowls. Top with the hot Parmesan broth, a drizzle of extra virgin olive oil, pepper, and more grated Parmesan, and serve.

Seafood
From the Lake to the Shore

Although I now live on the shore of New Jersey, I'll always be a Midwesterner at heart. In this chapter, I've included a brief homage to the lake culture that I grew up with while also showcasing the fresh seafood I have come to love so dearly while living on the East Coast.

Pan-Seared Branzino
with Anchovy and Herbs

SERVES 2

Frisée and Branzino

1 medium head frisée (about 12 ounces/340 g), core removed and leaves separated

2 skin-on branzino fillets (about 5 ounces/142 g each), pin bones and scales removed (see Tip)

Kosher salt and freshly cracked black pepper, to taste

Canola oil, for frying

All-purpose flour, for dusting

Anchovy-Herb Sauce

½ cup (120 ml) olive oil

¼ cup (15 g) finely chopped fresh dill fronds

¼ cup (15 g) finely chopped fresh parsley

3 tablespoons red wine vinegar

6 oil-packed anchovy fillets, minced

3 scallions, thinly sliced

1 garlic clove, finely grated

Freshly cracked black pepper, to taste

Pairing salty, punchy anchovies with a delicate fish like branzino may sound kinda contradictory, but stick with me. The addition of a bunch of fresh herbs and vinegar brings the two together beautifully. The anchovy-herb sauce is spooned over the crispy fish and served with bitter frisée to make a lovely light meal. If you are looking for something heartier, the dish pairs perfectly with some steamed white rice to pick up even more of that vibrant sauce. If you're having trouble finding frisée, any sort of bitter green works here. Escarole, Belgian endive leaves, or even radicchio would be nice swaps. Really any lettuce would be lovely.

1. **Prepare the frisée:** Place the frisée in a large ice bath for a few minutes to crisp. Remove from the ice bath and dry in a salad spinner, or lay out on a kitchen towel to dry completely.

2. **Make the sauce:** Whisk the olive oil, dill, parsley, vinegar, anchovies, scallions, garlic, and pepper in a medium bowl until combined.

3. **Make the branzino:** Using a very sharp knife, score just the skin of each branzino fillet (being very careful not to cut into the flesh) with two or three diagonal slashes down the length of the fillet. This helps prevent the fish from curling while cooking.

4. Season the fillets with salt and pepper, and set aside.

5. Heat about ¼ inch (6 mm) of canola oil in a 12-inch (30 cm) stainless-steel pan over medium heat. To test if the oil is hot enough, add a small pinch of flour to see if it sizzles.

6. Working with one fillet at a time, dust the fish in flour until fully coated, shaking off any excess. Carefully place the fillet in the pan, skin-side down, and immediately press down on the fish gently with a fish spatula to prevent curling. When you feel the fish relax and flatten out, you can release the gentle press.

7. Fry until the fish is golden and crispy and releases itself from the pan, 3 or 4 minutes. If you feel like the fish is sticking to the pan while you're frying, don't panic; just leave it undisturbed to cook. It will release itself from the pan when it's ready.

8. Carefully flip the fish (away from your body), and cook the second side until golden, 2 or 3 minutes. Transfer the fish to a sheet pan lined with a wire rack.

9. Fry the second fillet. You shouldn't need to add more oil, but if bits of flour in the pan look black or smell burnt, pour out the oil into a heatproof bowl and add fresh oil to the pan. Either way, after cooking, let the used oil cool and then discard it.

10. Serve the crispy fish, skin side up, with the frisée on the side, and top everything with the anchovy sauce right before serving. Serve any remaining sauce on the side for extra topping.

TIP Don't be shy about asking your fishmonger to remove the pin bones and scales for you!

Halibut Fines Herbes

SERVES 4

Four 5-ounce (142 g) skinless halibut fillets (about 1 inch/ 2.5 cm thick)

Kosher salt and freshly cracked black pepper, to taste

3 tablespoons unsalted butter

1 large shallot, minced

3 garlic cloves, minced

½ cup (120 ml) dry white wine

½ cup (120 ml) heavy cream

1 tablespoon thinly sliced fresh chives

1 tablespoon finely chopped fresh parsley

1 tablespoon finely chopped fresh tarragon

Extra virgin olive oil, for drizzling

1 lemon, cut into wedges for serving

I never would have seen myself shallow-poaching fish outside of culinary school. It was one of those dishes that was on every practical exam, but I was never a fan. It just seemed fussy for no reason. This recipe is much simpler than the classic shallow-poached fish we learned in school but uses the basic technique of gently cooking fish in a small amount of liquid and then building on that liquid to make a delicious sauce. The fish comes out incredibly moist and renders a flavorful base for another culinary school classic: fines herbes sauce. Fines herbes is usually a mix of finely chopped chives, parsley, tarragon, and chervil, but I skip the chervil because it tends to be hard to find and tarragon lends a similar flavor anyway. If you happen to stumble upon some, though, feel free to add it! This dish has made me a shallow-poach convert. I love eating it with some steamed white rice to sop up the yummy sauce and complete the meal. Or maybe even with a bit of Belgian endive lightly dressed in lemon juice and olive oil. Yum!

1. Place the halibut on a plate, and season all over with salt and pepper.

2. Melt the butter in a large sauté pan over medium-low heat. Add the shallot and garlic, season with salt, and cook until softened, 3 or 4 minutes.

3. Add the wine and fish. Bring to a simmer, cover the pan, and cook until the fish is cooked through, 7 to 9 minutes. The fish will be opaque and should easily flake with a fork. Carefully transfer the fish to a serving platter.

4. Add the cream to the pan, and simmer until slightly thickened, 4 or 5 minutes. The sauce should just lightly coat the back of a spoon.

5. Turn off the heat, and stir in the chives, parsley, and tarragon. Season with salt and pepper.

6. Spoon the sauce over the top of the fish, drizzle with olive oil, and serve with the lemon wedges on the side.

Slow-Roasted Salmon
with Vermouth-Fennel Soubise

SERVES 4

Salmon

1½ teaspoons kosher salt

1 teaspoon packed dark brown sugar

½ teaspoon fennel seeds, crushed in a mortar and pestle or spice grinder

½ teaspoon freshly cracked black pepper

One 1½-pound (680 g) center-cut salmon fillet, pin bones and skin removed (see Note)

1 lemon, thinly sliced and seeds removed

¼ cup (60 ml) olive oil

Vermouth-Fennel Soubise

2 tablespoons unsalted butter

1 large yellow onion, thinly sliced

½ large fennel bulb, cored and thinly sliced (fronds reserved)

⅓ cup (80 ml) dry vermouth

Kosher salt, to taste

⅓ cup (80 ml) heavy cream

For Serving

½ large fennel bulb, cored and thinly sliced on a mandoline

1 lemon

Kosher salt, to taste

Soubise is a velvety French sauce made of pureed, slowly cooked buttery onions. As a self-proclaimed allium lover, I think this sauce is a dream. (I dream of one day writing an allium-only cookbook!) Its delicate flavor pairs so well with fish, especially this variation that includes a touch of vermouth and fennel for their distinct herbaceousness. The salmon itself is seasoned with a salt-sugar rub, which almost gives it a quick cure before slow roasting. This recipe is best made with a thick, center-cut portion of salmon rather than a thin, tail-end piece. Just ask your fishmonger, and they will get you what you need! They will also likely remove the skin and pin bones if you ask kindly. I like this salmon cooked to medium doneness, but feel free to adjust the cook time to your preference. A light salad and some sourdough or the Sourdough Discard Flatbread (page 223) make great serving options.

1. **Prepare the salmon:** Mix the salt, brown sugar, fennel seeds, and pepper in a small bowl.

2. Place the salmon on a small sheet tray, season all over (top and bottom) with the spice rub, and then place in the refrigerator while you make the sauce.

3. **Make the soubise:** Melt the butter in a small saucepan over medium heat. Add the onion, fennel, and vermouth, and season with salt. Reduce the heat to medium-low, cover, and cook, uncovering to stir every now and then, until the onions and fennel are very soft but not brown and the pan is nearly dry, 40 to 45 minutes. Reduce the heat if needed to prevent any browning.

4. Preheat the oven to 275°F (135°C) with a rack positioned in the center.

5. Transfer the onion mixture to a blender along with the cream. Carefully (the mixture will be hot), with the blender vented, blend until very smooth.

6. Lay the lemon slices on the bottom of a small (at least 1-quart/1 L) baking dish. Place the salmon on top of the lemon slices, and drizzle with the olive oil.

7. Bake the salmon for 35 to 45 minutes, until the thickest part reads 125°F to 130°F (52°C to 54°C) on an instant-read thermometer for medium doneness. The cook time will heavily depend on the thickness of your salmon, so keep an eye on it.

8. When the salmon is just about done, toss the fennel in a small bowl with the juice of half of the lemon and some salt to taste. Cut the remaining half of the lemon into wedges to serve on the side. I like to do this just a few minutes before the salmon is done so the fennel stays nice and crisp.

9. To serve, add as much soubise as you like to the bottom of a platter. Gently break the salmon into about four large pieces, and place on top. Top with the dressed fennel, some reserved fronds, and the lemon wedges alongside, and serve.

NOTE You also can use smaller, center-cut fillets of salmon that equal 1½ pounds (680 g).

Midwestern Fish Fry

SERVES 4

Tartar Sauce

¼ cup (7 g) loosely packed fresh dill, roughly chopped

¼ cup (7 g) loosely packed fresh parsley leaves, roughly chopped

1 egg

1 garlic clove, smashed

Zest and juice of ½ lemon

1 cup (240 ml) canola oil

3 tablespoons finely chopped cornichons

1 tablespoon capers, drained and roughly chopped

1 tablespoon whole-grain mustard

Kosher salt and freshly cracked black pepper, to taste

Slaw

4 heaping cups (260 g) thinly sliced (on a mandoline) red cabbage (about ½ medium head)

1 bunch red radishes (about 8), greens removed and thinly sliced on a mandoline

½ small red onion, thinly sliced and rinsed (see Tip 1 on page 80)

2 tablespoons red wine vinegar

1 tablespoon honey

½ teaspoon caraway seeds

Kosher salt and freshly cracked black pepper, to taste

Fish

Canola oil, for frying

¾ cup (100 g) plus ½ cup (65 g) all-purpose flour

½ cup (65 g) medium rye flour

½ teaspoon baking powder

One 12-ounce (335 ml) can lager-style beer, cold

Four 4- or 5-ounce (113 to 142 g) cod fillets, pin bones and skin removed (thinner cod fillets are best for this)

continued >>

I grew up visiting Wisconsin in the summertime with my family, and whether it was Door County or Hayward, we always made our way to a fish fry. It was what I looked forward to most about those trips (along with all the ice cream and cheese, of course). There was always coleslaw, tartar sauce, a potato of sorts, bread and butter, and of course, beer-battered fried lake fish. The bread served was often seeded rye, which is the inspiration for adding some caraway seeds to this slaw and the rye flour to the batter. The rye flour also promotes a nicely golden crust. I call for cod in this recipe because it is more readily available than the typical walleye or perch of the Midwest, but you can definitely sub those in if you can find them! Serve this with a good ol' baked potato or your favorite fries for the complete Midwestern experience.

1. **Make the sauce:** Place the dill, parsley, egg, garlic, lemon zest, and lemon juice in a high-sided container (like a jar or quart/1 L container). Use an immersion blender to blend until smooth (see Note). There will still be bits of herbs.

2. With the blender running, slowly stream in the canola oil to create a smooth emulsion. Stir in the cornichons, capers, and mustard, and season with salt and pepper.

3. **Make the slaw:** Place the cabbage, radishes, onion, vinegar, honey, and caraway seeds in a large bowl, and toss to combine. Season with salt and pepper. Place in the refrigerator while you prepare the fish.

4. **Make the fish:** Add 2 inches (5 cm) of canola oil to a large pot, and attach a candy thermometer to the side. Heat the oil over medium-high heat until the temperature reaches 365°F (185°C).

5. While the oil heats, prepare the batter. Add ¾ cup (100 g) all-purpose flour, the rye flour, and the baking powder to a large bowl, and whisk in the beer until combined. (A few lumps are okay!) Place in the refrigerator until you're ready to batter the fish.

6. Place the remaining ½ cup (65 g) of all-purpose flour in a shallow dish.

7. When the oil is hot, pat all the cod fillets completely dry with a paper towel, and season both sides with salt and pepper.

8. Working with one fillet at a time, dredge the fish in the flour and shake off any excess. Dip the fillet into the batter, and fully coat on all sides. Shake to remove any excess batter. Carefully add the fish to the hot oil using your hands, holding onto the fillet and letting it "swim" for a few seconds before dropping it fully into the oil. (This prevents the fish from sticking to the bottom of the pot.) Repeat with a second fillet. Return the batter to the refrigerator until you need it for the next batch.

9. Fry until golden and crispy on both sides, flipping halfway through, 5 or 6 minutes. Adjust the heat as needed to maintain the oil temperature (365°F/185°C).

Kosher salt and freshly
  cracked black pepper,
  to taste

Flake salt, for finishing

Lemon wedges, to taste

10. Using a spider or fish spatula, transfer the fish from
    the oil to a wire rack or paper towel–lined plate, and
    sprinkle lightly with flake salt.

11. Repeat steps 7 through 10 with the remaining fillets.

12. Serve, with the tartar sauce, slaw, and lemon wedges
    on the side.

NOTE The tartar sauce can
also be made in a food
processor or blender. Transfer
to a small bowl before stirring
in the cornichons, capers, and
mustard.

Clam Boil Toast

SERVES 4

5 dozen littleneck clams

¼ cup (40 g) kosher salt, for cleaning the clams, plus more as needed

¼ cup (40 g) cornmeal, plus more as needed

Olive oil, for toasting and browning

4 thick slices sourdough bread (see page 218)

8 ounces (227 g) smoked andouille sausage (2 or 3 links), thinly sliced

2 celery stalks, thinly sliced on a bias (celery leaves reserved)

2 large shallots, thinly sliced

5 garlic cloves, thinly sliced

Freshly cracked black pepper, to taste

2 teaspoons chopped jarred Calabrian chiles in oil

2 teaspoons Old Bay Seasoning

One 12-ounce (335 ml) can lager-style beer

4 tablespoons unsalted butter

1 lemon

3 scallions, thinly sliced

½ cup (20 g) chopped fresh parsley

Vinegary hot sauce, to taste (I love Crystal for this)

Although Lake Michigan might look like a small ocean at first glance, we didn't have access to much fresh seafood growing up in the Chicago suburbs. I probably had clams only a handful of times on family vacations, and I didn't think too much of them. But after years of living on the East Coast, my admiration for them has grown greatly. They are so simple to cook and just an all-around fun and tasty food to share with friends. I love nothing more than crushing a large bowl of clams with a big group of people. These clam toasts are inspired by the classic flavors of a clam boil, served up on a big hunk of sourdough bread to absorb all the goodness. Eat the clams with your hands, use a fork and knife to cut the bread, slurp up the broth with a spoon—it's an interactive eating experience! This is a perfect use for any day-old sourdough bread you may have lying around.

1. Place the clams in a large bowl. Rinse and scrub off any visible dirt or grit. Cover with cold water, and add ¼ cup (40 g) salt and ¼ cup (40 g) cornmeal. Let sit for 30 minutes to purge the clams of their sand. Lift the clams out of the water and transfer to a colander. (If there is still sand remaining in the water, change out the water and repeat the purging-and-soaking process until no sand remains.) Rinse off any remaining cornmeal, and discard any cracked or chipped clams along with any open ones that don't close with a gentle nudge.

2. While the clams soak, make the toast. Coat the bottom of a large skillet with olive oil, and set over medium heat. Add the bread, 2 slices at a time, and toast on both sides, 2 or 3 minutes per side. Transfer to a small sheet tray or plate, and set aside. Repeat with the remaining slices of bread, adding more oil as needed to toast.

3. To cook the clams, coat the bottom of a large pot with a thin layer of olive oil, and heat over medium heat. Add the sausage and cook, stirring occasionally, until brown and rendered, 3 to 5 minutes.

4. Add the celery, shallots, and garlic, and season with salt and pepper. Cook until slightly softened, 2 or 3 minutes. Stir in the chiles and Old Bay. Add the beer, and stir, scraping up any bits from the bottom of the pot, 1 minute.

5. Add half of the clams, increase the heat to medium-high, and bring to a boil. Cover, reduce the heat to medium-low, and steam the clams until they open, 6 or 7 minutes. Discard any clams that do not open. Transfer the clams to a large bowl using a slotted spoon. Add the remaining clams to the same cooking liquid, and repeat the steaming process. Transfer the clams to the large bowl with the first batch.

6. Reduce the heat to low, add the butter to the brothy mixture, and melt. Turn off the heat, and stir in the juice of half a lemon (cut the remaining half into wedges for serving) and the scallions and parsley. Season with salt if desired and pepper to taste.

7. Return the clams to the hot broth, and gently stir.

8. Place each slice of toast in an individual shallow serving bowl, and top with some clams and broth. Garnish with a few splashes of hot sauce, some reserved celery leaves, and a lemon wedge on the side, and serve immediately.

Salmon Tartare
with Potato Chips

SERVES 6 TO 8

Tartare

8 ounces (227 g) sashimi-grade salmon

1 finger chile, minced

1 small Meyer lemon, seeded and minced (see Tip)

1 small shallot, minced

3 tablespoons thinly sliced fresh chives

1 tablespoon capers, drained and chopped

1 tablespoon extra virgin olive oil

½ teaspoon fish sauce

Kosher salt and freshly cracked black pepper, to taste

Potato Chips

2 large russet potatoes (about 10 ounces/283 g each), skin on, scrubbed clean, and sliced paper-thin on a mandoline

1 tablespoon white vinegar

Canola oil, for frying

Kosher salt, to taste

I love a good tartare, and the best ones are always the simplest. In this salmon tartare, the dressing is essentially created by dicing up an entire Meyer lemon, rind and all. If you can't source a Meyer lemon, a conventional lemon will work, but there really is something so special about the Meyer in this! Because the tartare itself is such a simple recipe, I thought this would be a fun place for a potato chip tutorial as well, but feel free to buy some kettle chips from the store in a pinch. This is a perfect, easy, and elegant appetizer for a dinner party or holiday meal. If you plan on leaving the tartare out for an extended period of time, serve it over a bowl of ice so it stays nice and chilled. I also think it looks quite cute served that way!

1. Dice the salmon very small, and add to a medium bowl. Place in the refrigerator to chill until you are ready to mix the tartare.

2. **Make the potato chips:** Place the potato slices in a large pot, and rinse under cold water until the water runs clear, three or four times.

3. Fill the pot with cold water to cover the potatoes by about 1 inch (2.5 cm), and add the vinegar.

4. Set the pot over high heat, bring to a boil, and then immediately strain. Divide the potatoes between two large, paper towel–lined sheet trays, spread out evenly, and pat completely dry. Wipe out the pot until it is completely dry.

5. Heat 1½ inches (4 cm) canola oil in the pot over medium heat to 350°F (180°C).

6. Carefully lower the chips, in three batches, into the hot oil using a slotted spoon or spider. Fry the chips, adjusting the heat as needed to maintain 350°F (180°C), until lightly golden and crispy, 3 or 4 minutes. (You can tell the chips are done when the sizzling from the potatoes drastically decreases.) Use a slotted spoon or a spider to transfer the chips from the hot oil to a paper towel–lined sheet tray, and immediately sprinkle with salt.

7. **Make the tartare:** Combine the chile, lemon, shallot, chives, capers, olive oil, and fish sauce in a medium bowl. Add the chilled salmon, and gently toss. Season with salt and pepper.

8. Serve immediately alongside the potato chips.

TIP Be sure to remove any seeds and use all the juices that accumulate from mincing when prepping the tartare.

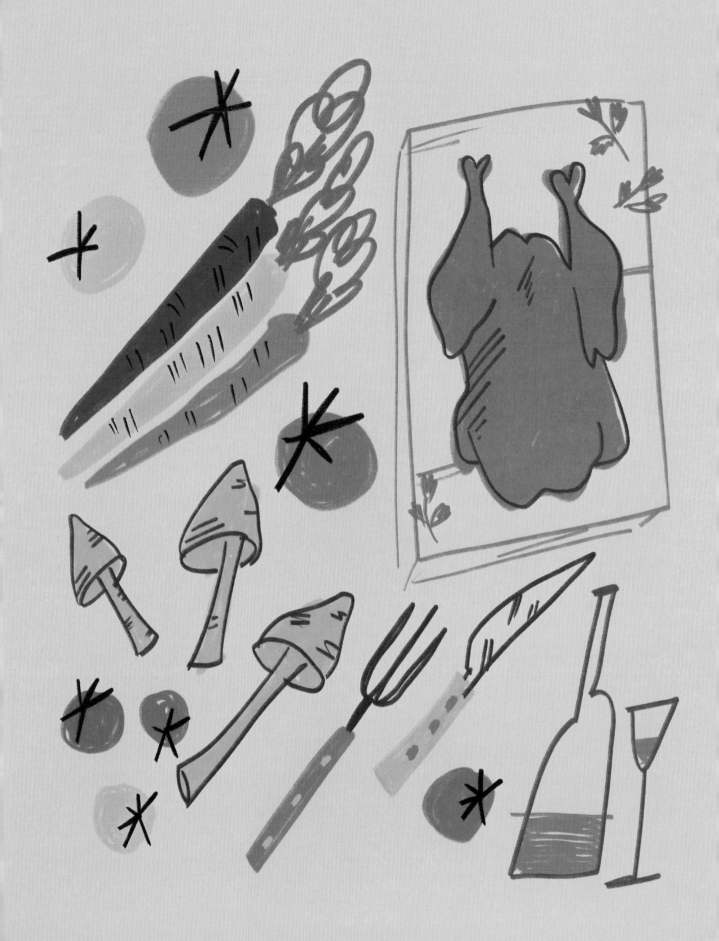

A Few Meat Dishes

While I do enjoy meat, it's not usually at the forefront of my creative process when it comes to recipe development. I tend to sprinkle it in around whatever seasonal produce I want to showcase. But in this chapter, meat is the main event. Here, we have a few staple dishes that I truly love and that are all about the protein.

Roast Chicken
with Red Wine Vinegar and Honey

SERVES 4

One 4-pound (1.8 kg)
  whole chicken

1 tablespoon black
  peppercorns

2 teaspoons fennel seeds

1 tablespoon porcini
  mushroom powder (see
  Tip on page 66)

4 teaspoons kosher salt,
  plus more to taste

2 teaspoons dried oregano

1 teaspoon sweet smoked
  paprika

Olive oil, for searing

5 large shallots (about
  1 pound/454 g), peeled
  and halved

3 tablespoons unsalted
  butter

5 garlic cloves, thinly sliced

3 tablespoons red wine
  vinegar

2 tablespoons honey

Torn fresh parsley leaves,
  to taste

Everyone should have a simple roast chicken recipe in their back pocket, one you can feel just as confident making during the week as you would for a dinner party. I love how a roast chicken can feel equally as homey and casual as it can feel elegant and special. Spatchcocking and seasoning the chicken a day ahead makes for a super-moist, well-seasoned, and evenly cooked bird. If you don't remember to prep the chicken a day ahead, no sweat; it will still be quite delicious made the day of. This recipe uses mostly pantry ingredients, so after making it once, you'll have almost everything on hand to make it over and over again. Serve this with some steamed white rice or some fresh crusty bread and the Little Gem Salad with Garlicky White Bean Spread (page 83), and you're in for a stunning meal.

1. The day before you plan to roast it, prep and season the chicken. To spatchcock the chicken, position it on a cutting board, breast side down. Pat the chicken dry, and be sure the cavity is empty. Using kitchen shears, cut along each side of the backbone to remove it. (Freeze the backbone for the next time you make broth!) Flip over the chicken, and firmly press down between the two breasts to break the breastplate and fully flatten the chicken. Place the chicken on a sheet pan lined with a wire rack.

2. Add the peppercorns and fennel seeds to a mortar, and use a pestle to grind them to a coarse powder. (Or use a spice grinder.) Transfer to a small bowl, and mix in the mushroom powder, salt, oregano, and paprika. Reserve 2 tablespoons of the spice mix for finishing the sauce later on.

3. Season the chicken all over with the remaining spice rub. Place in the refrigerator, uncovered, overnight for at least 8 hours or up to 24.

4. The next day, when you're ready to roast, preheat the oven to 400°F (200°C) with a rack positioned in the center. While the oven preheats, remove the chicken from the refrigerator to temper.

5. Heat a 12-inch (30 cm) cast-iron pan over medium heat, and coat the bottom with olive oil. Add the chicken, skin side down, and place another heavy pan on top to press. Sear, without disturbing the chicken, until the skin is golden brown, 7 to 10 minutes.

6. Remove the second pan, and carefully flip over the chicken. Sear for another 2 minutes, this time without the second pan on top. Transfer the chicken, breast side up, to a sheet tray or large plate.

7. Add the shallots, cut side down, to the pan, and sear until deeply charred, 5 or 6 minutes. Leave the shallots cut side down, and place the chicken, breast side up, on top of the shallots.

8. Transfer the pan to the oven, and roast for 40 to 50 minutes, until the internal temperature of the thickest part of the breast is 160°F (71°C) and the thighs are at least 180°F (82°C). The internal temperature will increase as the chicken rests.

9. Transfer the chicken to a cutting board, and let it rest for at least 15 minutes or up to 45 minutes. Remove the shallots to a serving platter.

10. Meanwhile, return the pan to medium heat, and add the butter to melt. Add the reserved spice mix and the garlic, and cook, stirring, until the garlic has softened and the spices have toasted and browned, 3 or 4 minutes.

11. Turn off the heat, and stir in the vinegar and honey. Fear not, this is meant to be a broken sauce! Season with salt.

12. To cut the chicken, remove the leg quarters and then cut between the thighs and legs to separate. Cut through the breastbone to separate the two breasts and then cut each breast in half horizontally. (I like to keep the wing attached to the breast.)

13. Pile all the chicken on the platter with the shallots, and spoon the warm sauce over the top (reheating it if needed before spooning). Garnish with a lot of torn fresh parsley leaves, and serve.

Chicken Milanese
with Shaved Celery and Mushroom Salad

SERVES 4

Salad

8 ounces (227 g) cremini mushrooms, very thinly sliced on a mandoline

2 celery stalks, thinly sliced on a bias on a mandoline (some tender inner leaves reserved)

¼ small red onion, thinly sliced on a mandoline and rinsed (see Tip 1 on page 80)

1 ounce (28 g) shaved pecorino Romano

¼ cup (10 g) chopped fresh parsley

Zest of 1 lemon

Juice of ½ lemon

2 tablespoons extra virgin olive oil

Kosher salt and freshly cracked black pepper, to taste

Chicken

2 boneless, skinless chicken breasts (8 to 10 ounces/227 to 283 g each), halved horizontally (see Tip)

Kosher salt and freshly cracked black pepper, to taste

⅔ cup (87 g) all-purpose flour

2 eggs, beaten

1 cup (90 g) panko breadcrumbs

¾ cup (83 g) finely grated pecorino Romano

Olive oil, for pan-frying

TIP Using a sharp knife, cut the chicken in half horizontally by carefully dragging the knife through the meat in long strokes. Repeat that motion until the chicken is fully cut in half. If this seems too tricky, you can look for "thinly sliced chicken breasts" (also sometimes labeled cutlets) at the grocery store and pound them as directed in step 2 if needed.

Crispy chicken cutlets and a fresh, acidic salad is a classic pairing that's a go-to of mine for a quick weeknight meal. It's also a perfect framework to highlight fresh, seasonal vegetables, which we love! What's so cool about this crispy chicken and salad combo is that it can be made year-round without compromising freshness or flavor. You can almost always find a good cremini mushroom and a bunch of crisp celery at the grocery store. This celery and mushroom salad is classically made with shaved Parmesan, but I'm using pecorino Romano here because I just can't shake my love for it. Be sure to use very fresh cremini mushrooms because soggy ones that are on their last leg will not hold up well in the salad.

1. **Make the salad:** Place the mushrooms, celery, onion, shaved pecorino Romano, and parsley in a large bowl. Set aside in the refrigerator.

2. **Make the chicken:** Working with one piece of chicken at a time, place the chicken between two pieces of plastic wrap, and use a meat mallet or heavy-bottomed pan to pound it to an even ¼ inch (6 mm) thickness. Transfer the pounded chicken to a small sheet pan lined with a wire rack or a plate, and repeat with the remaining chicken. Season both sides of the chicken with salt and pepper.

3. Prepare the breading station: Place the flour in a shallow bowl. Place the eggs in another shallow bowl. Mix the panko and grated pecorino Romano in a third shallow bowl.

4. Coat the chicken in the flour, then the egg, and then the panko mixture, making sure to evenly coat in each step. Place the breaded chicken back on the wire rack or plate, and repeat with the remaining cutlets.

5. Heat ¼ inch (6 mm) olive oil in a large skillet over medium heat until hot. (You can check by adding a bit of panko to see if it sizzles.)

6. Working with two cutlets at a time, carefully add the breaded chicken to the pan by laying it away from you to avoid oil splashes. Cook until golden on one side, 3 or 4 minutes. Flip over and cook on the second side, another 3 or 4 minutes, carefully basting with the hot oil if there are any pale spots. Remove the chicken to a sheet tray lined with a wire rack, and repeat with the remaining cutlets, adding more oil to the pan as needed to keep it ¼ inch (6 mm) up the sides. After cooking, let the oil cool completely and then discard it.

7. Remove the salad from the refrigerator, and gently toss with the lemon zest, lemon juice, olive oil, salt, and pepper. Be careful not to break up the mushrooms too much as you toss.

8. Serve the chicken cutlets topped with the salad and celery leaves.

Steak Night Dinner
Anchovy-Basted Rib Eye with Dilly Creamed Spinach

SERVES 2

Steak

One 2-inch-thick (5 cm) bone-in rib eye (about 1½ pounds/680 g)

Kosher salt and freshly cracked black pepper, to taste

Olive oil, for searing

4 tablespoons unsalted butter

4 oil-packed anchovy fillets, chopped

4 garlic cloves, smashed

5 fresh thyme sprigs

2 dried bay leaves

Spinach

1 tablespoon olive oil

15 ounces (425 g) baby spinach

2 tablespoons unsalted butter

2 large shallots, minced

2 garlic cloves, minced

½ cup (120 ml) heavy cream

2 ounces (57 g) garlic and herb Boursin cheese (see Tip)

¼ cup (28 g) grated Parmesan

Pinch of ground nutmeg

Kosher salt and freshly cracked black pepper, to taste

¼ cup (10 g) loosely packed fresh dill, roughly chopped

TIP Truffle Boursin is so good in this, too, if you can find it!

I love going out to eat as much as the next gal, but there's nothing quite like knowing how to cook your own steak at home and skipping the steakhouse and all of its à la carte sides. This steak is prepared using the reverse-sear method, where it is cooked at a very low heat in the oven and then seared off in a cast-iron pan to finish. Using a probe thermometer makes this method almost foolproof! This recipe yields a medium-rare steak, but for a medium doneness, bake the steak a bit longer to 125°F (52°C) and then sear as directed. Serve this with the Mustardy Herb-Buttered Potatoes (page 117) or simply with some sourdough bread (see page 218) for mopping up the anchovy butter and dipping into the creamed spinach! Oh, and maybe a nice shaken gin martini, too.

1. **Make the steak:** Season the steak liberally all over with salt and pepper. Place on a sheet tray lined with a wire rack, and set aside at room temperature while you preheat the oven. (You also can season the steak the night before and leave it uncovered in the refrigerator until you are ready to cook.)

2. Preheat the oven to 250°F (120°C).

3. Bake the steak on the wire rack–lined sheet tray for 60 to 65 minutes, until the internal temperature of the thickest part reaches 115°F (46°C). The cook time will depend on the thickness of your steak, so just keep an eye on it.

4. **Meanwhile, make the spinach:** Heat the olive oil in a medium pot over medium heat. Add the spinach, and stir to coat in the oil. Cover and cook, uncovering and stirring occasionally, until the spinach is wilted, 2 or 3 minutes.

5. Transfer the spinach to a strainer over a bowl. Using a spoon, press the spinach in the strainer to remove as much liquid as you can. Discard the liquid, and roughly chop the spinach.

6. Wipe out the skillet, add the butter, and melt over medium heat. Add the shallots and minced garlic, and cook until translucent, 3 or 4 minutes.

7. Add the cream, Boursin, and Parmesan, and reduce the heat to medium-low. Cook, stirring, until the cheeses melt and the mixture is bubbly, 1 or 2 minutes. Stir in the reserved spinach, and cook, stirring, until slightly thickened, 2 or 3 minutes. The cream mixture should lightly coat the back of a spoon.

8. Season with nutmeg, salt, and pepper. Remove from the heat, and cover while the steak finishes.

9. Remove the steak from the oven. Coat the bottom of a large cast-iron pan with olive oil, and heat over medium-high heat. Add the steak, and sear until golden, 3 to 5 minutes. Using tongs, hold the steak up on its fatty side (the fat cap), and sear until golden and slightly rendered, 1 or 2 minutes.

10. Flip the steak onto its second side, and add the butter, anchovies, smashed garlic, thyme, and bay leaves. Sear the steak on the second side, basting with the anchovy butter (the anchovies will melt into the butter as you baste), until the internal temperature is between 120°F and 125°F (49°C and 52°C), 2 or 3 minutes.

11. Transfer the steak to a wire rack on top of a sheet tray or a plate, and let rest for 10 minutes. While the steak rests, reheat the creamed spinach over medium heat until warm. Stir in the dill.

12. Slice the steak against the grain, and serve with the warm anchovy butter (discard the bay leaves) spooned on top and the creamed spinach on the side.

Garlic Coriander Pork Chops
with Crunchy Iceberg Salad

SERVES 2

Pork

1 teaspoon black peppercorns

1 teaspoon coriander seeds

2 bone-in center-cut pork chops (1½ to 2 pounds/680 to 907 g), about 1 inch (2.5 cm) thick

Kosher salt, to taste

2 tablespoons Worcestershire sauce

1 tablespoon plus 1 teaspoon soy sauce

1 tablespoon maple syrup

1 tablespoon mirin

¼ cup (60 ml) plus 2 tablespoons canola oil

4 garlic cloves, thinly sliced on a mandoline

3 tablespoons unsalted butter

Dressing

2 inches (5 cm) ginger, peeled and thinly sliced

2 scallions, whites only, roughly chopped

1 small carrot, thinly sliced

2 tablespoons maple syrup

2 tablespoons soy sauce

2 tablespoons unseasoned rice vinegar

½ teaspoon ground turmeric

Kosher salt and freshly cracked black pepper, to taste

Salad

1 small head iceberg lettuce, cored and cut into small wedges (leaves separated slightly)

2 scallions, greens only, thinly sliced

1 medium carrot, julienned

My mom didn't cook a lot of meat when I was growing up, but she did have a few go-tos. There was her pork tenderloin, her meatloaf, and, when it came to summer grilling, her coriander pork chops. The smell of the heavily Worcestershire'd coriander chops on the grill is such a nostalgic scent of summer for me. This recipe combines my mom's pork chops and Japanese tonteki, pork fried in garlic oil and then glazed with a sweet Worcestershire and soy sauce. Tonteki is usually served with shredded cabbage, but here, I opted for a crunchy iceberg salad for a bit more of a crisp, watery crunch. Some steamed white rice on the side is also lovely!

1. **Prepare the pork:** Use a mortar and pestle or spice grinder to crush the peppercorns and coriander into a coarse powder. Season the pork all over with salt and then the spice mix.

2. Mix the Worcestershire sauce, soy sauce, syrup, and mirin in a small bowl. Set aside.

3. Add the canola oil and garlic to a large skillet, set over medium-low heat, and fry the garlic, stirring often, until lightly golden brown, 3 to 5 minutes. The garlic won't seem very crisp at this point, but it will crisp up when fully cool. Transfer the garlic to a paper towel to drain, and sprinkle with a touch of salt.

4. Remove all but about 1 tablespoon of the garlic oil from the pan, and reserve the rest (about ¼ cup/60 ml) to use in the dressing. You'll use this pan to cook the pork, so don't get rid of it! (But do turn off the heat.)

5. **Make the dressing:** Place the ginger, scallion whites, carrot, the reserved ¼ cup (60 ml) garlic oil, and the syrup, soy sauce, vinegar, and turmeric in a blender, and blend until very smooth. Season with salt and pepper.

6. **Cook the pork:** Heat the skillet over medium heat. Add the pork chops, and sear the first side until golden brown, 4 or 5 minutes. Flip the chops onto the fat cap, and sear until they are golden and the fat has rendered a bit, 1 or 2 minutes.

7. Flip over and cook the second side until the chops are golden and the internal temperature is about 125°F (52°C), 3 or 4 minutes. Transfer the pork chops to a plate. (They will not be fully cooked at this point.)

8. Remove all the oil from the skillet. Reduce the heat to low, and add the reserved Worcestershire sauce mixture and butter. Cook, stirring to scrape up any fond, until the butter is melted and everything is combined and bubbly, 1 or 2 minutes.

9. Return the pork to the skillet, and cook, basting with the sauce, until the internal temperature is about 140°F (60°C), 1 or 2 minutes. Turn off the heat.

10. **Make the salad:** Arrange the iceberg on a platter, and drizzle with the ginger dressing. Top with the scallion greens and carrots.

11. Slice the pork off the bone, top with more sauce from the pan and the fried garlic, and serve with the salad on the side.

Pot Roast au Poivre
with Charred Onions

SERVES 6 TO 8

Pot Roast

2 teaspoons black peppercorns

3 tablespoons shiitake mushroom powder (see Note)

1 tablespoon kosher salt

One 3½-pound (1.5 kg) chuck roast, tied with butcher's twine to keep snug while cooking

Olive oil, for searing

4 medium yellow onions, peeled and halved

8 garlic cloves, peeled and smashed

½ cup (120 ml) cognac or brandy

2 cups (480 ml) unsalted beef stock, homemade (see page 90) or store-bought

1 small bunch fresh thyme, tied together with butcher's twine

2 dried bay leaves

Sauce

2 tablespoons unsalted butter

3 small shallots, minced

2 tablespoons green peppercorns in brine, drained and roughly chopped

½ cup (120 ml) cognac or brandy

½ cup (120 ml) heavy cream

Kosher salt and freshly cracked black pepper, to taste

Thinly sliced fresh chives, to taste

NOTE Make the shiitake mushroom powder by blending about ½ ounce (14 g) of dried shiitakes until powdery.

The humble pot roast is a classic comfort meal, but I find it can be just as elegant and special as a big fancy steak or prime rib roast. Au poivre, the inspiration for this dish, is a French steak preparation where the steak is coated in peppercorns and served with a creamy, peppery sauce. I'm not a huge fan of adding too many different vegetables to cook with the pot roast itself, but feel free to make any of your favorite pot roast veggies on the side if you'd like. The onions I add to this braise come out deliciously soft and are a great stand-alone side dish. I also love serving this alongside any kind of potato and/or a little acidic salad. This dish is as perfect for a cozy Sunday night meal as it is for a special occasion or holiday.

1. **Make the roast:** The night before you want to cook the roast, crush the black peppercorns into a coarse powder with a mortar and pestle or spice grinder. Transfer to a small bowl along with the mushroom powder and salt, and mix.

2. Season the roast all over with the spice mix. Transfer to a wire rack on top of a sheet tray, and let sit, uncovered, in the refrigerator for at least 8 hours or up to 24 hours.

3. The next day, preheat the oven to 325°F (165°C) with a rack positioned in the lower third.

4. Coat the bottom of a large Dutch oven with olive oil, and heat over medium heat. Add the roast, and sear on all sides until deep golden, 5 to 7 minutes per side. Adjust the heat as needed to ensure that the bits at the bottom of the pot don't burn. Transfer the meat to a large plate.

5. Add the onions, cut side down, to the Dutch oven, and sear until deep golden, 2 or 3 minutes. (The onions won't be fully cooked at this point, just charred.) Add the garlic, and cook for 1 minute.

6. Remove the pot from the heat (leaving the onions and garlic in the pot), and deglaze with the cognac, scraping up any brown bits from the bottom of the pot. Reduce the cognac by half using the residual heat, 1 or 2 minutes.

7. Return the pot to medium heat, and add the beef stock, thyme, and bay leaves. Bring to a simmer and then return the roast to the pot along with any accumulated juices. The liquid should come about halfway up the side of the meat. (If not, add some water.)

8. Cover and bake for 3 for 4 hours, until fork-tender. Transfer the meat to a platter, remove the twine, and cover with foil to keep warm.

9. Scoop out the onions and garlic using a slotted spoon (they will be very soft), place them on a small plate, and set aside.

10. **Make the sauce:** Strain the braising liquid into a large bowl. Skim off any excess fat from the top with a spoon and discard.

11. Wipe out the Dutch oven, and heat over medium heat. Add the butter and melt. Toss in the shallots, and sweat until soft, 3 or 4 minutes.

12. Stir in the green peppercorns. Turn off the heat, and deglaze with the cognac. Reduce the cognac by half using the residual heat, 1 or 2 minutes.

13. Set the pot over medium-high heat, and add 1½ cups (360 ml) of the reserved braising liquid. (Discard any remaining liquid.) Reduce until the liquid lightly coats the back of a spoon, 6 to 8 minutes.

14. Add the cream and continue to reduce the sauce until it fully coats the back of the spoon, 4 to 6 minutes. Season with salt and pepper, if needed.

15. Top the beef with the sauce, and garnish with chives. Serve the charred onions alongside the beef on the platter.

Lamb Goulash Pot Pie
with Horseradish Gremolata

SERVES 4

Pot Pie

1¼ pounds (567 g) boneless lamb stew meat, cut into bite-size cubes (about ½ inch/1 cm)

Kosher salt and freshly cracked black pepper, to taste

Olive oil, for searing

1 red bell pepper, ribs and seeds removed, and diced

1 medium yellow onion, diced

3 garlic cloves, minced

2 tablespoons tomato paste

2 tablespoons sweet smoked paprika

2 teaspoons caraway seeds

2¼ cups (540 ml) unsalted beef stock, homemade (see page 90) or store-bought

1 small bunch fresh thyme, tied together with butcher's twine

1 dried bay leaf

2 medium carrots, diced

1 large Yukon Gold potato (about 8 ounces/227 g), diced

3 tablespoons unsalted butter, very soft

3 tablespoons all-purpose flour, plus more for dusting

1 egg

1 tablespoon water

¾ cup (113 g) frozen peas

One 14-ounce (397 g) sheet puff pastry, thawed overnight in the refrigerator (see Note 1)

Flake salt, to taste

continued >>

When I visited Australia in my early twenties, I experienced firsthand their appreciation for a good meat pie. Before that, I didn't think much of savory pies outside of chicken pot pie, but I was truly missing out. Stew-y lamb covered in a deeply golden, buttery pastry is something quite special. This one has a bunch of paprika and caraway seeds added to channel Hungarian goulash, along with the classic pot pie vegetables. Be sure to cut the lamb into small enough pieces so that they braise as quickly as the recipe calls for. I would usually use a cast-iron pan for a pot pie, but I suggest stainless steel or enamel-coated cast iron here because the tomato stew can strip the coating of cast iron.

1. **Make the pot pie:** Season the lamb all over with salt and pepper.

2. Coat the bottom of a 12-inch (30 cm) ovenproof skillet with olive oil, and heat over medium heat. When hot, add half of the lamb and sear on all sides until golden brown, 6 to 8 minutes. Transfer to a plate. Add the rest of the lamb, adding more oil if the pan seems dry, and sear on all sides. Transfer to the plate, leaving any reduced fat and juices in the pan.

3. Add the bell pepper, onion, and garlic, and season with salt and pepper. Cook, stirring often, until softened, 5 or 6 minutes.

4. Stir in the tomato paste, paprika, and caraway seeds. Cook, stirring, until the tomato paste browns slightly, 1 or 2 minutes.

5. Pour in the stock, scraping up any brown bits from the bottom of the pan. Add the thyme and bay leaf along with the seared lamb and any accumulated drippings. Bring to a boil and then reduce the heat to low. Simmer until the meat starts to get tender, about 40 minutes. Maintain a low simmer here; you don't want to boil away the stock because you need it to create a sauce later.

6. Add the carrots and potato, and stir. Cover, increase the heat to medium-low, and cook, uncovering and stirring every now and then to ensure nothing is sticking to the bottom of the pan, until the lamb and vegetables are tender, 30 to 35 minutes.

7. While the meat simmers, mix the butter and flour in a small bowl to make a beurre manié (see Note 2). Whisk the egg and water together in another small bowl to make an egg wash.

8. Preheat the oven to 425°F (220°C).

9. When the lamb is tender, remove and discard the thyme and bay leaf. Stir in the beurre manié until it melts into the sauce. Bring the mixture to a boil, stirring, and cook until thickened, 1 or 2 minutes.

10. Stir in the peas. Turn off the heat, and season with salt and pepper. Place the skillet on a sheet tray.

11. Roll out the puff pastry, dusting with flour as needed and keeping a rough rectangular shape, to fully cover the skillet with about a 1-inch (2.5 cm) overhang. (The pastry will shrink up a bit when it bakes.) Place the pastry over the skillet, nestling in the overhanging edges so they don't fall over the edges of the pan.

Gremolata

1 cup (28 g) loosely packed fresh
  parsley leaves, finely chopped

½ cup (14 g) loosely packed
  fresh dill, finely chopped

Zest of 2 lemons

1½-inch (4 cm) piece fresh
  horseradish root, finely grated,
  or 2 to 3 teaspoons prepared

1 garlic clove, finely grated

Kosher salt, to taste

12. Use a pastry brush to brush the egg wash all
  over the pastry, and sprinkle with flake salt
  and pepper.

13. Transfer the pan to the oven, and bake for 30
  to 35 minutes, until deep golden brown.

14. **As the pot pie bakes, make the gremolata:**
  Mix the parsley, dill, lemon zest, horseradish,
  and garlic in a small bowl. Season with salt.

15. Serve the pot pie by scooping out big, rustic
  portions and topping generously with
  gremolata.

NOTES

1. My favorite puff pastry is Dufour,
which is sold as one 14-ounce
(397 g) sheet. Some other brands
are sold with two 8-ounce (227 g)
sheets. If yours comes in two
8-ounce (227 g) sheets, simply roll
out a sheet to fit over the pan. The
pastry will just be a touch less thick
but still equally delish!

2. To make a beurre manié, simply
mash the softened butter with the
flour to make a paste. This is
essentially a raw roux.

Pizza Night

There's no need for excessively fancy equipment to make a great pizza in your standard home oven. Here's to simple, straightforward pizza party success. Thick or thin, I've got you covered here.

Basic Sheet-Pan Pizza Dough

MAKES ENOUGH
DOUGH FOR 1 LARGE
(13×18-INCH/33×46 CM)
SHEET-PAN PIZZA

475 grams (3½ cups) bread flour

1 tablespoon kosher salt

1 teaspoon instant yeast (I like Saf-instant brand)

370 grams (1½ cups) room-temperature water

Olive oil, for drizzling

This is my go-to dough for any sheet-pan pizza. It's simple to mix up and can be made ahead, which we love! Top it as directed on page 177 under the Fried Garlic Pizza Sauce recipe for a basic cheese pie, or use it in the fun Potato and Anchovy Sheet-Pan Pizza (page 178) or Broccoli and Soppressata Sheet-Pan Pizza (page 181) recipes, where you will also find the forming and baking directions. Any 13×18-inch (33×46 cm) sheet pan will work here, but for best crust results, I like to use a LloydPans sheet pan. I recommend using the gram measurements in this recipe to yield the most precise and accurate dough. This recipe calls for instant yeast, not active dry, so be sure you are using the right one!

1. The day before (or up to 3 days before) you want to make a pizza, prepare the dough: Whisk the flour, salt, and yeast in a large bowl until fully combined. Add the water, and mix. The dough will look lumpy, but there should be no dry pockets of flour.

2. Cover with plastic wrap, and let the dough rest at room temperature for 30 minutes.

3. Uncover the dough. Using damp hands, stretch and fold it: Gently pick up the north side of the dough, stretching it until you feel resistance, and fold it over to the south side of the bowl. Rotate the bowl 90 degrees, and repeat three times, until four sides have been stretched and folded.

4. Cover with plastic wrap, and let rest for another 30 minutes.

5. Repeat the folding process from step 3.

6. Drizzle the top of the dough with a bit of olive oil, and cover with plastic wrap. Place in the refrigerator to rest for at least 8 hours or up to 3 days.

7. See the steps for forming and baking the pizza on pages 178 and 181.

Thin Bar Pie–Style Pizza Dough

MAKES ENOUGH
DOUGH FOR TWO
12-INCH (30 CM)
BAR PIES

200 grams (1½ cups) bread flour

50 grams (¼ cup plus
1 tablespoon) semolina flour

2 teaspoons kosher salt

1 teaspoon instant yeast (I like
Saf-instant brand)

150 grams (½ cup plus
2 tablespoons) room-
temperature water

2 tablespoons unsalted butter,
melted and cooled slightly

Olive oil, for coating the bowl
and dough

Bar pies hold a special place in my heart. In the Chicagoland area, we are more often known for our deep dish, but some of my favorite pies in the area are actually thin, bar-style ones. After I moved to New Jersey, my love for bar-style pizza grew, with so many different places to get a really good, almost cracker-like pizza. This style of pizza is easy to eat, not too messy, and seriously smashable. However you slice it, in squares or in triangles, it's always a good time sharing a bar pie with friends. This recipe will work in any pizza pan you have, but for optimal results, I always recommend a LloydPans pan. It is the best investment you can make if you want crispy-bottomed pizzas at home. I use this dough in the White Clam Bar-Style Pizza (page 185) and Mushroom and Dill Bar-Style Pizza (page 182), where you will find the shaping and baking method, but also check out the Fried Garlic Pizza Sauce (page 177) for directions on how to make a great classic cheese pie using this crust!

1. The day before (or up to 3 days before) you want to make a pizza, prepare the dough: Whisk the bread flour, semolina flour, salt, and yeast in a large bowl until fully combined. Add the water and melted butter, and mix with your hands to form a shaggy dough.

2. Cover with plastic wrap, and let the dough rest at room temperature for 30 minutes. The dough will have puffed up a bit but not risen significantly.

3. Uncover the dough. Using damp hands, stretch and fold it: Gently pick up the north side of the dough, stretching it until you feel resistance, and fold it over to the south side of the bowl. Rotate the bowl 90 degrees, and repeat three times, until four sides have been stretched and folded. It will be a fairly stiff dough.

4. Cover with plastic wrap, and let rest for another 30 minutes.

5. Repeat the folding process from step 3.

6. Cover with plastic wrap, and let rest for another 30 minutes. Once again, the dough will not have risen significantly.

7. Divide the dough in half (about 227 g/8 ounces each), and shape each half into a ball. Place each dough ball in its own oiled small bowl (or similar-sized airtight container; I love using quart/1 L containers for this), and roll the dough around to coat it in oil. Cover with plastic wrap or a lid, and place in the refrigerator to rest for at least 12 hours or up to 3 days. Once again, the dough will not have risen much. The resting time here is mainly for the dough to develop flavor.

8. See the steps for forming and baking the pizza on pages 182 and 185.

Fried Garlic Pizza Sauce

MAKES ABOUT 3 CUPS (700 G), ENOUGH FOR 2 SHEET-PAN PIZZAS OR 4 BAR PIES

One 28-ounce (794 g) can whole peeled San Marzano tomatoes

¼ cup (60 ml) olive oil

5 large garlic cloves, thinly sliced on a mandoline

3 tablespoons tomato paste

1 teaspoon dried oregano

Kosher salt and freshly cracked black pepper, to taste

When it comes to pizza sauce, I find the simpler the better. The tomato flavor should shine through without being masked by too many other ingredients. That being said, I think a bit of garlic and oregano add that quintessential pizza taste. Frying the garlic and then blending it into the sauce provides a mellow yet toasty flavor that really makes this shine. It may seem out of the ordinary that this sauce isn't cooked, but it maintains a sense of freshness that I really enjoy. At the bottom of this recipe, you will also find directions for how to use this sauce with both the Basic Sheet-Pan Pizza Dough (page 174) and the Thin Bar Pie–Style Pizza Dough (page 175).

1. Add the tomatoes to a blender, and blend until they're broken down slightly but still chunky.

2. Add the olive oil and garlic to a small sauté pan. Set over medium-low heat, and fry the garlic, stirring constantly, until lightly golden brown, 3 to 5 minutes.

3. Pour the garlic and oil into the blender with the tomatoes. Stir with a spoon to incorporate the oil with the tomatoes. (Blending before stirring may cause the sauce to shoot out of the blender.)

4. Add the tomato paste and oregano, and blend until smooth.

5. Season with salt and pepper.

6. This sauce can be made up to 3 days in advance and stored in an airtight container in the refrigerator. It also can be stored in the freezer for up to 4 months.

Basic Sheet-Pan Cheese Pizza

Follow the basic instructions for making the dough on page 174 and forming the dough on page 178. Top the pizza with ¾ cup (180 ml) Fried Garlic Pizza Sauce, 12 ounces (340 g) shredded whole-milk low-moisture mozzarella, and ¼ cup (28 g) finely grated pecorino Romano. I leave about a ½-inch (1 cm) border for the crust. See the steps for baking the pizza on page 178.

Basic Bar-Style Cheese Pizza

Follow the basic instructions for making the dough on page 175 and forming the dough on page 182. Top each pizza with ⅓ cup (80 ml) Fried Garlic Pizza Sauce, 6 ounces (170 g) shredded low-moisture whole-milk mozzarella, and 2 tablespoons finely grated pecorino Romano. I leave about a ¼-inch (6 mm) border for the crust. For a true Chicago delight, top it with some of the Chicago-Style Fennel Giardiniera (page 46). See the steps for baking the pizza on page 182.

Potato and Anchovy Sheet-Pan Pizza

SERVES 6 TO 8

Pizza

1 tablespoon unsalted butter

5 tablespoons olive oil, divided

1 recipe Basic Sheet-Pan Pizza Dough (page 174)

1 pound (454 g) Yukon Gold potatoes (2 or 3 medium), sliced paper-thin on a mandoline

Kosher salt and freshly cracked black pepper, to taste

2 teaspoons finely chopped fresh thyme leaves

One 2-ounce (57 g) tin oil-packed anchovy fillets, drained and torn into smaller pieces

Salad

5 ounces (142 g) baby arugula

½ small red onion, thinly sliced and rinsed (see Tip 1 on page 80)

Extra virgin olive oil, for drizzling

Fresh lemon juice, to taste

Kosher salt and freshly cracked black pepper, to taste

There's nothing wrong with a little carb-on-carb action every now and then, and potatoes on pizza is one of the tastiest ways to enjoy that indulgence. Potato might seem like a nontraditional pizza topping, but it is actually quite common in Italy, and like many Italian dishes, it is beautiful in its simplicity. I love loading up any slice of pizza with a big handful of salad, so we are channeling that energy here by topping this pizza with a simple lemony arugula salad that I find it so desperately calls for. If you feel like you want a little cheese here, grating some fresh Parmesan over everything before serving is a nice option. This pizza can also easily be made vegan by removing the anchovies. I would top the pizza with some flake salt after baking to make up for the lack of saltiness the anchovies impart.

1. **Make the pizza:** Preheat the oven to 500°F (260°C) with a pizza stone (if you have one) in the lower third (see Note). Grease a half-sheet pan (13×18 inches/ 33×46 cm) very well all over with the butter and 2 tablespoons olive oil.

2. With oiled hands, place the Basic Sheet-Pan Pizza Dough on the tray, and press and stretch out the dough as far as you can. (It won't fit the entire sheet tray at this point.) Oil the top with 1 tablespoon olive oil, and place a sheet of plastic wrap on top of the dough. Let the dough rest for 45 minutes at room temperature.

3. Press and stretch out the dough again, this time to fill the entire tray. If the dough still won't quite stretch out the entire way, cover and let it rest another 15 minutes and try again.

4. Add the potatoes to a large bowl, drizzle with the remaining 2 tablespoons olive oil, and season with salt and pepper. Toss to coat.

5. Spread the potatoes evenly all over the pizza, edge to edge. (No need for a crust edge here.) Sprinkle with the thyme.

6. Bake in the lower third of the oven (on top of the pizza stone, if using) for 20 to 25 minutes, until the potatoes are golden brown with some crispy edges.

7. Immediately transfer the pizza to a wire rack by lifting the pizza with a spatula and sliding the rack right under it. (This prevents the bottom crust from getting soggy.) Top with torn anchovies across the entire pie.

8. **Make the salad:** Add the arugula and onion to a large bowl. Drizzle with extra virgin olive oil, lemon juice, and a touch of salt and pepper, and toss gently to coat. I like a delicately dressed salad here.

9. Cut the pizza into squares, top with the salad, and serve.

NOTE Preheating the oven this early, before the dough has rested, might seem odd, but for the best results, I like to do so to ensure the oven is very hot and totally preheated before the pizza goes in.

Broccoli and Soppressata Sheet-Pan Pizza

SERVES 8 TO 10

1 tablespoon unsalted butter

6 tablespoons olive oil

1 recipe Basic Sheet-Pan Pizza Dough (page 174)

Kosher salt and freshly cracked black pepper, to taste

12 ounces (340 g/about 2 crowns) broccoli, tough ends trimmed, chopped into ¼-inch (6 mm) pieces (tender stems and all)

3 garlic cloves, minced

¾ cup (6 ounces/170 g) whole-milk ricotta

Zest of 1 lemon, plus more for topping, optional

8 ounces (227 g) fontina, shredded

8 ounces (227 g) low-moisture whole-milk mozzarella, shredded

8 ounces (227 g) spicy soppressata, thinly sliced

Hot honey, to taste (I like Mike's or Zab's)

Torn fresh basil leaves, to taste

Super-soft, garlicky broccoli tossed with pasta is one of my favorite simple pasta dishes. It embraces the beauty of a soft vegetable in a world that tells us green vegetables have to be served tender-crisp and bright green. Here, that same style of mushy broccoli is mixed into some ricotta to make a silky base for this sheet-pan pizza. I love the soppressata as a spicy counterpart to the luscious broccoli, but subbing in some sun-dried tomatoes instead would make a perfect vegetarian option. I cut my sheet-pan pizzas into squares with scissors because that's what my mom always did. It's both practical and nostalgic, and I love it.

1. Preheat the oven to 500°F (260°C) with a pizza stone (if you have one) in the lower third (see Note on page 178). Grease a half-sheet pan (13 ×18 inches/ 33×46 cm) very well all over with the butter and 2 tablespoons olive oil.

2. With oiled hands, place the Basic Sheet-Pan Pizza Dough on the tray, and press and stretch out the dough as far as you can. (It won't fit the entire sheet tray at this point.) Oil the top with 1 tablespoon olive oil, and place a sheet of plastic wrap on top of the dough. Let the dough rest for 45 minutes at room temperature.

3. Meanwhile, bring a medium pot to a boil over high heat. Generously season with salt. Add the broccoli, and boil until very soft, 6 to 8 minutes. Drain into a colander, and set aside.

4. Dry out the pot and add the remaining 3 tablespoons olive oil and the garlic. Reduce the heat to medium, and cook, stirring, until the garlic is slightly golden, 2 or 3 minutes.

5. Add the broccoli, and stir to coat. Reduce the heat to medium-low, and continue to cook, stirring occasionally, until the broccoli is super soft and mushy, 5 or 6 minutes.

6. Turn off the heat, and mash the broccoli even further to form a chunky paste. Add to a medium bowl, and mix with the ricotta and lemon zest. Season with salt and pepper.

7. After the dough has rested, press and stretch it out again, this time to fill the entire tray. If the dough still won't quite stretch out the entire way, cover and let it rest another 15 minutes and try again.

8. Add dollops of the broccoli mixture all over the dough, and spread out evenly, leaving about a ½-inch (1 cm) border for the crust. Sprinkle the fontina and mozzarella all over, and top with the soppressata.

9. Bake in the lower third of the oven (on top of the pizza stone, if using) for 20 to 25 minutes, until golden and bubbly.

10. Immediately transfer the pizza to a wire rack by lifting the pizza with a spatula and sliding the rack right under it. (This prevents the bottom crust from getting soggy.) Drizzle with hot honey, and top with torn fresh basil leaves and lemon zest, if using.

11. Cut the pizza into squares, and serve.

Mushroom and Dill Bar-Style Pizza

Cornmeal, for dusting

1 recipe Thin Bar Pie–Style
Pizza Dough (page 175)

Olive oil, for drizzling

1 cup (240 ml) heavy cream

1 ounce (28 g) dried porcini
mushrooms

Kosher salt and freshly cracked
black pepper, to taste

12 ounces (340 g) low-moisture
whole-milk mozzarella,
shredded

6 ounces (170 g) cremini
mushrooms, sliced paper-thin
on a mandoline

½ cup (20 g) loosely packed
fresh dill, roughly chopped

This vegetarian pizza is an ode to mushrooms and their undeniable ability to pack a serious umami punch. I love utilizing dried mushrooms in the sauce and fresh mushrooms on top for two types of mushroom fun. The amount of sliced mushrooms on top may seem like way too much before baking, but trust the process; they cook down considerably in the oven. If you want to add some meat to this, Italian sausage would be delightful. Just add small bits of raw bulk Italian sausage to the pie after topping with the creminis, and bake as directed.

1. Preheat the oven to 500°F (260°C) with a pizza stone (if you have one) in the lower third (see Note on page 178). Dust two 12-inch (30 cm) round pizza pans with cornmeal (see Note 1).

2. Place one ball of Thin Bar Pie–Style Pizza Dough on each pizza pan, and press and stretch out the dough as far as possible with your hands. The dough will not fit the whole pan at this point.

3. Lightly oil the top of each pizza dough, and cover lightly with plastic wrap. Let both pizzas rest for 45 to 60 minutes at room temperature.

4. Meanwhile, make the mushroom cream sauce. Add the heavy cream and porcinis to a small saucepan, and set over medium heat. Bring to a boil, reduce the heat to low, and simmer until the porcinis are rehydrated and very soft, 10 to 15 minutes.

5. Transfer the mixture to a blender, and blend (with the top lid vented) until smooth. Start the blender on low and then increase to high because the mixture will be hot and you don't want the sauce to shoot out of the blender. Add a small splash or two of water, if needed, to get the blender going. Season with salt.

6. After the doughs have rested, press and stretch them out again, this time to fill out the entire pan. If the doughs still won't quite stretch out the entire way, cover and let them rest another 15 minutes and try again. Prick the doughs all over with a fork.

7. Top each pizza with half of the mushroom sauce and spread it out, leaving about a ¼-inch (6 mm) border of dough exposed for the crust. Top each with half of the mozzarella and half of cremini mushrooms. Drizzle the mushrooms with olive oil, and season with salt and pepper.

8. Bake one pizza at a time (see Note 2) in the lower third of the oven (on top of the pizza stone, if using) for 12 to 15 minutes, until golden and bubbly.

9. Transfer the pizza to a cutting board. Top with half of the fresh dill, slice, and serve. (I find these pies are best eaten fresh from the oven.)

10. Repeat steps 8 and 9 with the second pizza.

NOTES

1. Although I find the 12-inch (30 cm) round pizza pans by LloydPans to be the best option for all the thin bar pies in this book, a 12-inch (30 cm) cast-iron pan or standard half sheet tray are great substitutes. If you opt for a sheet tray, you won't "fill out" the whole pan with the dough as directed in step 6; instead, you'll press and stretch the dough into a rough 12-inch (30 cm) circle. No matter what pan you end up using, a sprinkling of cornmeal on the bottom is always essential.

2. I like to bake just one pizza at a time here because I find that baking it in the lower third of the oven without overcrowding creates the crispiest-bottom crust. And really, it's all about a crispy bottom here!

White Clam Bar-Style Pizza

SERVES 4 (MAKES TWO 12-INCH/30 CM PIZZAS)

Cornmeal, for dusting

2 heads garlic, tops trimmed to expose the cloves

Olive oil, for drizzling

Kosher salt and freshly cracked black pepper, to taste

1 recipe Thin Bar Pie–Style Pizza Dough (page 175)

12 ounces (340 g) low-moisture whole-milk mozzarella, shredded

One 6.5-ounce (184 g) can whole clams, drained (see Note)

6 tablespoons finely grated pecorino Romano

Vinegary hot sauce, to taste (I love Crystal for this)

Thinly sliced fresh chives, to taste

Lemon wedges, for serving

No clam pizza can quite compete with the ones out of New Haven, Connecticut. Terroir is a big part of what makes a pizza taste a certain way, and that's a very special thing. It's the water, it's the oven—it's so many things. In any case, a salty, chewy clam on a thin, crispy crust is a thing of pizza beauty, and that beauty is captured here in a relatively simple at-home version. Although many clam pies don't include mozzarella, I like adding it here. What can I say? I'm still a Midwesterner at heart: I love cheese.

1. Preheat the oven to 425°F (220°C) with a pizza stone (if you have one) in the lower third. Dust two 12-inch (30 cm) round pizza pans with cornmeal (see Note 1 on page 182 for other pan options).

2. Drizzle the heads of garlic with olive oil, and season with salt. Wrap each head tightly in foil, and place on a sheet tray. Roast for 40 to 45 minutes, until soft and golden. Let cool enough to handle and then squeeze out the cloves.

3. While the garlic roasts, place one ball of Thin Bar Pie–Style Pizza Dough on each pizza pan, and press and stretch out the dough as far as possible with your hands. The dough will not fit the whole pan at this point.

4. Lightly oil the top of each pizza dough, and cover lightly with plastic wrap. Let both pizzas rest for 45 to 60 minutes at room temperature.

5. When the garlic is out of the oven, increase the oven temperature to 500°F (260°C).

6. After the doughs have rested, press and stretch them out again, this time to fill the entire pan. If the doughs still won't quite stretch out the entire way, cover and let them rest another 15 minutes and try again.

7. Prick the doughs all over with a fork.

8. Divide the roasted garlic, mozzarella, clams, and pecorino Romano evenly between the two pizzas, leaving about a ¼-inch (6 mm) border of dough exposed for the crust. Drizzle the top of each with a bit of olive oil, and season heavily with pepper.

9. Bake one pizza at a time (see Note 2 on page 182) in the lower third of the oven (on top of the pizza stone, if using) for 12 to 15 minutes, until golden and bubbly.

10. Transfer the pizza to a cutting board. Top with hot sauce and chives, slice, and serve with lemon wedges on the side. (I find these pies are best eaten fresh from the oven.)

11. Repeat steps 9 and 10 with the second pizza.

NOTE Bar Harbor makes a great canned clam and is my go-to for this, for both accessibility and the number of clams per can. Island Creek Oysters also makes great canned clams in many varieties, all of which would work here as well. Any high-quality canned clam is going to be great in this recipe.

Inspired by Tina

Tina

Italian American Favorites

My grandma Tina first showed me the joy of bringing people together through food. This collection of Italian American recipes is an homage to many of her classic flavors, with a bit of a spin.

Tina's Meatballs

Meatball Mix

½ cup (55 g) finely grated
  pecorino Romano

½ cup (45 g) panko
  breadcrumbs

2 eggs, beaten

1 small yellow onion,
  shredded on the large
  holes of a box grater

4 garlic cloves, finely grated

¼ cup (15 g) finely chopped
  fresh parsley

1½ teaspoons kosher salt

½ teaspoon freshly cracked
  black pepper

8 ounces (227 g) ground
  beef (80/20)

8 ounces (227 g) ground
  pork

Olive oil, for greasing your
  hands and searing

Sauce

One 24-ounce (680 g) jar
  passata

½ cup (120 ml) water

2 tablespoons granulated
  sugar

2 Parmesan rinds (if you
  have them)

1 dried bay leaf

Kosher salt and freshly
  cracked black pepper,
  to taste

These are the meatballs I grew up eating and loving. Watching my grandma Tina make these meatballs was my first introduction to the importance of tasting your food and seasoning as you go. She would always try a bit of the raw meat mixture to adjust the seasoning before forming all the meatballs, and although it made me a little squeamish at the time, I remember thinking how much sense it made. As much as I love my grandma, I don't suggest trying raw meatball mix for seasoning; instead, you can cook a small bit in a pan and taste it that way. All that being said, I have done all the taste testing ahead of time, and this is my ideal meatball. There's nothing crazy happening in this recipe, but these meatballs are guaranteed to be tender, flavorful, and nostalgic. Is there a better combo of adjectives for a meatball? I think not. Combining everything but the meat first and then gently mixing in the meat prevents the meatballs from becoming overworked and tough. Tina rarely added veal to her meatballs, and I skip it, too, but feel free to use a combo of beef, pork, and veal in this recipe if you'd like. When searing the meatballs, don't worry too much about maintaining a perfect, round shape; it's almost impossible, and in my opinion, if a meatball is perfectly round, it's probably not a very good meatball. This recipe makes the perfect amount of meatballs and sauce for serving over 1 pound (454 g) of pasta, but I also love enjoying these topped simply with grated pecorino Romano, torn fresh basil, and some focaccia on the side for dipping.

1. **Make the meatballs:** Add the pecorino Romano, panko, eggs, onion, garlic, parsley, salt, and pepper to a large bowl, and mix with a spoon to combine. Add the beef and pork, and mix with your hands just until combined. Try not to overwork the meat!

2. Using oiled hands, form the meatball mixture into 1½-inch (4 cm) meatballs (35 to 40 g each). Place the finished meatballs on a sheet tray or large plate. You should yield 16 to 18 meatballs.

3. Coat the bottom of a large pot with olive oil, and heat over medium-high heat. Working in two batches, add half of the meatballs to the pot, and sear on one side until golden, 4 or 5 minutes.

4. Use a small spoon or offset spatula to carefully flip over the meatballs and brown the other side for another 1 or 2 minutes. (The meatballs will not be fully cooked at this point; they will finish in the sauce.) Transfer the meatballs to a plate, set aside, and repeat with the second half of the meatballs, adding more oil to the pot as needed.

5. **Make the sauce:** Reduce the heat under the pot to low, and carefully add the passata. Add the water to the passata jar, cover, shake to fully clean out the jar, and pour into the pot. Stir, scraping up any brown bits from the bottom of the pot.

6. Add the sugar, Parmesan rinds, if using, and bay leaf, and season with salt and pepper. Add the meatballs and any accumulated juices, and gently stir to cover the meatballs in sauce.

7. Bring the sauce to a simmer and then reduce the heat to low. Cover and cook, uncovering every now and then to stir, for 25 minutes.

8. Uncover and cook, stirring occasionally, for another 10 minutes.

9. Season with more salt and pepper, remove the bay leaf, and serve.

Sunday Gravy

SERVES 6 TO 8

Gravy

1 pound (454 g) lamb neck bones (these should be meaty), cut into 2-inch (5 cm) pieces

Kosher salt and freshly cracked black pepper, to taste

Olive oil, for searing

2 medium yellow onions, small diced

8 garlic cloves, minced

3 tablespoons tomato paste

Two 24-ounce (680 g) jars passata

2 dried bay leaves

1 tablespoon granulated sugar

½ teaspoon red pepper flakes

1 batch Tina's Meatballs (page 190), prepared through step 2

1 pound (454 g) hot Italian sausage (4 or 5 links)

Braciole

½ cup (55 g) finely grated pecorino Romano

½ cup (45 g) panko breadcrumbs

¼ cup (15 g) finely chopped fresh parsley

2 tablespoons olive oil

3 garlic cloves, finely grated

1 egg

Kosher salt and freshly cracked black pepper, to taste

8 very thin slices (1 to 1½ pounds/454 to 680 g) top round steak (see Note)

Butcher's twine, for securing the braciole

½ cup (120 ml) water, divided

continued >>

Grandma Tina's gravy was probably the first dish that made me realize how much I love food. My grandpa Sam would always lovingly tease me about the amount of gravy-smothered pasta I could eat. There was so much I loved about eating pasta at Tina's house: I loved the smell of the gravy simmering on the stove, coupled with the potent aroma of the bowl of grated pecorino Romano at the center of the table. I loved being with my family, eating something we all enjoyed. I loved the slight sense of chaos of having the whole family in the house at once and the extremely loud yet comforting sound of everyone's voices as we all talked over each other. I didn't know it then, but everything about Sunday supper at my grandma's is what led to me to love food and cooking the way I do now. All that being said, this is Tina's beloved gravy recipe. It's the utmost definition of a labor of love but so, so worth it. It makes enough for 1½ to 2 pounds (680 to 907 g) of pasta, depending on how saucy you like things. Tina always served this with penne, but boil any short-cut pasta shape you desire. Be sure to top your bowl with a bunch of pecorino Romano, and complete the meal with the Vinegary Iceberg Salad (page 194). We always had a liter of RC Cola on the table, which I highly recommend here as well.

1. **Make the gravy:** Season the lamb neck bones all over with salt and black pepper. Heat a large, heavy-bottomed pot over medium heat. Coat the bottom of the pot with a thin layer of olive oil. Add the neck bones, and sear all over until golden brown, 4 to 6 minutes per side. Transfer the bones to a plate, and set aside.

2. Add the onions and garlic to the pan, and cook, stirring occasionally, until softened, 5 or 6 minutes. Add the tomato paste, and cook, stirring constantly, until slightly browned, 1 or 2 minutes.

3. Add the passata, bay leaves, sugar, and red pepper flakes. Season with a big pinch of salt and a good amount of black pepper. Nestle the lamb neck bones in the sauce, and bring to a simmer. Reduce the heat to low, cover, and cook, stirring occasionally to prevent scorching on the bottom, for 1 hour.

4. **Meanwhile, make the braciole:** Mix the pecorino Romano, panko, parsley, olive oil, garlic, and egg in a medium bowl. Season with salt and black pepper.

5. Lightly season one side of the beef slices with salt and black pepper. Spread a thin layer of filling over each slice of beef to cover. Starting at one of the shorter ends, roll up the beef to make a small roll. Repeat with the remaining beef and stuffing.

6. Tie the rolls with two pieces of butcher's twine to secure. Lightly season the outside of the braciole with salt and pepper.

7. Heat a large cast-iron pan over medium heat, and coat the bottom of the pan with a thin layer of olive oil. Working in two batches, add the braciole and sear on all sides until golden, 4 or 5 minutes per side. Transfer to the pot with the gravy.

8. Deglaze the cast-iron pan with about ¼ cup (60 ml) water, and add the drippings to the pot of gravy. (Skip this step if the fond smells or looks at all burnt.)

9. Reduce the heat to low, and simmer, covered, uncovering and stirring occasionally to prevent scorching, for 2 hours.

For Serving

1½ pounds (680 g) dry pasta of choice, cooked to al dente

Freshly grated pecorino Romano, to taste

NOTE Your steak slices should be ⅛ inch (3 mm) thick and about 6 × 4 inches (15 × 10 cm) in size. Most of the time, you can find this cut ready to go at the butcher or in the meat section of the grocery store. If you can't find it, the butcher usually can prepare it for you if you ask kindly. If all else fails, you can buy a chunk of top round, slice it about ¼ inch (6 mm) thick, and then pound it with a meat mallet to the correct size and thickness.

10. Clean the cast-iron pan, and heat over medium-high heat. Coat the pan with a thin layer of olive oil. Add the meatballs, and sear on one side until golden, 4 or 5 minutes.

11. Use a small spoon or offset spatula to carefully flip over the meatballs, and brown the other side for another 1 or 2 minutes. (The meatballs will not be fully cooked at this point; they will finish in the sauce.) Transfer the meatballs to a plate, and set aside.

12. Deglaze the pan with ¼ cup (60 ml) water, and add the drippings to the pot of gravy.

13. Clean the cast-iron pan, and heat over medium heat. Coat the bottom of the pan with a thin layer of olive oil. Add the sausage, and sear until golden on both sides, 3 or 4 minutes per side. Set the browned sausage aside. (There won't be any worthwhile fond here, so no need to deglaze!)

14. After the braciole has cooked in the gravy for 2 hours, gently nestle in the seared meatballs and sausage. This will be a snug mixture! Simmer the sauce over very low heat, uncovered, stirring every now and then, until the sauce has reduced a bit and the meatballs and sausage are cooked through, about 1 hour.

15. Remove the sausage links, cut them into 2-inch (5 cm) pieces (Tina always did this, so I do it, too!), and return them to the pot. Remove the twine from the braciole, and return them to the gravy. Tina always left the lamb bones in the gravy to serve because their meat is really tasty as well.

16. Season the gravy with salt and black pepper to taste, remove the bay leaves, and enjoy the fruits of your labor over a big bowl of pasta, with a mountain of freshly grated pecorino Romano on top. I like serving this family style so people can pick and choose whatever meat they want from the pot.

Vinegary Iceberg Salad

SERVES 6

Dressing

¼ cup (60 ml) red wine vinegar

1 tablespoon granulated sugar

1½ teaspoons kosher salt

1 teaspoon dried oregano

½ teaspoon freshly cracked
black pepper

½ cup (120 ml) extra virgin
olive oil, plus more for
topping

Salad

1 medium head iceberg lettuce,
quartered, cored, leaves
separated, and torn into large
bite-size pieces

5 large red radishes, thinly
sliced on a mandoline

3 mini seedless cucumbers, cut
into random bite-size pieces

1 small carrot, peeled and thinly
sliced on a mandoline

Kosher salt and freshly cracked
black pepper, to taste

4 Campari tomatoes, cut into
small wedges

Torn fresh basil leaves, to taste

This is the first salad I learned to make. Every Sunday supper at Grandma Tina's included this vinegary, crunchy iceberg salad. From my memory, it was my aunt Grace's job to dress the salad just before we ate. I would always volunteer as taste tester, and I have such fond memories of tasting the salad and helping her decide if it needed more vinegar, oil, salt, or sugar to get the perfect balance. The salad was so vinegary that there often would be a good few tablespoons of vinegar left in the bottom of the bowl after it was eaten. I used to drink that leftover vinegar right out of the bowl, which I remember everyone being somewhat shocked by—but hey, to this day, I still love me some vinegar. It was probably some sort of sign. I also must note that the colder the iceberg, the better the salad here! This recipe is an essential accompaniment to the Sunday Gravy (page 192). Adding some grated pecorino Romano on top, if it happens to be on the table with the gravy, is also a delightful finish.

1. **Prepare the dressing:** Add the vinegar, sugar, salt, oregano, and pepper to a medium bowl, and whisk to combine. Stream in the olive oil while whisking continuously. (The dressing doesn't have to be perfectly emulsified; a broken vinaigrette is just fine here.)

2. **Make the salad:** Add the iceberg, radishes, cucumbers, and carrot to a large bowl. Toss with your desired amount of dressing, saving any extra for another salad or for serving on the side. Season with salt and pepper.

3. Transfer the salad to a large platter, and top with the tomatoes and basil. Drizzle with a bit more olive oil, sprinkle with a few cracks of pepper, and serve.

Garlicky Escarole
with Guanciale Breadcrumbs

SERVES 4 TO 6

Kosher salt and freshly cracked black pepper, to taste

2 large bunches escarole (about 2 pounds/907 g), cores trimmed, roughly chopped, and washed (it can be quite gritty!)

4 ounces (113 g) guanciale (see Tip), small diced

¾ cup (68 g) panko breadcrumbs

3 tablespoons olive oil

4 garlic cloves, thinly sliced

¼ teaspoon red pepper flakes

Although escarole falls into the bitter green family, I find it has a much mellower flavor, closer to the mildness of green leaf lettuce. It is considerably less bitter than some other bitter greens, like radicchio or dandelion greens (which I also adore; no shade to them!). Grandma Tina often would crisp some bacon when she sautéed bitter greens, and that simple addition always made them feel more special. The guanciale breadcrumbs here act in the same way, adding an extra bit of crunchy, umami pizzazz.

1. Bring a large pot of water to a boil over high heat. Season the water with a pinch of salt. Add the escarole, and boil until just tender, 3 or 4 minutes.

2. Strain the escarole through a colander, and gently press the greens with the back of a spoon to remove more excess moisture. Let the escarole continue to drain in the colander while you prepare the topping.

3. Add the guanciale to a large sauté pan, set over medium-low heat, and cook, stirring, until golden brown and crispy, 10 to 12 minutes.

4. Using a slotted spoon, transfer the guanciale to a paper towel–lined plate. Pour out all but 2 tablespoons of fat from the pan.

5. Add the panko to the pan, and toast, stirring constantly, until golden brown, 4 or 5 minutes. Transfer to a small bowl.

6. Finely chop the crispy guanciale, add it to the bowl with the panko, and toss. Season with salt and black pepper.

7. Clean the sauté pan, add the olive oil and garlic, and return to medium-low heat. Cook the garlic, stirring constantly, until lightly golden, 3 or 4 minutes.

8. Add the red pepper flakes and escarole, toss to coat the greens in the garlic and oil, and cook just to meld all the flavors and heat the escarole, 1 or 2 minutes. Season with salt and black pepper.

9. Transfer the escarole to a serving bowl. Right before serving, top it with some of the guanciale breadcrumbs. Don't do this too early because they will get soggy! Serve the remaining breadcrumbs at the table so people can add more as they eat.

TIP You likely will have extra guanciale fat leftover, which you could use in place of olive oil in this recipe if you'd like. I prefer using olive oil so the whole dish doesn't just taste like guanciale. Regardless, be sure to save any fat that you don't use for future cooking—sautéing, roasting, or making sauce.

Artichoke Gratin

Artichokes are such a big part of my childhood. Whenever they made an appearance at my grandma's as a part of Sunday supper, or when my dad would bring home a huge bag from the grocery store, it was a sign of spring and the feeling of new beginnings or an indication of a special event. My mom learned to make stuffed artichokes from Tina, and then she taught me. I hold recipes like this so close to my heart because I don't remember one specific moment I was "taught" to make them. They were learned over time, through many occasions of cooking and eating as a family, and that's so special to me. This gratin is a take on those stuffed artichokes from my childhood. It has all the flavors, just presented in a slightly different way. The artichokes are halved, and the chokes are removed, making them much easier (and a bit less messy) to eat and get to the best part: the heart! This would be a great addition to a holiday spread or served alongside a roast chicken or a perfect steak dinner.

SERVES 8

2 lemons

5 large artichokes (about 1 pound/454 g each) with long
   stems attached (see Note 1)

½ cup (45 g) plain breadcrumbs

¼ cup (15 g) finely chopped fresh parsley

2 oil-packed anchovy fillets, finely chopped

2 garlic cloves, finely grated

2 tablespoons olive oil, plus more for greasing

Kosher salt and freshly cracked black pepper, to taste

¾ cup (180 ml) heavy cream

¾ cup (180 ml) whole milk

1 cup (110 g) finely grated pecorino Romano

1. Zest the lemons, and reserve the zest for topping the gratin. Halve the lemons, and squeeze their juice into a large bowl. Throw the lemon halves into the bowl as well. Fill the bowl with cold water, and set aside.

2. Trim about 1½ inches (4 cm) off the top of one artichoke with a serrated knife and discard. Using your hands, peel off the tough outer dark-green leaves, leaf by leaf, until you reach the more tender inner pale-green ones. Discard the outer leaves (see Note 2).

3. Using a peeler, peel away any remaining dark leafy pieces left on the heart. Peel the stem to remove the fibrous outside and reveal the tender, very pale-green interior. (The inside stem is an extension of the heart!) Trim the stem to 3 inches (8 cm) long, if needed. (If your artichokes don't have stems, ignore this trimming step.)

4. Using a serrated knife, cut the artichoke in half lengthwise and place it in the lemon water to prevent oxidation. Repeat steps 2 to 4 with the remaining artichokes.

5. Preheat the oven 400°F (200°C) with a rack positioned in the center. Set up a steamer over medium heat, and bring to a low boil. Grease a 12-inch (30 cm) cast-iron skillet or 3-quart (3 L) baking dish with olive oil.

6. Remove the artichokes from the lemon water (discard the water), place them in the steamer, and cook until the hearts are very tender, 25 to 35 minutes, depending on size.

7. While the artichokes steam, add the breadcrumbs, parsley, anchovies, garlic, and olive oil to a small bowl, and stir to combine. Season with salt and pepper. Set aside.

8. Transfer the cooked artichokes to a large plate or sheet tray. Carefully, to avoid breaking the artichokes, scoop out the fuzzy choke at the top of the heart, any purple leaves, and any remaining prickly inner leaves with a small spoon. Discard the chokes and prickly inner leaves. Place the artichokes, scooped side up, in the prepared baking dish.

9. Bring the cream and milk to a simmer in a small saucepan over medium heat. Add the pecorino Romano, and whisk.

10. Reduce the heat to medium-low, and simmer, whisking continuously, until the cheese is melted and the sauce is slightly thickened, 3 or 4 minutes. Season with pepper. Pour the cheese sauce all over the artichokes, and tightly cover the baking dish with foil.

11. Bake for 25 minutes, until bubbling and starting to brown. Uncover, and top with the reserved breadcrumb mixture all over.

12. Broil on high for 3 to 5 minutes, until the breadcrumbs are golden brown and crispy. Top with the reserved lemon zest, and serve.

13. Eat the artichokes by picking off any outer fibrous leaves and using your teeth to scrape off the tender meat from the fibrous leaf. Discard the remainder of the leaf. When you get to the very inner leaves, they will be tender and you can eat the entire leaf. After you're through all the leaves, you will have made it to the heart, which is totally edible, including the stem!

NOTES

1. If you can't find artichokes with stems, you can still make the recipe, ignoring any steps involving the stems. The ones with stems are preferable because the stems are an extension of the heart, which is my favorite part!

2. Wear gloves when prepping the artichokes to prevent staining or pricking your hands.

PasTINA and Mini Meatball Soup

SERVES 4 TO 6

½ recipe meatball mix from Tina's Meatballs (page 190)

Olive oil, for searing and drizzling

3 garlic cloves, finely minced

2 celery stalks, small diced

1 small fennel bulb, cored and small diced (fronds reserved for topping)

1 medium yellow onion, small diced

Kosher salt and freshly cracked black pepper, to taste

2 tablespoons tomato paste

6 cups (1.4 L) chicken broth, homemade (see page 92) or store-bought

2 dried bay leaves

½ cup (90 g) dry pastina

1 medium bunch (about 12 ounces/340 g) dandelion greens, tough stem end removed and roughly chopped

Grated pecorino Romano, to taste

Lemon zest, to taste

Might one just call this Italian wedding soup? Maybe, but that's not the point. Grandma Tina didn't call it that, so neither will I. Italian wedding soup also usually uses acini de pepe pasta, and here, we are using the beloved pastina. Tiny and often star-shaped, pastina is also commonly referred to as Italian penicillin to reference its nostalgic coziness that makes it a perfect sick-day meal. The touch of tomato paste in this recipe also sets it apart from most Italian wedding soups. My grandpa Sam was notorious for foraging his own dandelion greens from around the Chicago area, and they often made their way into Tina's cooking. As homage, I wilted in some dandelion greens at the end, but any green like kale, Swiss chard, or even spinach would be lovely.

1. Using oiled hands, form the Tina's Meatballs mixture into very tiny meatballs, about 1 teaspoon (7 g) each.

2. Coat the bottom of a large pot with olive oil, and heat over medium-high heat. Working in two batches, add half of the meatballs to the pot, and sear on one side until golden, 2 to 4 minutes. Use a small spoon or offset spatula to carefully flip over the meatballs, and brown the other side for another 1 or 2 minutes. Transfer the meatballs to a plate. (The meatballs will not be fully cooked at this point; they will finish in the soup.) Repeat with the second half of the meatballs, adding more oil to the pot as needed.

3. Reduce the heat to medium, and add more oil to the pot, if needed. Add the garlic, celery, fennel, and onion, and cook until softened, 5 to 7 minutes. Season with salt and pepper.

4. Stir in the tomato paste, and cook until slightly brown, 1 or 2 minutes. Add the chicken broth and bay leaves. Bring to a boil and then reduce the heat to medium-low for a light simmer. Add the meatballs, and simmer for 10 minutes.

5. Increase the heat to medium, and bring the soup back to a boil. Stir in the pastina, and cook, maintaining a steady but not rapid boil, until the pastina is cooked through, 6 or 7 minutes. Stir every now and then to ensure the pastina isn't sticking to the bottom of the pot. Remove the bay leaves.

6. Reduce the heat to low, and add the dandelion greens. Cook until the greens wilt, 2 or 3 minutes. Season with salt and pepper.

7. Serve topped with pecorino Romano, lemon zest, the reserved fennel fronds, pepper, and a drizzle of olive oil.

TIP The pasta will continue to soak up liquid as the pot sits off the heat, so feel free to add a splash of water or stock if you have any leftovers or when reheating.

Lemony Cauliflower Chicken and Rice Soup

SERVES 6 TO 8

2½ pounds (1.1 kg) bone-in, skin-on chicken thighs (6 to 8 thighs)

Kosher salt and freshly cracked black pepper, to taste

Olive oil, for searing

1 large yellow onion, small diced

3 celery stalks, small diced

1 small fennel bulb, cored and small diced

5 garlic cloves, minced

8 cups (1.9 L) unsalted chicken broth, homemade (see page 92) or store-bought

1 small head cauliflower (about 2 pounds/907 g), cored and cut into bite-size florets

2 Parmesan rinds (if you have them)

2 dried bay leaves

4 eggs

Zest and juice of 2 lemons (zest reserved for serving)

For Serving

Cooked jasmine rice, to taste (see Note)

Fresh dill fronds, to taste

Freshly grated pecorino Romano, to taste

Because my mom mainly learned to cook from my grandma Tina, I grew up eating renditions of Tina's recipes quite frequently. A Tina classic that always made the weekly rotation at our house was cauliflower and rice. It was a very simple soupy, porridge-y mix of cauliflower and rice cooked down in chicken stock. There wasn't much to it, but it always provided a homey sense of comfort. This soup combines those same cozy flavors with avgolemono, the classic Greek lemon and chicken soup. I like to cook the rice separately from the soup here because I prefer a slightly less-starchy broth that will stay nice and soupy even in leftover form.

1. Preheat the oven to 325°F (165°C). Line a sheet tray with parchment paper.

2. Generously season the chicken thighs all over with salt and pepper. Coat the bottom of a large, heavy-bottomed pot with olive oil, and heat over medium heat until the oil begins to ripple. Add the chicken thighs, skin side down, and sear until they are deeply golden and the chicken naturally releases from the pan, 10 to 14 minutes. Flip over the thighs, and cook the second side until lightly seared, 2 or 3 minutes.

3. Transfer the chicken thighs to a plate, and carefully (they will be hot!) peel off the skin using tongs. Place the chicken skins on the sheet tray.

4. Bake the chicken skins for 40 to 45 minutes, until shatteringly crispy. Set aside to cool and then break into irregular shards and reserve for topping the soup.

5. Meanwhile, add the onion, celery, fennel, and garlic to the pot with the chicken drippings. Season with a good pinch of salt and a few grinds of pepper, and cook until softened, 5 or 6 minutes. Pour in the broth, and scrape up any brown bits from the bottom of the pan.

6. Return the chicken and any accumulated drippings to the pot along with the cauliflower, Parmesan rinds, and bay leaves. Bring the mixture to a boil and then reduce the heat to low. Simmer, uncovered, until the chicken is cooked, shreddable, and has an internal temperature of at least 185°F (85°C) and the cauliflower is very soft and falling apart, 40 to 45 minutes.

7. Remove the bay leaves and Parmesan rinds. Transfer the chicken thighs to a plate, and shred the meat off the bone using two forks.

8. Whisk the eggs and lemon juice in a medium bowl until homogeneous. While quickly whisking the eggs, add a few ladles of the hot soup to the egg mixture to temper the mixture and bring it up to temperature without scrambling the eggs.

9. Whisk the tempered egg mixture into the pot of soup. Bring to a simmer, and cook, stirring, until slightly thickened, 4 or 5 minutes. Stir in the reserved shredded chicken.

10. To serve, add a small scoop of the cooked rice to each serving bowl and then pour the hot soup over the top. Drizzle with a touch of olive oil, and top with some dill, pecorino Romano, pepper, lemon zest, and crushed pieces of the reserved crispy chicken skin.

NOTE I cooked 1½ cups (270 g) dry rice in my rice cooker to yield about 3 cups (420 g) cooked rice, but you can make more or less depending on your preference.

Chicago-Style Braised Italian Beef Sandwiches

MAKES FOUR 6-INCH (15 CM) SUBS

4 pounds (1.8 kg) beef shanks (3 or 4 pieces, 1½ inch/4 cm thick)

2 teaspoons porcini mushroom powder (see Tip on page 66)

Kosher salt and freshly cracked black pepper, to taste

Olive oil, for searing

6 garlic cloves, smashed

3 celery stalks, roughly chopped

2 large yellow onions, roughly chopped

1 tablespoon dried oregano

2 teaspoons garlic powder

2 teaspoons onion powder

1 teaspoon red pepper flakes

One 12-ounce (360 ml) bottle amber ale of choice

2 cups (480 ml) unsalted beef stock, homemade (see page 90) or store-bought

1 dried bay leaf

½ bunch fresh thyme sprigs

For Serving

3 green bell peppers, stems removed, halved, and ribs and seeds removed

Olive oil, for drizzling

Kosher salt and freshly cracked black pepper, to taste

Four 6- to 8-inch (15 to 20 cm) Italian sub rolls, split

Chicago-style giardiniera, homemade (see page 46) or store-bought, to taste

This sandwich is my childhood all wrapped up in a beef jus–soaked Italian sub roll. There's nothing quite like a Chicago-style beef, whether it be from my grandma's kitchen or from the best fast-food chain to exist, Portillo's. (I am forever patiently waiting for an East Coast location.) The classic sandwich is made with thinly shaved roast beef, but you probably don't have a deli slicer at home, unless your husband owns a grocery store, like Tina's did. I find this braised beef version to be much more feasible than, and just as tasty as, the original, with no slicing required. I opt for beef shanks here because the bone and its marrow add a great depth of flavor to the braising liquid that's then used as the jus for dipping. I'm not the biggest fan of green peppers on the regular, but here, I find them as essential to the sandwich as the spicy giardiniera. You can find Chicago-style giardiniera online or make the Chicago-Style Fennel Giardiniera (page 46) for even more fun.

1. Preheat the oven to 325°F (165°C) with a rack positioned in the lower third.

2. Season the beef all over with the mushroom powder and a generous amount of salt and black pepper.

3. Coat the bottom of a large, heavy-bottomed oven-safe pot with olive oil, and heat over medium heat until the oil begins to ripple. Add the beef in batches, and sear until deeply golden, 5 to 7 minutes per side. Transfer to a plate.

4. Add the garlic, celery, and onions, and cook, stirring occasionally, until lightly browned and slightly softened, 7 to 9 minutes. Add the oregano, garlic powder, onion powder, and red pepper flakes, and cook until aromatic, 30 seconds.

5. Deglaze the pan with the beer, scraping up the brown bits from the bottom of the pan, and reduce by half, 2 or 3 minutes. Add the beef stock, bay leaf, and thyme, along with the reserved beef and any accumulated juices, bring to a simmer, and cover.

6. Transfer the pot to the oven, and bake for 3 to 3½ hours, until the meat is tender and shreds easily with a fork.

7. Remove the pot from the oven. Increase the oven temperature to 400°F (200°C).

8. Place the peppers on a sheet tray, toss with a generous drizzle of olive oil, and season with salt and black pepper. Turn the peppers cut side down, and bake for 30 to 40 minutes, until very, very soft. Let cool slightly. Remove the skins and then slice into 1½-inch (4 cm) strips.

9. Meanwhile, transfer the beef to a cutting board. Use a fork to gently break up the meat into bite-size pieces. (Don't completely shred the meat. You want nice, small chunks.) Discard any large bones.

10. Strain the liquid from the pot through a fine-mesh strainer into a medium pot. This is the jus for the sandwich. Bring the jus to a soft simmer over medium heat. Season with salt and black pepper. Return the meat to the jus, reduce the heat to very low, and keep warm until ready to serve.

11. To serve, use a slotted spoon to scoop up some meat from the jus and pile it on a roll. Quickly dip the base of the roll in the jus to soak slightly. Top with the soft green peppers and some giardiniera, and serve.

Tina's Chicken Bake

SERVES 4 TO 6

Chicken Bake

1½ pounds (680 g/3 or 4 large) Yukon Gold potatoes, cut into wedges 1 inch (2.5 cm) thick

1 pound (454 g/3 or 4 medium) Roma tomatoes, cut into wedges 1 inch (2.5 cm) thick

One 14-ounce (397 g) can quartered artichoke hearts, drained

6 large shallots, halved

4 large garlic cloves, grated

3 tablespoons olive oil, plus more for drizzling

Kosher salt and freshly cracked black pepper, to taste

2½ to 3 pounds (1.1 to 1.3 kg) bone-in, skin-on chicken thighs (6 to 8 thighs)

2 teaspoons dried oregano

Freshly grated pecorino Romano, for topping, optional

Herb Sauce

½ cup (14 g) loosely packed fresh basil leaves

½ cup (14 g) loosely packed fresh dill fronds

½ cup (14 g) loosely packed fresh parsley leaves

¼ cup (60 ml) extra virgin olive oil

3 tablespoons fresh lemon juice (from about 1 lemon)

1 teaspoon honey

Kosher salt and freshly cracked black pepper, to taste

Admittedly, I have never eaten this dish made by my grandma herself, but when I was doing R&D for this cookbook, I asked around the family for some of their favorite things Tina used to make. I spoke mostly with my mom and dad and my aunt Cathy, who is actually a chef herself and yet another strong female figure in the culinary world I have always looked up to. She mentioned a chicken, potato, and artichoke bake, and I instantly knew I wanted to include a version in this book. There is something so exceptionally special about a potato that has soaked up a bunch of luscious chicken fat. Tina often added basil to this dish, so I made a quick herb puree with basil, dill, and parsley as a nice, fresh component to eat alongside this lovely roasted meal.

1. **Make the chicken:** Preheat the oven to 425°F (220°C).

2. Add the potatoes, tomatoes, artichoke hearts, shallots, and garlic to a 9×13-inch (23×33 cm) baking dish (or 3.5-quart/3.3 L baking dish). Toss with the olive oil, and season with salt and pepper.

3. Pat the chicken dry, and season all over with salt, pepper, and oregano. Place the chicken on top of the vegetables, and drizzle the chicken skin with a bit of olive oil.

4. Bake for 50 to 60 minutes, until the potatoes are tender, the chicken is golden, and the internal temperature of the chicken is at least 185°F (85°C).

5. **About 15 minutes before the chicken is done, make the herb sauce:** Add the basil, dill, parsley, extra virgin olive oil, lemon juice, honey, salt, and pepper to a high-powered blender, and blend until smooth.

6. Transfer the chicken to a plate, and tent with foil to keep warm.

7. Turn the broiler to high, and broil the vegetables in the baking dish until they start to char, 6 to 8 minutes. (Broilers vary in strength, so keep an eye on the vegetables as they may brown more quickly!)

8. Serve the chicken and vegetables topped with some of the pan juices, the herb sauce, and pecorino Romano, if using.

Cannoli Crunch Ice Cream Cake

SERVES 6 TO 8

Cake

Unsalted butter, for greasing

100 grams (½ cup plus 3 tablespoons) cake flour, plus more for dusting

100 grams (½ cup) granulated sugar

1 teaspoon kosher salt

¾ teaspoon baking powder

60 grams (¼ cup) whole milk, at room temperature

50 grams (¼ cup) olive oil

2 egg yolks, at room temperature

1 egg, at room temperature

1 teaspoon vanilla bean paste

⅛ teaspoon pure almond extract

Cannoli Crunch

60 grams (⅓ cup) mini chocolate chips

45 grams (½ cup) roughly crushed cannoli shells

45 grams (⅓ cup) roughly chopped roasted salted pistachios

No-Churn Ricotta Ice Cream

260 grams (1 cup) whole-milk ricotta

200 grams (½ cup plus 2 tablespoons) sweetened condensed milk

120 grams (½ cup) heavy cream

2 tablespoons sweet Marsala wine or brandy

1 teaspoon vanilla bean paste

¾ teaspoon kosher salt

Pinch of ground cinnamon

NOTE A 9×13-inch (23×33 cm) baking dish will also work for this cake.

This cake is an ode to the cannoli that often made an appearance for Sunday supper at Tina's. It's also a tribute to cannoli cake, which, whether you requested it or not, was the standard birthday cake if you were celebrating at her house. There are a few components to this dessert, but the cake is quick to mix up (and can be made ahead!), and the ice cream layer is no-churn, so it's pretty simple! Cannoli shells are relatively easy to find at any Italian grocery store or bakery, but if you're having trouble sourcing them, crushed waffle cones make a great substitute.

1. Preheat the oven to 350°F (180°C) with a rack positioned in the center. Butter the bottom of a 9½×13-inch (24×33 cm) sheet tray (see Note), and line with parchment paper. Grease the pan all over with more butter, and dust with flour.

2. **Make the cake:** Add the sugar, flour, salt, and baking powder to a large bowl, and whisk to combine and break up any clumps. In a medium bowl, whisk the whole milk, olive oil, egg yolks, egg, vanilla, and almond extract. Pour the wet ingredients into the dry, and mix with a rubber spatula until just combined. Don't overmix; a few lumps are okay! Pour into the prepared pan.

3. Bake for 12 to 15 minutes, until the cake springs back when gently pressed and doesn't leave an imprint. Cool in the pan for 10 minutes and then carefully invert onto a wire rack to cool completely. (This cake layer can be made a day ahead, cooled, wrapped in plastic wrap, and stored at room temperature.)

4. Place the cooled cake on a cutting board with one of the longer sides facing you. Cut the cake vertically into even thirds.

5. **Make the cannoli crunch:** Mix the chocolate chips, cannoli shells, and pistachios in a small bowl.

6. **Make the no-churn ice cream layer:** Line a 9×5×3-inch (23×13×8 cm) loaf pan with two long pieces of plastic wrap arranged like a plus sign, with overhang on all sides.

7. Add the ricotta to a food processor, and process until light and fluffy, 1 minute. Transfer the whipped ricotta to a medium bowl along with the condensed milk, cream, Marsala, vanilla, salt, and cinnamon. Use an electric mixer on medium to whip until the mixture thickens and soft peaks form, 6 to 8 minutes.

8. **Assemble the cake:** Add one-third of the ice cream (about 1 cup/58 g), to the bottom of the lined loaf pan. Add one-third of the cake, then another one-third of the cream, then half (about ½ cup/72 g) of the cannoli crunch. Add another third of the cake. Layer on the remaining cream, and finally, the last piece of cake. Cover the top with plastic wrap, and freeze overnight or for at least 12 hours.

9. When you're ready to serve, let the cake sit at room temperature for 5 to 10 minutes and then invert it onto a serving platter. Carefully remove the loaf pan and peel away the plastic. Top the cake with the remaining cannoli crunch, slice, and serve. Store any remaining cake wrapped in plastic in the freezer for up to 2 weeks.

Olive Oil Pineapple Upside-Down Cake

SERVES 6 TO 8

Topping

3 tablespoons unsalted butter, plus more for greasing the pan

67 grams (⅓ cup) granulated sugar

2 tablespoons heavy cream, at room temperature

¾ teaspoon kosher salt

½ teaspoon vanilla bean paste

One 20-ounce (567 g) can pineapple slices in 100 percent pineapple juice, drained and patted dry

7 or 8 maraschino cherries, destemmed

Cake

130 grams (1 cup) all-purpose flour, plus more for dusting the pan

200 grams (1 cup) granulated sugar

120 grams (½ cup) full-fat Greek yogurt, at room temperature

105 grams (½ cup) olive oil, plus more for serving

2 eggs, at room temperature

2 teaspoons vanilla bean paste

⅛ teaspoon pure almond extract

65 grams (½ cup) super-fine blanched almond flour, lightly packed

2 teaspoons baking powder

1 teaspoon kosher salt

When I was a child, my excitement for a big bowl of my grandma's gravy and pasta at Sunday supper was equally matched by my excitement for dessert. My Aunt Grace would routinely arrive with dessert in hand from a local Italian bakery; this was usually either a box of cannoli or a pineapple upside-down cake. I adore both of these desserts now, but as a kid, I secretly hoped for the latter because I would never think to murmur that I didn't love cannoli in a Sicilian household. The fruity olive oil in this cake goes so well with the pineapple and makes for a fun Italian twist. I stick to the classic canned pineapple here; I find fresh pineapple can bake somewhat stringy, dry, and inconsistent. I love a honeyed whipped cream (see page 270) on the side, but a scoop of vanilla ice cream drizzled with some more olive oil would also be stunning.

1. Preheat the oven to 375°F (190°C). Cut a circle of parchment paper to fit the bottom of a 9-inch (23 cm) round cake pan. Grease the pan with a little butter to help the parchment stick to the bottom. Then grease the pan all over with butter and dust with all-purpose flour.

2. **Make the topping:** Heat the sugar in a small saucepan over low heat. Cook, stirring, until the sugar melts and then turns a deep amber color, 5 to 7 minutes. (The sugar will clump at first but will then melt and caramelize.)

3. Remove the pan from the heat, and slowly whisk in the butter and cream. (It will bubble up quite a bit!)

4. Return the pot to low heat, and cook, whisking, until everything is bubbly and combined, about 1 more minute. Turn off the heat, and stir in the salt and vanilla bean paste. Immediately pour the caramel into the prepared cake pan, and tilt the pan to cover the bottom with the caramel.

5. Arrange slices of pineapple on top of the caramel. Cut pieces of pineapple as needed to cover the whole pan (except the holes in the center of the pineapple rings). Add cherries in the holes of the pineapple slices. Set the pan aside.

6. **Make the batter:** Whisk the sugar, yogurt, olive oil, eggs, vanilla, and almond extract in a medium bowl until combined.

7. Add the all-purpose flour, almond flour, baking powder, and salt to a large bowl. Whisk to combine and break up any clumps. Pour in the wet ingredients, and whisk until just combined. Don't overmix; a few lumps are okay!

8. Pour the batter over the pineapple, and spread out evenly. Bake for 30 to 35 minutes, until a toothpick inserted into the cake comes out mostly clean with a few moist crumbs.

9. Let the cake cool in the pan for 10 minutes and then carefully invert the cake onto a wire rack positioned over a sheet pan or cutting board to catch any drips. If any small pieces of pineapple don't release, simply press them back onto the cake.

10. Slice and serve the cake warm. Store any cooled leftovers at room temperature in an airtight container for up to 2 days.

Sourdough

Crash Course

Sourdough baking is as much of an exact science as it is an intuitive art. The measurements of the ingredients are all very precise because they are based on baker's percentages (essentially, the weight of the flour determines the weight of the other ingredients), while a lot of the recipe method is based on feel and instinct. This is a brief and condensed look into the world of sourdough to help you get your feet wet and produce a beautiful boule.

Sourdough Starter

**MAKES ENOUGH
STARTER TO GET
STARTED**

Initial Starter Mix

60 grams (¼ cup) room-
temperature water

40 grams (5 tablespoons)
whole-wheat flour

10 grams (1 tablespoon
plus 1 teaspoon) bread
flour

First and Daily Starter
Feedings

12 grams (1 tablespoon)
sourdough starter

50 grams (3 tablespoons)
room-temperature water

25 grams (3 tablespoons)
bread flour

25 grams (3 tablespoons)
whole-wheat flour

I wouldn't call this a recipe for a sourdough starter but more a method. In my mind, a "recipe" implies something more exact, and making a starter from scratch is quite variable-dependent. This method is a great guide! A lot of starter methods will direct you to discard some starter and add flour directly into the same container to feed, but I prefer to remove the starter from its original container into a bowl, mix in the new flour and water, and then transfer the mixture to a new, clean container. It may seem like this method creates unnecessary dishes, but I find it to be overall less confusing. It also keeps the containers nice and clean and free of dried flour junk. I always use clear containers (I love using a plastic pint container or glass jar) to store my starter so I can easily see its growth and bubbles. You can also place a rubber band around the outside of the container at the top of the mixture so you have a clear indicator of the original height and can gauge the growth. The starter will take at least 12 days of daily feeding (for a total of 16 days from start to finish) to be established enough to make bread, but it may take more time, depending on the climate of your kitchen. The hotter and more humid it is, the quicker things will move along. If you still aren't seeing any movement after 12 days of daily feeding, let the starter sit at room temperature without feeding for 2 days and then return to the daily feeds. Sometimes starters just need a little space to breathe. Although I have included imperial measurements here, I highly recommend getting a digital scale and using the metric measurements, not only for precision but also to avoid coating measuring spoons or cups in sticky starter. Keep the sourdough discard in an airtight container in the fridge, and use it for discard recipes like the Sourdough Discard Flatbread (page 223).

1. **Make the initial mix:** Add the water, whole-wheat flour, and bread flour to a small bowl, and mix until fully combined.

2. Transfer to a clear container with a lid. Cover, but don't completely seal so the starter can breathe a bit. Let sit at room temperature for 2 days (see Tip 1). A bit of thin, grayish liquid (called "hooch") may develop at the top of your starter. Fear not; this is normal and can just be stirred back into your starter.

3. After 2 days, the starter should seem slightly bubbly, have risen a bit, and have a yeasty, fermented smell. Now the starter is ready to begin feeding.

4. **Feed the starter:** For the first feeding, add 12 grams (1 tablespoon) of the initial starter to a small bowl. Discard or save the remaining starter (aka sourdough discard) in another container (see Tip 2). Add the water, bread flour, and whole-wheat flour, and mix to combine.

5. Transfer the fed starter to a clear container with the lid left slightly ajar and let it sit at room temperature for another 2 days without feeding.

6. After 2 days, the starter will have risen again, appear slightly bubbly, and have a yeasty smell. Now the starter is ready for the **daily** feedings.

7. For the daily feedings, repeat step 4. Transfer to a clear container with the lid left slightly ajar, and let sit at room temperature for 24 hours.

8. Repeat these daily feedings (discarding or saving excess starter each time) until the starter more than doubles (almost triples) in the span of 8 to 10 hours.

TIPS

1. I find a 13-ounce (384 ml) repurposed glass jar to be the perfect size for making the starter. Any clear container will work, but I don't suggest anything smaller than that.

2. Sourdough discard is any excess starter that you don't need as you feed your starter. It can be saved in an airtight container in the refrigerator and used in many different recipes to add flavor and reduce waste.

This should happen around the twelfth day of daily feedings. The number of days depends on many variables (mainly heat and humidity levels), but it shouldn't take more than 14 days of daily feeding to establish an active starter.

9. When your starter is active, you're ready to make bread and can continue to page 218 to make a loaf of sourdough. Yay! If you aren't making bread right away, continue the daily feedings for 2 or 3 more days to really strengthen the starter. From there, continue daily feeds if you plan to make bread frequently; if not, place it in the refrigerator to store. If you opt to let it chill in the refrigerator for later use, feed it at least every 2 weeks to keep the starter strong. Pull the starter out of the refrigerator 2 or 3 days before you want to make bread. Feed the starter daily to restrengthen it before making the pre-bread mix (leaven) and then the loaf. The more you use and feed the starter, the stronger it will get and the better your final loaves will become, so don't give up!

A Loaf of Sourdough Bread

This is my go-to method for making a beautiful sourdough loaf. Sourdough can seem complicated, but really, it's just a very personal process. Everyone has a certain way they like to do it, and there truly is no one way to produce a successful loaf. This is a fairly streamlined process that I also find to be quite forgiving. It's not the end of the world if the shaping isn't perfect or you let the dough rest a bit longer than suggested. At the end of the day, you are going to have a lovely loaf of fresh, warm bread, and there's nothing bad about that. This recipe yields an even, medium crumb, perfect for eating freshly baked and for toasts and sandwiches alike. The more you make bread, the better your loaves will become! It's just one of those things. I don't usually suggest investing in special equipment to make specific recipes, but here, I do think a kitchen scale, a proofing basket, and a lame are well worth it.

MAKES 1 STANDARD LOAF

Pre-Bread Mix (aka Leaven)

100 grams (¼ cup plus 3 tablespoons) room-temperature water

90 grams (⅔ cup) bread flour

25 grams (2 tablespoons) established Sourdough Starter (page 216)

10 grams (1 tablespoon plus 1 teaspoon) whole-wheat flour

Dough

400 grams (1⅔ cups) room-temperature water

100 grams (½ cup) active leaven (from previous column)

400 grams (3 cups) bread flour, plus more for dusting

100 grams (¾ cup) whole-wheat flour

14 grams (1 tablespoon plus 1 teaspoon) kosher salt

1. **Make the pre-bread mix (leaven):** The night before you want to mix a loaf of sourdough, mix the water, bread flour, sourdough starter, and whole-wheat flour in a small bowl. At this point, you can also feed your starter as you normally would (see step 7 on page 216).

2. Transfer to a clear container (I like using a 1-quart/1 L plastic container or glass jar) with the lid left slightly ajar. Let sit at room temperature for 8 to 12 hours, until the leaven is bubbly and has more than doubled (almost tripled).

3. Be sure your leaven is active: Place a small pinch of the leaven into a cup of cold water. If it floats, it's ready. The starter also should be bubbly, airy, and fermented smelling. If it doesn't float and hasn't risen much, it likely needs to sit at room temperature for a bit longer.

4. **Make the dough:** Whisk the water and active leaven in a large bowl until the leaven dissolves. Add the bread flour and whole-wheat flour, and mix with your hands until completely combined. It will still look a bit shaggy at this point.

5. Scrape down the sides and bottom of the bowl with a rubber spatula to incorporate all the dry bits. Cover with plastic wrap, and let rest for 30 minutes to let the gluten relax. The dough will not rise here.

6. Sprinkle the salt evenly over the dough, and mix with your hands, using a pinching motion, until completely combined. Be thorough so that you don't end up with pockets of salt in your bread. Cover with plastic wrap, and let rest for 1 hour. The dough will not rise much at this point, but it should feel a bit more aerated.

7. Using damp hands, stretch and fold the dough: Gently pick up the north side of the dough, stretching it until you feel resistance, and fold it over to the south side of the bowl. Rotate the bowl 90 degrees, and repeat three times, until four sides have been stretched and folded. Cover and let rest for 1 hour.

8. Repeat the folds in step 7. Cover and let rest for 1 hour.

9. Repeat the folds in step 7 again. The dough should be slightly aerated and might have a few small bubbles on the surface. Cover and let rest for 2 or 3 hours, depending on the climate of your kitchen. (The hotter and more humid it is, the quicker things will move along.) The dough should almost double in size, and when you shake the bowl, it should be jiggly and fluffy, with potentially a few small bubbles on the surface.

10. Generously flour a work surface and use a floured bench scraper to carefully transfer the dough to the surface. Using cupped, floured hands, and working in a circular motion, roughly shape the dough into a ball.

11. Lightly flour the top of the dough and cover with a kitchen towel. Let rest on the counter for 30 minutes.

12. Uncover the dough (it should look like it has relaxed a bit), and dust the top with a touch more flour. Using a bench scraper, flip over the dough so the side you just floured is facing down.

13. Shape the dough by folding the side of the dough closest to you up to the center and then the left and right sides of the dough toward each other, overlapping in the middle. Then fold the farthest side of the dough toward you, all the way over. Flip over the entire piece of dough so the seam sides are now on the work surface.

14. Using cupped hands and working in a circular motion, shape the dough into a tight, uniform ball. It's important to form as tight of a ball as possible to create surface tension.

15. Flour a 9-inch (23 cm) round proofing basket or line a 9-inch (23 cm) wide bowl with a kitchen towel and then heavily flour the towel. Use a bench scraper to transfer the dough, smooth side down, to the basket or bowl.

16. Pinch the dough in all four quadrants, and pull into the center to help create even more tension and a tighter loaf. Lightly dust the top with more flour. Cover the basket with a kitchen towel, and refrigerate for at least 8 hours or up to 24 hours.

17. When you are ready to bake, place a 6-quart (5.7 L) Dutch oven with a lid in the oven on the middle rack. Preheat the oven to 475°F (245°C). Continue to preheat the Dutch oven (and ensure the oven is very hot) for 20 to 30 minutes after the oven has come to temperature.

18. Remove the loaf from the refrigerator. Gently tip the dough out of the basket onto a piece of parchment paper. Score the loaf using a lame or razor with one quick, long slash going down the middle. (A very sharp paring knife will work in a pinch.)

19. Remove the hot Dutch oven from the oven and carefully lower the bread inside using the ends of the parchment paper. Cover with the lid.

20. Bake for 25 to 30 minutes, until the bread has risen and is pale golden. Carefully remove the lid, and return the Dutch oven to the oven. Bake for 20 to 25 minutes, until the bread is deeply golden brown.

21. Use a spatula to carefully transfer the bread to a wire rack to cool completely, at least 1 hour, before slicing and serving.

Sourdough Discard Flatbread

MAKES 8 FLATBREADS

228 grams (1¾ cups) all-purpose flour, plus more for dusting

2 tablespoons whole-wheat flour

2 teaspoons kosher salt

2 teaspoons instant yeast (I like Saf-instant brand)

100 grams (⅓ cup) sourdough discard (from Sourdough Starter; page 216)

75 grams (⅓ cup) room-temperature water

60 grams (¼ cup) whole-milk Greek yogurt

3 tablespoons unsalted butter, very soft

15 grams (2 teaspoons) honey

Olive oil, for greasing the bowl and frying

Flake salt, for finishing

Our brief trip through Sourdough Land wouldn't be complete without at least one sourdough discard recipe! I thought a flatbread would be so great to include because it can be served with many of the other recipes in the book. It's a relatively simple bread to prepare and rounds out any meal. Enjoy it alongside any dip (from the book or otherwise), or slather it with any of the flavored butters in the next chapter. Fresh bread always turns a good meal into a truly special one. The use of discard in this recipe is more for the sour flavor it imparts than actual leavening, hence the addition of commercial yeast as well.

1. Whisk the all-purpose flour, whole-wheat flour, salt, and yeast in a medium bowl.

2. Add the sourdough discard, water, yogurt, butter, and honey to the bowl, and mix, starting with a fork and then switching to your hands, until fully combined.

3. Transfer to a lightly floured work surface, and knead the dough to form a cohesive ball, about 1 minute.

4. Transfer to a lightly oiled bowl, cover with plastic wrap or a kitchen towel, and let rest at room temperature until the dough has risen by about one-third, about 2 hours.

5. Transfer the dough to the lightly floured surface, and divide it into 8 equal pieces (about 70 grams/2.5 ounces each). Roll each portion into a rough ball, and cover lightly with a kitchen towel while you roll the rest.

6. Preheat a large cast-iron pan over medium-high heat until very hot and nearly smoking.

7. While the pan heats, lightly flour the work surface again and use a lightly floured rolling pin to roll out one ball of dough at a time to a rough 7-inch (18 cm) circle. (They don't have to be perfect circles! I actually prefer a more rustic, misshapen look.)

8. When the pan is hot, reduce the heat to medium-low and coat with 1 tablespoon olive oil.

9. Place 1 flatbread at a time in the hot pan, and cook until puffed and golden, about 1 minute. Flip over the flatbread, and cook until golden on the second side, about 1 more minute.

10. Transfer to a plate, immediately sprinkle with flake salt, and cover with a kitchen towel to keep warm while you roll and cook the remaining bread (see Tip).

11. Repeat the rolling and cooking method (wiping out any charred bits that stick to the pan and adding more oil by the teaspoon to keep the pan coated), until you have cooked all the flatbread. Serve warm!

TIP You can also keep the flatbreads warm on a sheet tray in a 200°F (95°C) oven as you cook the rest.

Breads and Butters

Bread of all kinds, accompanied by butter of all kinds.
Some sweet, some savory, and some that can do both.

A Very Olive-y Focaccia

400 grams (3 cups) bread
  flour

1 tablespoon plus
  ½ teaspoon kosher salt

1¼ teaspoons instant yeast
  (I like Saf-instant brand)

320 grams (1⅓ cups)
  room-temperature water

1 tablespoon olive oil, plus
  more for coating the bowl
  and pan and for topping
  the bread

Unsalted butter, for
  greasing

2 tablespoons olive brine
  from the jar

113 grams (1 cup) whole
  pitted Castelvetrano
  olives

Freshly cracked black
  pepper, for topping

I've always enjoyed a good focaccia, but I developed a much deeper appreciation for the bread while working at a restaurant called Cellar Door Provisions in Chicago. We would bake the most delicious, airy focaccia in the biggest cast-iron pan I have ever witnessed. It must have been at least 18 inches (46 cm) in diameter. Truly majestic. The focaccia we baked was a Ligurian-style focaccia, meaning we topped it with a salt brine (shout-out to Samin Nosrat's Salt, Fat, Acid, Heat, *the show from which I first learned of this style!), which gave it the most amazing taste and texture. Here, I'm subbing in the brine from a jar of olives to make an olive lover's dream focaccia. I like using Castelvetrano olives in this bread, but substitute with any briny olive you desire. This focaccia is lovely sliced and served as is to round out a meal, but it's also thick enough to be split in half and used to make a great sandwich.*

1. Whisk the bread flour, salt, and yeast in a medium bowl. Add the water and olive oil, and mix until thoroughly combined. (I find using my hands is easiest.) The dough might look a little lumpy, but there shouldn't be any dry pockets of flour. Scrape down the sides of the bowl.

2. Cover the bowl with plastic wrap, and let the dough rest at room temperature for 45 minutes.

3. Using damp hands, stretch and fold the dough: Gently pick up the north side of the dough, stretching it until you feel resistance, and then fold it over to the south side of the bowl. Rotate the bowl 90 degrees, and repeat three times, until four sides have been stretched and folded.

4. Cover, let rest for another 45 minutes, and then repeat the folding process from step 3.

5. Heavily grease a large bowl with olive oil, and transfer the dough to the bowl. Flip the dough over so it's all coated in oil.

6. Cover with plastic wrap, and place the dough in the refrigerator for at least 12 hours or up to 2 days.

7. When you are ready to bake, remove the dough from the refrigerator. Lightly butter (about 1 tablespoon) and heavily oil (about 2 tablespoons) a 12-inch (30 cm) cast-iron pan.

8. Spray a clean work surface with water, and transfer the dough to the damp surface.

9. With damp hands, shape the dough by folding the side of the dough closest to you up to the center, bringing the left and right sides of the dough in toward each other, and then folding the farthest side of the dough toward you. Flip the end closest to you all the way over so that the bottom of the dough is now the top. Using cupped hands and working in a circular motion, shape the dough into a uniform ball.

10. Transfer the dough to the cast-iron pan. Drizzle the top with a touch of olive oil.

11. Cover with plastic wrap, and let rest at room temperature for 1 hour.

12. Preheat the oven to 500°F (260°C) with a rack positioned in the lower third. Continue to let the dough rest as the oven preheats.

13. When the oven is hot, using oiled hands, dimple and press out the dough to fill the pan. Pour the olive brine all over the top of the dough, and generously drizzle with

more olive oil. Arrange the olives across the dough, and gently press them into the dough. Add a few cracks of pepper.

14. Bake for 25 to 30 minutes, rotating halfway through the cooking time, until deeply golden. Let cool in the pan for 5 minutes.

15. Using a spatula, carefully transfer the focaccia to a wire rack to help preserve the crunchy bottom crust. Serve warm. Keep any cooled leftovers wrapped in plastic or a ziplock bag, and store at room temperature for up to 3 days.

Hearty Seeded Rye Bread

MAKES ONE 9×4-INCH
(23×10 CM) LOAF

Unsalted butter, for greasing

235 grams (1¾ cups) bread flour

160 grams (1¼ cups) rye flour

150 grams (1 cup) pepitas, toasted (see Tip on page 54), plus more for topping

35 grams (¼ cup) sesame seeds, toasted (see Tip on page 234), plus more for topping

1 tablespoon baking soda

1 tablespoon kosher salt

400 grams (1⅔ cups) buttermilk

2 tablespoons honey

2 tablespoons dark molasses

This bread is a seeded rendition of kavring, a classic Swedish rye bread. Kavring is a beautifully dense bread with the deep, toasty flavors of rye, and when paired with pepitas and sesame seeds, it makes for an ideal hearty loaf. It's also a quick bread, which means it's super easy to throw together with no kneading or proofing required. Who doesn't love a bit of instant gratification every now and then, especially when it comes to fresh homemade bread? Because this bread is so hearty, I prefer to slice it on the thinner side for ideal enjoyment. I especially love it toasted alongside some runny eggs or topped with a lovely jam. Any of the butters later in this chapter would be delightful with it, too. For a truly special breakfast, top it with a thin spread of cream cheese and then layer on some cucumber, red onion, capers, smoked salmon, and dill. The toast toppings here are endless. I use a 9×4-inch (23×10 cm) Pullman loaf pan, which yields a slightly taller loaf, but feel free to use a 9×5-inch (23×13 cm) pan if you have it on hand. Just note it may take about 5 minutes fewer to bake.

1. Preheat the oven to 350°F (180°C) with a rack positioned in the center. Butter a 9×4-inch (23×10 cm) loaf pan all over.

2. Whisk the bread flour, rye flour, pepitas, sesame seeds, baking soda, and salt in a large bowl.

3. Add the buttermilk, honey, and molasses, and stir until all the dry ingredients are combined with the wet. This will be a very thick mixture.

4. Add the dough to the pan, and spread out evenly. Top with more pepitas and sesame seeds all over.

5. Bake for 60 to 65 minutes, until the bread has risen and a cake tester inserted into the center comes out clean. The bread should be 195°F to 200°F (90°C to 95°C) when tested with an instant-read thermometer.

6. Let the bread cool in the pan for 10 minutes and then invert the bread onto a wire rack to cool completely before slicing and serving.

Oniony Poppy Seed Dinner Rolls

MAKES 15 ROLLS

Onions

3 tablespoons unsalted butter

1 large yellow onion, small diced

Kosher salt, to taste

Dough

228 grams (1¾ cups) all-purpose flour

225 grams (1½ cups plus 2 tablespoons) bread flour

1 tablespoon plus 2 teaspoons granulated sugar

1 tablespoon kosher salt

1¼ teaspoons instant yeast (I like Saf-instant brand)

250 grams (1 cup) whole milk

5 tablespoons unsalted butter, at room temperature, plus more for greasing

1 tablespoon plus 1 teaspoon poppy seeds, plus more for garnish

Unsalted butter, for greasing

1 egg

1 tablespoon water

For Finishing

57 grams (¼ cup) unsalted butter, melted

Flake salt, for topping

Warm, pillowy, and buttery, these rolls are a joy to pass around any dinner table. If you are a beginner bread baker, this is a great recipe to start with. It will get you familiar with proofing, shaping, and working with dough in general, all while being straightforward enough to yield delicious results no matter what. The more you make these rolls, the more you will know exactly what to look for in each step and the more bread-skilled you will become! You can prep these rolls through step 8 and then cover and refrigerate overnight. The next day, when you're ready to bake, pull them out of the fridge and continue with step 9. Step 9 (the second rise) will take longer (closer to 3 or 3½ hours) because the dough will be cold.

1. **Make the onions:** Melt the butter in a medium saucepan over medium heat. Add the onion, and season with a generous pinch of salt. Cook, stirring occasionally, until the onion is very soft with minimal browning, 8 to 10 minutes. Set aside to cool to room temperature.

2. **Make the dough:** Add the all-purpose flour, bread flour, sugar, salt, yeast, milk, butter, and poppy seeds to the bowl of a stand mixer fitted with a dough hook. Mix on low to combine.

3. Increase the speed to medium, and mix until the dough is smooth and has pulled away from the sides of the bowl, about 4 minutes. Increase the speed to medium-high, and mix until the dough can be stretched out fairly thin without tearing, 8 to 10 minutes. You may need to hold onto the mixer to stabilize it during this process!

4. Add in about two-thirds (about 5 tablespoons) of the cooled onion mixture, and mix on medium until the onions are fully incorporated, 3 or 4 minutes.

5. Grease a large bowl with butter, transfer the dough to the bowl, cover with plastic wrap, and let rise until it doubles in size, about 2 hours. (This time will depend on how warm your kitchen is, but it shouldn't take longer than 2½ hours.)

6. Place the dough on a clean surface (not dusted with flour), and divide it into 15 equal pieces. (For perfectly even rolls, weigh the entire batch of dough in grams to get the total weight and then divide that number by 15. That will give you the exact gram measurement for each roll.)

7. Form each piece of dough into a roll by cupping your hand over the dough and using a quick circular motion to form a tight ball.

8. Place the rolls in a buttered 9×13-inch (23×33 cm) baking dish (metal is ideal, but glass also works!), leaving a bit of space in between each roll.

9. Lightly cover the dish with a kitchen towel, and let the rolls rise until they puff up and nearly double in size, 45 minutes to 1 hour; the rolls will be just about touching. (This time will also depend on how warm your kitchen is, but it shouldn't take longer than 1½ hours.)

10. Meanwhile, preheat the oven to 375°F (190°C) with a rack positioned in the center.

11. Make the egg wash by whisking together the egg and water in a small bowl until completely homogeneous. Brush the risen rolls all over with the egg wash, and sprinkle the tops with the remainder of the cooked onions (the butter will have solidified, but that is okay!) and a bit more poppy seeds.

12. Bake the rolls for 35 to 45 minutes, until very golden. Brush the hot rolls with the melted butter, being careful not to brush off the onions on top. Sprinkle with flake salt.

13. Let the rolls cool for 5 to 10 minutes before enjoying warm. Store any leftovers in an airtight container for up to 2 days. Toast or reheat in a a 350°F (175°C) oven before enjoying.

Spiced Date and Pecan Sticky Buns

MAKES 9 BUNS

Dough

195 grams (1½ cups) all-purpose flour, plus more for dusting

200 grams (1½ cups) bread flour

2 tablespoons granulated sugar

1 tablespoon kosher salt

1½ teaspoons instant yeast (I like Saf-instant brand)

260 grams (1 cup plus 1 tablespoon) whole milk

4 tablespoons unsalted butter, at room temperature, plus more for greasing

Filling

145 grams (about 8 large) Medjool dates, pitted

3 tablespoons unsalted butter, at room temperature

3 tablespoons honey

2 teaspoons ground cinnamon

½ teaspoon ground cardamom

½ teaspoon kosher salt

Caramel

120 grams (½ cup) heavy cream

55 grams (¼ cup) packed dark brown sugar

3 tablespoons honey

1 teaspoon kosher salt

1 teaspoon vanilla bean paste

120 grams (1 cup) finely chopped pecans, toasted (see Tip)

Flake salt, for topping

Cinnamon rolls are good and all, but for me, a sticky bun will always reign supreme. The best part of a cinnamon roll is that last bite at the center, but a sticky bun is ooey-gooey and delicious throughout. Here, dates are added to the filling for a rich and deep dried fruit flavor that pairs so well with the nuts in the caramel. I like pecans for their buttery texture in this bun, but walnuts, hazelnuts, or pistachios would be equally delightful. These rolls can be prepped a day ahead up through step 10, covered with plastic wrap, and refrigerated overnight. The next day, when you're ready to bake, pull them out of the fridge and continue on as directed. The second rise (step 11) will just take a bit longer (closer to 3 or 3½ hours) because the dough will be proofing from cold.

1. **Make the dough:** Add the all-purpose flour, bread flour, sugar, salt, yeast, milk, and butter to the bowl of a stand mixer fitted with a dough hook. Mix on low to combine.

2. Increase the speed to medium, and mix until the dough is smooth and has pulled away from the sides of the bowl, about 4 minutes. Increase the speed to medium-high, and mix until the dough can be stretched out fairly thin without tearing, 8 to 10 minutes. You may need to hold onto the mixer to stabilize it during this process!

3. Transfer the dough to a large, greased bowl, cover with plastic wrap, and let rise until it doubles in size, about 2 hours. (This time will depend on how warm your kitchen is, but it shouldn't take longer than 2½ hours.)

4. **Meanwhile, make the filling:** Add the dates to a small bowl, and cover with hot water to soak until softened, 15 minutes. Drain.

5. Add the soaked dates, butter, honey, cinnamon, cardamom, and salt to a food processor, and process until mostly smooth. A few small chunks are okay!

6. Grease a 9-inch (23 cm) square baking dish all over with butter.

7. **Make the caramel:** Heat the cream, brown sugar, honey, salt, and vanilla in a small saucepan over medium heat. Cook, whisking, until bubbly and slightly thick, 3 to 5 minutes. Stir in the pecans and then pour the caramel into the baking dish and spread to cover the bottom. Set aside while you prepare and shape the rolls.

8. When the dough has risen, roll it out to an 11×14-inch (28×35.5 cm) rectangle on a lightly floured surface.

9. Add the filling, and spread it out edge to edge. Starting with the longest side, roll up the dough as tight as you can into a log. Using a sharp knife (serrated works great), cut the log into thirds. Cut each third into thirds to form 9 even buns.

10. Place the buns on top of the caramel in the baking dish, and lightly cover with a kitchen towel.

11. Let the buns rise until doubled in size and touching, 1 to 1½ hours.

12. Preheat the oven to 375°F (190°C) with a rack positioned in the center.

13. Bake for 35 to 45 minutes, until the buns are deeply golden brown and an instant-read thermometer reads 195°F (90°C) in the center of the bun.

TIP Toast the pecans on a sheet tray at 375°F (190°C) until golden and aromatic, 8 to 12 minutes.

14. Let cool for 10 minutes and then carefully invert the buns onto a serving plate. Serve warm, sprinkled with a touch of flake salt. Store any leftovers in an airtight container for up to 2 days at room temperature. Reheat on a sheet tray in a 350°F (175°C) oven for 10 to 15 minutes. You also can do a quick reheat in the microwave.

Chocolate-Chunk Sesame Scones

MAKES 6 BIG SCONES

113 grams (½ cup) crème fraîche, cold (see Note 1)

60 grams (¼ cup) buttermilk, cold

228 grams (1¾ cups) all-purpose flour, plus more for dusting

35 grams (¼ cup) whole-wheat flour

100 grams (½ cup) granulated sugar

2 teaspoons baking powder

1 teaspoon baking soda

2 teaspoons kosher salt

113 grams (½ cup/1 stick) unsalted butter, cold and cut into ½-inch (1 cm) cubes

One 4-ounce (113 g) bar semisweet chocolate, roughly chopped

30 grams (3 tablespoons) sesame seeds, toasted (see Note 2), plus more for topping

1 egg

1 tablespoon water

Demerara sugar, for sprinkling (or more granulated if you can't find demerara)

NOTES

1. If you are in the mood for a project, you can make the crème fraîche from scratch using the method for making cultured cream (up to step 2) in the Cultured Butter recipe on page 238.

2. Toast the sesame seeds in a small, dry sauté pan over medium heat until aromatic and lightly browned, 3 to 5 minutes.

"Trust the process" is the overall theme for these scones. For the flakiest and most tender scones, these three steps are key: Use just barely enough wet ingredients to hydrate the dry ingredients, be extra careful not to overmix the dough, and keep the dough cold. The dough is going to seem "wrong" for a good part of this recipe. Only during the last few steps will it come together into something that seems like a scone can be shaped from it. I developed a true appreciation for scones while working at Cellar Door Provisions in Chicago. They produced the best scones I'd ever had, and I was able to hone my own scone-making skills while working there. This recipe is a crack at bringing that iconic scone to the home baker. A bench scraper is super helpful to have for handling and shaping the dough, but using just your hands will work, too! The final 4-hour chill time might seem long, but I find it to be necessary for the dough to hydrate properly. It's even better if you prep the scones through step 10, chill them overnight, and then cut and bake them in the morning. There's nothing like a fresh, warm scone to start the day!

1. Mix the crème fraîche and buttermilk in a small bowl. Place in the refrigerator.

2. Whisk the all-purpose flour, whole-wheat flour, granulated sugar, baking powder, baking soda, and salt in a large bowl.

3. Add the butter, and toss to coat in the flour mixture. Use your fingers to press the butter pieces, one at a time, into flat shingles and then drop them back into the flour mixture. Toss again with your hands to coat the butter in the flour. Add the chocolate and sesame seeds, and gently toss with your hands to combine.

4. Pour in the crème fraîche mixture. Stir with a rubber spatula until the wet ingredients start to mix with the dry.

5. Switch to mixing with your hands to gently incorporate everything and form a very rough and shaggy dough. It will seem very dry, which is what you want! Don't mix so much that it forms a cohesive dough.

6. Turn out the dough onto a parchment paper–lined sheet tray. Press the dough together into a rough 8-inch (20 cm) square (about ¾ inch/2 cm thick), using your hands and/or a bench scraper. The dough will still feel dry in spots and should barely hold together. Place the sheet tray of dough in the freezer to chill for 30 minutes.

7. Remove the dough from the freezer, and use the parchment paper to lift the dough and fold it in half like a book. Press any pieces of butter, dry flour, or chocolate that may have fallen off back into the dough.

8. Using a lightly floured rolling pin, roll out the dough to a rough 8-inch (20 cm) square (about ¾ inch/2 cm thick). Press the dough together with your hands as needed to form an even square, as it will likely still be quite crumbly.

9. Fold the square of dough in half like a book again, using the parchment paper to lift the dough. The dough should be a rough 8×4-inch (20×10 cm) rectangle (about 1¼ inches/3 cm thick), but use your hands as needed to press the dough together and make the rectangle as even as possible. The dough should no longer feel dry or crumbly.

10. Transfer the dough (along with the parchment) to a sheet tray, and wrap the sheet tray lightly with plastic wrap. Place the dough in the refrigerator, and chill for at least 4 hours or overnight.

11. When you are ready to bake, preheat the oven to 425°F (220°C). Line a sheet tray with parchment paper.

12. Whisk the egg and water in a small bowl until homogeneous to make an egg wash.

13. Remove the dough from the refrigerator, and transfer to a cutting board. With the long side of the dough positioned closest to you, cut the log into thirds to make approximately 2⅔ × 4-inch (7 × 10 cm) rectangles. Cut each third in half diagonally to make 6 triangular scones.

14. Brush the top of each scone with the egg wash, and generously sprinkle with demerara sugar and sesame seeds. Place the scones on the sheet tray with ample space in between.

15. Bake for 20 to 25 minutes, until very deeply golden brown.

16. Let cool on the tray for 5 minutes, and serve warm, or let cool completely and enjoy at room temperature. The scones are delicious both warm and fully cooled. Store any cooled leftovers in an airtight container at room temperature for up to 2 days.

Creamed Corn Drop Biscuits

MAKES 12 TO 14 BISCUITS

195 grams (1½ cups) all-purpose flour

80 grams (½ cup) medium yellow cornmeal

67 grams (⅓ cup) granulated sugar

1 tablespoon baking powder

1½ teaspoons kosher salt

1 stick (113 g/½ cup) unsalted butter, cold and cut into ½-inch (1 cm) cubes

One 8.5-ounce (241 g) can creamed corn

60 grams (¼ cup) sour cream

Calabrian Chile Honey Butter (page 242), for serving

Honey, for drizzling, optional

If you have ever made a cornbread with creamed corn, you know what a game changer it can be. It lends the most delicious, sweet corn richness and a tenderness that just can't be replicated. Adding creamed corn to these drop biscuits turns them into an addicting mash-up of a moist cornbread and a buttery biscuit. You could go through the trouble of making creamed corn from scratch, but I find the canned variety to be just as good; plus, it also significantly streamlines the recipe. These are best served warm right out of the oven, but if you happen to have leftovers, store them in an airtight container at room temperature and rewarm them in a low oven before enjoying.

1. Preheat the oven to 425°F (220°C) with a rack positioned in the lower third. Line a sheet tray with parchment paper.

2. Whisk the flour, cornmeal, sugar, baking powder, and salt in a large bowl. Add the cubed butter, and toss to coat each cube in the flour mixture. Use your fingers to press the butter pieces, one at a time, into flat shingles and then drop them back into the flour mixture. Toss again with your hands to coat the butter in the flour.

3. Add the creamed corn and sour cream, and mix with a spatula until just moistened with no dry pockets of flour. (Overmixing will toughen the final biscuits.)

4. Drop a heaping ¼ cup (60 g) of the biscuit dough onto the sheet tray, leaving about 1 inch (2.5 cm) in between each biscuit. (You also can use two spoons or a 2-ounce/57 g cookie scoop.) You should yield 12 to 14 biscuits.

5. Bake for 20 to 25 minutes, until the biscuits are puffed and the bottoms are golden brown.

6. Let cool for 5 minutes, and enjoy warm, slathered with the Calabrian Chile Honey Butter and/or drizzled with honey.

Cultured Butter

1 quart (1 L) heavy cream

½ cup (120 g) whole-milk Greek yogurt (or reserved cultured cream from a previous batch; see headnote)

Cultured butter is technically a fermentation, but don't let that scare you. Even a total fermentation novice can make this with great success, pride, and ease. Cultured butter starts with cultured cream, and the easiest way to make cultured cream is to use some sort of already-cultured dairy. My culture of choice is yogurt because it is much less expensive than crème fraîche, and I think it produces a more reliable result than the even more budget-friendly alternative, buttermilk. I also think yogurt produces the best-tasting final butter. The cool thing about making your own cultured cream is that once you've done it one time using a store-bought cultured product (e.g., the yogurt), you never have to buy one again! Just reserve ½ cup (120 ml) of the cultured cream before whipping it all into butter to use as the "starter" for your next batch. As with anything fermented at home, there is always a risk of bad bacterial growth, although I have never had an issue. Be sure all of your tools and equipment are very clean. If you see any mold or the cream develops a putrid smell, please don't eat it.

1. Whisk the cream and yogurt in a medium bowl. Pour the mixture into an airtight container, and leave at room temperature for at least 36 hours or up to 48 hours, until the mixture has thickened to a loose sour cream texture. If your kitchen climate is warm and humid, this could happen more quickly, so check the cream after 24 hours.

2. Refrigerate the mixture for at least 12 or up to 24 hours, until it is very well chilled.

3. Transfer the cream mixture to the bowl of a stand mixer fitted with a whisk attachment, and whip on medium until the mixture separates into butter and buttermilk, 10 to 15 minutes. This can also be done with an electric hand mixer. The mixture will first look whipped, then curdled, and then fully separate.

4. Reduce the mixer speed to low, and whip for another 1 or 2 minutes. This step ensures you get the highest yield of butter possible without the mixture splattering everywhere and making a big mess.

5. Strain the mixture through a fine-mesh strainer into a large bowl to separate the butter from the buttermilk. Squeeze the butter between your hands (you can wear gloves here if you'd like) to remove as much buttermilk as possible. Store the buttermilk in an airtight container in the refrigerator for up to 1 week or in the freezer for up to 3 months.

6. Add the butter to a fine-mesh strainer. "Wash" the butter by running it under very cold water and squeezing out any remaining buttermilk until the liquid runs clear.

7. Squeeze out as much water as you can and then store the butter in an airtight container in the refrigerator for up to 2 weeks or in the freezer for up to 3 months.

Bagna Cauda Butter

**MAKES ABOUT
⅔ CUP (175 G)**

2 tablespoons olive oil

4 garlic cloves, finely grated

6 oil-packed anchovy fillets, finely chopped

½ cup (1 stick/113 g) softened unsalted cultured butter, homemade (see page 238) or store-bought

¼ teaspoon freshly cracked black pepper

Kosher salt, to taste

Garlic and butter are, of course, an iconic duo, and the only thing that can make it even more iconic in my mind is an anchovy. Bagna cauda is a delicious, oily garlic and anchovy dip usually served warm alongside raw vegetables. Here, we are taking that classic dip and solidifying it into a compound butter. Spread some on sourdough toast and top with thinly sliced radishes for a very addictive, elegant snack time.

1. Add the olive oil and garlic to a small sauté pan, set over medium heat, and cook, stirring constantly, until the garlic is lightly golden, 2 or 3 minutes.

2. Remove the pan from the heat, and stir in the anchovies. The residual heat from the pan will "melt" the anchovies into the oil. Let the mixture cool to room temperature, 15 to 20 minutes.

3. Mix the butter, pepper, and cooled garlic-anchovy mixture in a medium bowl. Season with salt.

4. Store the butter in an airtight container in the refrigerator for up to 1 week. Bring to room temperature before serving.

CENTO FLAT FILLET ANCHOVIES

Ranch

Beet horseradish

Calabrian chili

Bagna cauda

Calabrian Chile Honey Butter

MAKES ABOUT ¾ CUP
(150 G)

½ cup (1 stick/113 g) softened unsalted cultured butter, homemade (see page 238) or store-bought

2 tablespoons honey

1 tablespoon chopped jarred Calabrian chiles in oil

1 teaspoon kosher salt

Freshly cracked black pepper, to taste

Sweet and spicy is a tale old as time as far as flavor combinations go, and some things just never get old. This butter is a depiction of just that while also being exceptionally simple to make. Think hot honey but in butter form! Be sure to have a vat of this on hand to serve alongside the Creamed Corn Drop Biscuits (page 236).

1. Add the butter, honey, chiles, salt, and a few grinds of pepper to a food processor, and process until the butter is smooth, with just a few small specks of chile.

2. Store the butter in an airtight container in the refrigerator for up to 1 week. Bring to room temperature before serving.

Beet Horseradish Butter

MAKES ABOUT
1 HEAPING CUP (240 G)

3 ounces (85 g) small red beets (about 2), cooked, peeled, and roughly chopped (see roasting instructions on page 109)

2 tablespoons olive oil

½ cup (1 stick/113 g) softened unsalted cultured butter, homemade (see page 238) or store-bought

1-inch (2.5 cm) piece fresh horseradish root, peeled and finely grated on a microplane (see Tip)

2 teaspoons honey

1 teaspoon kosher salt

½ teaspoon freshly cracked black pepper

This butter is beautifully light pink and so fun to have on hand. It's great for dipping crunchy crudités into or for spreading on a toasted everything bagel. I also love it slathered on a slice of the Hearty Seeded Rye Bread (page 229), topped with smoked salmon, Pink Pickles (page 37), and dill for a quick lunch. I use the roasting method from the Charred Cumin Beets (page 109) to cook the beets for this, but feel free to buy precooked beets from the grocery store to whip this up even more quickly.

1. Add the beets and olive oil to a food processor, and process until the beets begin to break down.

2. Add the butter, horseradish, honey, salt, and pepper, and process until almost completely smooth. (A few small chunks of beet are cute!)

3. Store the butter in an airtight container in the refrigerator for up to 1 week. Bring to room temperature before serving. Re-whip in the food processor if the butter seems separated.

TIP If you can't find fresh horseradish, substitute 2 to 3 teaspoons prepared horseradish.

Ranch Butter

MAKES ABOUT ⅔ CUP
(135 G)

½ cup (1 stick/113 g) softened unsalted cultured butter, homemade (see page 238) or store-bought

1 garlic clove, finely grated

1 teaspoon kosher salt

Zest of 1 lemon

Freshly cracked black pepper, to taste

2 tablespoons sliced fresh chives

1 tablespoon finely chopped fresh dill

1 tablespoon finely chopped fresh parsley

I feel like no flavored butter section would be complete without some sort of herb butter, and this ranch version is my dedicated submission. It has all the classic herbs you would find in a ranch dressing, with a subtle hint of garlic. I recommend using cultured butter for this recipe because it adds the extra "tang" that I associate with a good buttermilk ranch. Just like ranch, this butter is super versatile and good on just about anything. Slather it over any grilled protein for a quick flavor boost (it's great on chicken), or serve it with any warm bread your heart desires. I adore it with the Oniony Poppy Seed Dinner Rolls (page 230).

1. Mix the butter, garlic, salt, lemon zest, and a generous amount of pepper in a medium bowl until fully incorporated.

2. Add the chives, dill, and parsley, and gently fold to incorporate.

3. Store the butter in an airtight container in the refrigerator for up to 1 week. Bring to room temperature before serving.

Whipped Chai Maple Brown Butter

MAKES ⅔ CUP (140 G)

½ cup (1 stick/113 g) unsalted cultured butter, homemade (see page 238) or store-bought

1 bag English breakfast tea, string cut off and discarded if applicable

½ teaspoon ground cinnamon

¼ teaspoon ground cardamom

¼ teaspoon ground ginger

⅛ teaspoon ground cloves

⅛ teaspoon ground black pepper

3 tablespoons maple syrup

½ teaspoon kosher salt

One of my fondest food memories is of my mom making me cinnamon toast in the mornings before I headed off to school. It was such a treat. Every time she spread some salty butter on warm toast and sprinkled it with cinnamon and sugar, I knew it was going to be a good day. This slightly sweetened, heavily spiced butter is reminiscent of those nostalgic breakfasts and will evoke all the warm and cozy feelings. It's delicious spread on toast or banana bread or even served with the Chocolate-Chunk Sesame Scones (page 234).

1. Melt the butter in a small saucepan over medium-low heat, and whisk continuously until browned, 3 to 5 minutes. Keep an eye on it because this can happen quickly!

2. Immediately remove the butter to a small bowl, and add the tea bag, cinnamon, cardamom, ginger, cloves, and pepper. Infuse for 5 minutes and then remove the tea bag (gently pressing out any butter that may have been absorbed into the bag) and discard.

3. Transfer the butter mixture to a small bowl along with the maple syrup and salt.

4. Prepare a large ice bath.

5. Place the bowl of butter over the ice bath, and whisk until the butter becomes light in color and has a whipped consistency, 2 or 3 minutes. Feel free to take the bowl of butter in and out of the ice bath while whisking to ensure the butter cools and whips evenly.

6. Store the butter in an airtight container in the refrigerator for up to 1 week. Bring to room temperature before serving.

Fun Things Between Bread

There is no better simple delight than a few quality
ingredients sandwiched between good bread.

Mortadella, Egg, and Cheese (MEC)

MAKES 4 SANDWICHES
AND ABOUT 1¼ CUPS
(320 G) ONION-TOMATO
SPREAD

Jammy Onion-Tomato Spread

Olive oil, for browning

2 large yellow onions, thinly
sliced

Kosher salt and freshly cracked
black pepper, to taste

3 tablespoons tomato paste

¼ cup (60 ml) water

2 tablespoons lightly packed
dark brown sugar

1 tablespoon chopped jarred
Calabrian chiles in oil

1 tablespoon apple cider vinegar

½ teaspoon sweet smoked
paprika

Sandwich Assembly

4 sesame kaiser rolls, split in
half

3 tablespoons unsalted butter

12 ounces (340 g) very thinly
sliced mortadella

8 slices yellow American cheese

Olive oil, for frying

4 eggs

Kosher salt and freshly cracked
black pepper, to taste

There's a certain culture around breakfast sandwiches on the East Coast. They are a beloved part of everyday life, and the sheer accessibility to one on seemingly any corner is truly iconic. This culture is not something I knew much about before moving to New Jersey, but it is something I am now so happy to know and love. A very classic order in New Jersey specifically is a pork roll (or Taylor ham!), egg, and cheese with salt, pepper, and ketchup. This sandwich recipe is my ode to that classic. Here, I swap mortadella for the pork roll and a jammy onion and tomato spread for the ketchup. The result is a familiar taste with a bit of a fun Italian twist. American cheese is a nonnegotiable for any breakfast sandwich in my opinion, so that stays the same as the original. I prefer a fully cooked egg on my sandwich, so I break the yolk and just about fully cook the egg, but you can fry your eggs to your desired doneness. I call for kaiser rolls here, but if you happen to have them around, the Oniony Poppy Seed Dinner Rolls (page 230) make a delicious mini-sized option as well. If you have any onion-tomato spread remaining, store it in an airtight container in the fridge for up to 1 week. Use it on future breakfast sandwiches or anything your heart desires.

1. **Make the spread:** Heat a large skillet over medium heat, and coat the bottom with a thin layer of olive oil. Add the onions, and season with salt and pepper. Cook, stirring often, until very soft and slightly browned, 15 to 20 minutes.

2. Add the tomato paste, and cook, stirring constantly, until slightly darker in color, 2 or 3 minutes.

3. Stir in the water, brown sugar, chiles, vinegar, and paprika. Reduce the heat to low, and cook until the sugar dissolves and the mixture is thick and jamlike, 2 or 3 minutes. Season with more salt. Set aside to cool to room temperature.

4. **Assemble the sandwiches:** Lightly toast the kaiser rolls in a toaster or oven.

5. Heat a large 12-inch (30 cm) cast-iron pan over medium heat. When hot, add the butter and melt. Add the mortadella to the pan, layering slices on top of each other to create four mortadella mounds. Sear the mounds until they are browned and crispy on the first side, 2 or 3 minutes.

6. Flip over the mortadella mounds, and top each with 2 slices of American cheese. Cook until the second side is browned and the cheese is melted, 1 or 2 minutes more. Place a mound of mortadella on the bottom half of each roll.

7. If the pan seems dry, add a drizzle of olive oil and increase the heat to medium.

8. Crack the eggs into the pan (it's okay if they run into each other!), season with salt and pepper to taste, and fry to your liking. Place 1 egg on top of each mortadella mound.

9. Spread your desired amount of onion-tomato spread on the top buns, and top the sandwiches.

10. Cut each sandwich in half, and serve right away, or wrap in foil to let the sandwich steam and meld together a bit, if desired, 2 or 3 minutes.

Brie and Butter Sandwich
with Shallot-y Frisée

MAKES 4 SANDWICHES

½ medium head frisée (about 4 ounces/113 g)

1 small shallot, thinly sliced into rings

2 tablespoons olive oil

2 tablespoons champagne or rice vinegar

1 tablespoon honey

1 tablespoon whole-grain mustard

Kosher salt and freshly cracked black pepper, to taste

2 tablespoons thinly sliced fresh chives

6 tablespoons high-quality salted butter, at room temperature

1 fresh baguette (about 24 inches/61 cm), split in half lengthwise

8 ounces (227 g) Brie or Camembert, sliced into ¼-inch (6 mm) slices (rind on)

Admittedly, thinking about combining Brie and butter on a sandwich felt like dairy overkill. But after giving it a whirl, this classic French baguette sandwich was eye-opening. Maybe it's one of those things that feels so wrong, it's right. In any case, I am so here for it. In my version, I add heavily dressed frisée to pack a vinegary, mustardy punch that also makes the sandwich a bit more substantial. Because this sandwich is so simple, be sure to use high-quality French butter, cheese, and bread here. It really makes all the difference. If you can't find frisée, endive, escarole or shredded radicchio would make great swaps! This sandwich gets better as it sits, making it great for packing up to go. I have also been known to spread a bit of fig jam on one side of the bread. Do what you will with that information.

1. Prepare a large ice bath.

2. Place the frisée and shallot in the ice bath, and let sit for a few minutes to crisp the frisée and remove the astringency of the raw shallot.

3. Remove the vegetables from the ice bath and dry in a salad spinner, or lay out on a kitchen towel to dry completely.

4. Whisk the olive oil, vinegar, honey, mustard, salt, and pepper in a large bowl. Add the frisée-shallot mixture and the chives, and toss to combine. Season with more salt and pepper.

5. Spread the butter all over both halves of the baguette. Lay out the Brie across the whole length of the bottom half of the baguette.

6. Cover the Brie with the frisée mixture. (It will be a fairly tall pile!) Add the top of the baguette to close the sandwich.

7. Cut in half and then in half again, to make 4 sandwiches, and serve.

BL Double T

Sandwich Assembly

24 ounces (680 g) thick-sliced pepper bacon

8 slices potato bread

1 medium head iceberg lettuce, leaves separated, cold

3 large heirloom tomatoes (about 2 pounds/907 g), in a variety of colors, sliced ½ inch (1 cm) thick

Flake salt and freshly cracked black pepper, to taste

Torn fresh dill fronds, to taste

Toum

½ cup (75 g) peeled garlic cloves

3 tablespoons fresh lemon juice (from about 1 lemon)

2 teaspoons kosher salt

1½ cups (360 ml) canola oil, divided

2 tablespoons ice-cold water

I have a love-hate relationship with mayonnaise. I used to say I didn't like it, but that isn't really true. I am very specific in the ways I enjoy it, and there really is no rhyme or reason. I love a good mayo-y potato salad, and I have recently come to love dipping my fries in it as well, but for some reason I rarely like it spread on a sandwich. That being said, I love everything about a beautiful summer BLT except the mayo. Here, I substitute the mayo with toum, a luscious Lebanese emulsified garlic sauce. It's similar to mayo, but I much prefer it spread on a sandwich. Toum can be somewhat finicky to emulsify, but with a bit of patience, a touch of ice water, and an immersion blender, you should be set! I love soft potato bread for this BLT, but feel free to substitute with rye or country white.

1. Preheat the oven to 425°F (220°C). Line a sheet tray with parchment paper, and place a wire rack on top.

2. Lay out the bacon across the wire rack. Transfer to the oven, and bake for 25 to 35 minutes, until golden and crispy. Transfer the bacon to a paper towel to drain.

3. **While the bacon cooks, make the toum:** Place the garlic, lemon juice, and kosher salt in a quart (1 L) container or similar high-sided container (see Note), and use an immersion blender to blend until smooth and creamy.

4. With the immersion blender running, very slowly stream in ¾ cup (180 ml) of the canola oil, drop by drop. With the blender still running, slowly stream in the water. Stop the blender, and scrape down the sides as needed.

5. With the blender running, slowly stream in the remaining ¾ cup (180 ml) oil. The final result should be emulsified, thick, and mayo-y. Place in the refrigerator until you're ready to assemble your sandwich.

6. Toast the potato bread until very lightly golden.

7. **Assemble the sandwiches:** Spread a layer of toum on a slice of toast and top with 2 large lettuce leaves and 2 tomato slices. Season the tomato with flake salt and pepper. Add 3 slices of bacon (breaking them as needed to fit the bread), and top with a generous amount of fresh dill.

8. Spread another layer of toum on a second slice of toast, and top off the sandwich. Cut in half.

9. Repeat with the ingredients for the remaining three sandwiches, and serve. Store any leftover toum in an airtight container in the refrigerator for up to 2 weeks.

NOTE You can make the toum in a food processor, although this method tends to be a little less foolproof. If you end up with a broken, watery toum, remove three-fourths of the broken sauce from the food processor and add 1 egg white to the remaining sauce in the food processor. Process until smooth. With the processor running, slowly stream in the reserved broken toum, drop by drop, until thick and mayo-y.

Mean, Green Turkey Sandwich

SERVES 4 TO 8 (MAKES TWO 12-INCH/30 CM SUB SANDWICHES)

Barely Pickled Jalapeños

4 jalapeños, thinly sliced into rounds

⅓ cup (80 ml) white distilled vinegar

2 teaspoons kosher salt

1 teaspoon granulated sugar

Green Sunflower Spread

Kosher salt, to taste

2½ ounces (70 g) fresh cilantro leaves and tender stems (from 1 to 1½ large bunches)

1 batch Roasted Garlic Sunflower Seed Dip (just the dip; page 58)

Sandwich Assembly

Two 12-inch (30 cm) sub rolls, split open but still connected

12 ounces (340 g) thinly sliced smoked deli turkey

8 ounces (227 g) aged white cheddar slices

½ large English cucumber, thinly sliced on a mandoline

1 small white onion, thinly sliced on a mandoline and rinsed (see Tip 1 on page 80)

3 ounces (85 g) alfalfa or broccoli sprouts

Olive oil, for drizzling

Fresh lemon juice, to taste

Flake salt and freshly cracked black pepper, to taste

This turkey sandwich is a bit spicy, pleasantly crunchy, and bound together with a delicious cilantro variation of the Roasted Garlic Sunflower Seed Dip (page 58). The heat comes from lightly pickled jalapeños, which have a great vinegary tang while still remaining crisp and vibrant green. Thinly sliced cucumber and onions bring a fresh crunchiness that I find essential to a great sandwich. I use aged white cheddar here, but mild provolone or creamy Havarti would be equally delicious. It's a perfectly fresh and light sub for any occasion, but it's especially lovely wrapped up and enjoyed at the beach. To make this come together even quicker, you can skip making the sunflower dip and substitute with an 8-ounce (227 g) tub of roasted garlic hummus. It's not an exact swap, but it's definitely a suitable one!

1. **Make the jalapeños:** Mix the jalapeños, vinegar, kosher salt, and sugar in a small bowl. Let sit at room temperature while you prepare the rest of the sandwiches, at least 20 minutes. The jalapeños will not be totally submerged in the vinegar at first but will release liquid as they sit.

2. **Meanwhile, make the spread:** Bring a small pot of water to a boil over high heat. Prepare a large ice bath.

3. Season the boiling water with a generous amount of kosher salt. Add the cilantro, and blanch for 30 seconds. Immediately transfer with a slotted spoon to the ice bath to shock.

4. Squeeze out all the excess moisture in the cilantro, roughly chop it, and transfer it to a high-powered blender along with the Roasted Garlic Sunflower Seed Dip. Blend until the cilantro is fully blended into the dip and the mixture is very green.

5. **Assemble the sandwiches:** Spread 2 or 3 tablespoons of the dip on the bottom of each sub roll. Add the turkey and cheddar and then add a layer of cucumber, a layer of onion, and a layer of pickled jalapeños to each sandwich.

6. Top each with a generous handful of sprouts, a drizzle of olive oil, and a squeeze of lemon juice. Sprinkle with flake salt and pepper. There will be more dip left, so feel free to also spread some on the other side of the bread, but I prefer just one side! (Save any leftover spread for dipping crackers, chips, or raw veggies. Store in an airtight container in the refrigerator for up to 3 days.)

7. Close the subs, cut each into halves or quarters, and serve.

Shareable Sweets

These simple treats are always a delight to have around, whether you're sharing with friends or craving a sweet treat just for you.

Rooibos Spice Cake
with Brown Butter Frosting

MAKES ONE 9-INCH
(23 CM) CAKE

Cake

Unsalted butter, for greasing

215 grams (1⅔ cups) all-purpose flour, plus more for dusting

110 grams (½ cup) packed dark brown sugar

100 grams (½ cup) granulated sugar

2 teaspoons ground cinnamon

1½ teaspoons baking soda

1 teaspoon ground ginger

1 teaspoon kosher salt

½ teaspoon baking powder

½ teaspoon ground cardamom

¼ teaspoon ground cloves

¼ teaspoon freshly grated nutmeg

2 bags rooibos tea or 4 grams (2 teaspoons) loose rooibos tea (see Note)

240 grams (1 cup) boiling water

1 egg, at room temperature

120 grams (½ cup) sour cream, at room temperature

55 grams (¼ cup) canola oil

2 tablespoons molasses

2 teaspoons vanilla bean paste

Frosting

57 grams (¼ cup/½ stick) unsalted butter

2 bags rooibos tea

57 grams (¼ cup) cream cheese

150 grams (1½ cups) confectioners' sugar

1 teaspoon vanilla bean paste

½ teaspoon kosher salt

NOTE Use your favorite rooibos variety in this cake. I like vanilla!

Single-layer cakes just make sense to me. They allow for the perfect ratio of frosting to cake, and they don't involve any risky stacking or intricate frosting techniques. They're casual, fun, and unfussy. The spices in this cake are almost bloomed by the hot rooibos tea, which also imparts a subtle herbal note that I adore in baked goods. Rooibos has a naturally nutty, warm flavor that enhances all the warm flavors in this cake. Whenever I make a cake from scratch, my goal is a boxed cake–level moistness, and I think this recipe achieves that! This cake is perfect for fall or winter, but make it all year round if you want! I won't stop ya.

1. Preheat the oven to 350°F (180°C) with a rack positioned in the center. Butter the bottom of a 9-inch (23 cm) metal square (or round, if you prefer!) baking pan, and line with parchment paper. Grease the pan all over with butter, and dust with flour.

2. **Make the cake:** Whisk the flour, brown sugar, granulated sugar, cinnamon, baking soda, ginger, salt, baking powder, cardamom, cloves, and nutmeg in a large bowl until fully combined.

3. Place the tea bags in a small bowl and add the boiling water. Steep until dark and fragrant, 4 minutes. Remove the spent tea bags, pressing out all of the liquid (or strain the loose tea through a fine-mesh strainer), and discard.

4. Whisk the egg, sour cream, canola oil, molasses, and vanilla in a medium bowl until combined. Stir the egg mixture into the dry ingredients until just barely combined. The batter will be very thick, almost like cookie dough.

5. Add the hot tea, and whisk until combined. (A few small lumps are okay!)

6. Pour the batter into the baking pan. Bake for 30 to 35 minutes, rotating halfway through the baking time, until a toothpick inserted into the center comes out clean.

7. Let the cake cool fully in the pan. This cake is so moist that if you invert it to cool on a rack, you run the risk of it sticking to the rack!

8. **While the cake cools, make the frosting:** Melt the butter in a small saucepan over medium-low heat, and whisk continuously until browned, 3 or 4 minutes. (Keep an eye on it because this can happen quickly!)

9. Immediately transfer the butter to a large bowl, and stir in the tea bags. Let the tea infuse and the butter cool to room temperature, about 15 minutes. Remove the tea bags (gently pressing out any butter that may have been absorbed into the bags) and discard.

10. Place the bowl of butter in the refrigerator, and let it chill until solidified but not super hard, 10 to 15 minutes.

11. Remove from the refrigerator, add the cream cheese, and use an electric mixer on medium to whip until light, fluffy, and smooth, 1 or 2 minutes.

12. Add the confectioners' sugar, vanilla, and salt. Whip on low to incorporate the sugar. Increase the speed to medium and whip until fluffy, 1 or 2 minutes.

13. When the cake is completely cool, invert it onto a wire rack and then onto a plate or cake stand so that the top is facing up.

14. Top with the frosting and spread out edge to edge. Slice and serve.

Malted Milk Butter Cookies

MAKES ABOUT
2½ DOZEN COOKIES

227 grams (1 cup/2 sticks) unsalted butter, at room temperature

100 grams (½ cup) granulated sugar

2 eggs, at room temperature, yolks and whites separated (place the whites in the fridge until needed)

1 tablespoon vanilla bean paste

1½ teaspoons kosher salt

260 grams (2 cups) all-purpose flour

40 grams (¼ cup) malted milk powder

100 grams (½ cup) demerara sugar, for coating

1 tablespoon water

My mom is an avid baker, especially during the holidays. Every year she makes what seems like dozens of varieties of cookies for her yearly cookie platter, but she always includes a simple butter cookie rolled in colored sugar. Even alongside all of her extravagant creations, those are the cookies I find myself going back for. There is something so beautiful about a simple butter cookie. They are perfect any time of day, as a midday sweet treat or dipped in your morning cup of coffee. These are made with a bit of malt powder, which enhances the buttery vanilla flavor and makes them seriously addicting. I love crumbling one of these over a scoop of the No-Churn Cherry Vanilla Ice Cream (page 269) for a contrasting crunch.

1. Using an electric mixer on medium, cream the butter and sugar in a large bowl until smooth, 1 minute. (This can also be made in a stand mixer fitted with a paddle attachment.)

2. Add the egg yolks, vanilla, and salt, and beat on medium until combined, scraping down the bowl as needed.

3. Add the flour and milk powder, and mix on low speed until just combined.

4. Split the dough into two halves (about 326 g/11.5 ounces each), and place each half on a large piece of plastic wrap. Form each half into an 8-inch (20 cm) log, about 1½ inches (4 cm) wide, using the plastic wrap to make the log even and tight. Refrigerate the logs until completely chilled, at least 3 hours, or up to 3 days in advance.

5. When you are ready to bake, preheat the oven to 375°F (190°C) with a rack positioned in the center. Line a sheet tray with parchment paper. Place the demerara sugar on a sheet tray or plate.

6. Whisk the reserved egg whites and water in a small bowl to make an egg wash.

7. Use a pastry brush to egg wash the cookie logs all over and then roll them in the demerara sugar to cover.

8. Cut the cookies into ½-inch-thick (1 cm) discs. Place about 9 cookies on the sheet tray (see Note). Keep any remaining sliced cookie dough on a plate or sheet tray in the refrigerator.

9. Bake the cookies, one tray at a time, until lightly golden and set, 14 to 16 minutes.

10. Cool the cookies on the tray for 5 minutes. Transfer to a wire rack to cool completely, and bake the remaining cookies. (Feel free to reuse the same sheet tray and parchment for each batch.)

11. Store in an airtight container at room temperature for up to 5 days.

NOTE I like to bake these one tray at a time, rather than multiple, because they tend to come out more uniform in shape.

Chocolate Amaretti Crinkle Cookies

MAKES ABOUT 5 DOZEN COOKIES

150 grams (¾ cup) granulated sugar, plus more for coating

113 grams (½ cup/1 stick) unsalted butter, melted and cooled slightly

50 grams (½ cup) unsweetened natural cocoa powder (not Dutch process)

2 eggs

1 teaspoon baking powder

1 teaspoon kosher salt

½ teaspoon pure almond extract

220 grams (2 cups, lightly packed) almond flour

100 grams (1 cup) confectioners' sugar, for coating

These cookies are a fun mash-up of Italian amaretti cookies and chocolate crinkle cookies, a holiday cookie staple. Amaretti cookies are traditionally crinkled, so I thought it was only natural to bring these two together. They have the almondy flavor of an amaretti cookie with the brownie-like taste and chewy texture of a chocolate crinkle. This recipe makes a ton of small cookies, so you are bound to have enough to last you quite a few days of sweet snacking. This is a perfect recipe for a holiday cookie swap as well! On top of all that, they also happen to be gluten free.

1. Place the sugar, butter, cocoa powder, eggs, baking powder, salt, and almond extract in a large bowl, and whisk until smooth.

2. Add the almond flour, and mix with a spatula to combine. Cover and refrigerate the dough for at least 5 hours or up to 24 hours.

3. Preheat the oven to 350°F (180°C) with racks positioned in the upper and lower thirds. Line two sheet trays with parchment paper. Place the confectioners' sugar in a small bowl.

4. Weigh out 10-gram (1 rounded teaspoon) portions of dough, and roll them into smooth balls. Heavily coat them in the confectioners' sugar (see Tip), and place them on the sheet trays, leaving about ½ inch (1 cm) in between. (These do not need much space; they don't spread very much.) They should all fit on the two trays.

5. Bake both trays for 13 to 15 minutes, rotating the trays halfway through the baking time, until puffed and crackly.

6. Let cool on the sheet trays for 5 minutes and then transfer to a wire rack to cool completely.

7. Store in an airtight container at room temperature for up to 4 days.

TIP The heavier you coat the cookies in confectioners' sugar, the more crinkled they will come out. So don't be shy!

Vanilla Bean and Brown Butter
Chocolate-Chunk Cookie Bars

MAKES 16 BARS

227 grams (1 cup/2 sticks) unsalted butter, plus more for greasing the pan

1 vanilla bean, split and scraped (see Note 1)

163 grams (1¼ cups) all-purpose flour

100 grams (1 cup) oat flour (see Note 2)

2 teaspoons cornstarch

1½ teaspoon kosher salt

1 teaspoon baking soda

300 grams (1½ cups) lightly packed dark brown sugar

100 grams (½ cup) granulated sugar

2 eggs, at room temperature

One 4-ounce (113 g) bar bittersweet chocolate, roughly chopped

One 4-ounce (113 g) bar semisweet chocolate, roughly chopped (you can substitute with milk chocolate if you prefer!)

Flake salt, to taste

NOTE

1. If you can't find vanilla beans, you can use 1 tablespoon vanilla bean paste or vanilla extract. Just add the paste or extract to the brown butter after it cools for about 10 minutes.

2. You can buy premade oat flour or simply blend 100 grams (1¼ cups) old-fashioned rolled oats to a fine powder in a high-powered blender.

This cookie is an homage to a very special sweet treat that got me through some stressful days when I was a young line cook just trying to prep her station for dinner service. When Friday rolled around, I would have the craziest pre–dinner service jitters, coupled with an anxiety that was almost nausea inducing. You just never knew how a Friday night service might go. It could be smooth as ever, or you might accidentally drop a whole gallon of Cambro salsa on the floor mid-service and have to clean it up while still trying to plate all the orders that are rolling in. But there was one thing about Fridays that I always looked forward to that helped put my mind at ease: Our pastry chef, Chef Jen, would always make her famous chocolate-chip cookie sheet tray for family meal. This perfect, ooey-gooey chocolate-chip cookie was so comforting, and it was just the sugar rush that I needed to get through a daunting service. Nothing will compare to that cookie and the feeling it gave me, but here is my humble attempt! This cookie is great either cooled completely and cut into bars or served warm out of the oven, à la mode.

1. Heat the butter and vanilla bean (pod and all) in a medium sauté pan over medium-low heat. Whisk the butter continuously until browned, 8 to 10 minutes. (Keep an eye on it because this can happen quickly!) Immediately transfer to a large bowl, and set aside to cool to about room temperature, 20 minutes. Remove the vanilla pod and discard.

2. Preheat the oven to 375°F (190°C) with a rack positioned in the center. Butter the bottom of a 9-inch (23 cm) square baking pan and line with parchment paper with an overhang on two sides. Grease the paper all over with butter.

3. Whisk the all-purpose flour, oat flour, cornstarch, salt, and baking soda in a medium bowl.

4. Add the brown sugar and granulated sugar to the cooled browned butter, and mix with a rubber spatula to combine. Mix in the eggs, one egg at a time, fully incorporating before adding the next egg.

5. Add the dry ingredients, and stir to incorporate the wet with the dry. Fold in 85 grams (3 ounces) each of the bittersweet and semisweet chocolate.

6. Place the dough on the sheet tray, and spread out evenly using an offset spatula. Top the cookie with the remaining bittersweet and semisweet chocolate.

7. Bake for 35 to 40 minutes, until the cookie is puffed up slightly and the top is set and golden. Remove from the oven, and immediately sprinkle with flake salt.

8. If you want to cut perfectly square cookie bars, let the cookie cool completely before inverting onto a cutting board and cutting into 16 squares. If serving warm, let the cookie cool for 15 to 20 minutes and scoop out portions directly from the baking pan.

No-Churn Cherry Vanilla Ice Cream

SERVES 6 TO 8 (MAKES 5½ CUPS/825 G)

300 grams (2 heaping cups) frozen pitted dark cherries

7 tablespoons granulated sugar, divided

7 egg yolks

120 grams (½ cup) amaretto liquor

1 tablespoon vanilla bean paste

1 teaspoon kosher salt

360 grams (1½ cups) heavy cream

I love the idea of making ice cream at home, but although I do own an ice-cream maker, I rarely find myself wanting to lug it out of the cabinet. It's a nice thought, but it's seldom in the cards for me. What I am always up for is a good no-churn ice cream, and this one is cheery, it's cherry, and it makes me happy. I call for frozen cherries here because they are available year-round and are already pitted, but feel free to use fresh cherries when they're in season. Just be prepared for a lot of pitting! I also love throwing in some chopped dark chocolate along with the cherries in step 8 when I'm in the mood for a "Cherry Garcia" feel.

1. Place the cherries and 4 tablespoons sugar in a small saucepan. Set over medium heat, and cook, stirring occasionally, until reduced, syrupy, and slightly thickened, 12 to 15 minutes. Break up the cherries a bit with a wooden spoon. Set aside to cool completely.

2. Add about 2 inches (5 cm) of water to a small saucepan, set over medium-low heat, and bring to a simmer.

3. Prepare a large ice bath.

4. Place the remaining 3 tablespoons sugar and the egg yolks, amaretto, vanilla, and salt in a medium heatproof bowl, and whisk to combine.

5. Set the bowl on top of the pot of simmering water (making sure the bottom of the bowl doesn't touch the water) to make a double boiler. Whisk constantly to prevent scrambling, until the egg mixture is light in color, thick, doubled in size, and ribbony, 7 to 9 minutes (see Tip). Adjust the heat as needed so the water under the bowl maintains a soft simmer, and scrape down the sides of the bowl occasionally so the eggs don't cook on the sides.

6. Remove the bowl from the simmering water, and place directly in the ice bath. Whisk until the mixture is chilled, 5 to 7 minutes. Remove the bowl from the ice bath.

7. Whip the cream in a medium bowl to form medium peaks, about 4 minutes. Gently fold the whipped cream into the egg yolk mixture.

8. Add the cooled cherries, and gently fold to evenly disperse. Don't overmix here; it should look streaky and swirled.

9. Transfer the mixture to three plastic 1-pint (480 ml) containers or similar freezer-safe containers.

10. Freeze until solid, at least 8 hours and preferably overnight. Store in the freezer for up to 2 months.

TIP Step 5 requires quite a bit of elbow grease. If you happen to have an outlet anywhere near your stovetop, you can use a handheld electric mixer on medium for this instead of doing it all by hand. It will still take the same amount of time to cook the eggs, but it will be a little easier on your arm!

Chuck's Birthday Pie
Earl Grey French Silk Pie

MAKES ONE 9-INCH (23 CM) PIE

Crust

11 chocolate graham crackers (about 180 g)

7 tablespoons unsalted butter, melted

1 tablespoon unsweetened natural cocoa powder (not Dutch process)

1 tablespoon granulated sugar

½ teaspoon kosher salt

Mousse

1 bag Earl Grey tea or 2 grams (1 teaspoon) loose Earl Grey tea

60 grams (¼ cup) boiling water

One 4-ounce (113 g) bar 60 percent dark chocolate, roughly chopped

1 egg

1 egg yolk

50 grams (¼ cup) granulated sugar

1 teaspoon vanilla paste

1 teaspoon kosher salt

240 grams (1 cup) heavy cream

Honeyed Whipped Cream

240 grams (1 cup) heavy cream

1 tablespoon honey

1 teaspoon vanilla bean paste

Kosher salt, to taste

Topping

60 percent dark chocolate bar, grated, optional (but quite lovely!)

TIP The crust can also be made by adding the graham crackers to a ziplock bag and crushing them with a rolling pin or meat mallet. Simply add the crumbs to a bowl along with the butter, cocoa, sugar, and salt, and mix until combined.

Mousse pies have long been my favorite of all the pies, ever since I had my first slice of French silk pie as a child—shout out Bakers Square! If you grew up in the Midwest, you may know the pie-centric diner chain and its renowned French silk slice. My partner, Chuck, wasn't lucky enough to grow up eating Bakers Square French silk like I was, but once I introduced him to this smooth and creamy chocolate mousse pie, there was no going back. It's been his birthday dessert of choice ever since. A classic French silk is made with a standard flaky piecrust, but I love a chocolaty, press-in crumb crust instead. It's less fussy and, in my opinion, just better for this type of pie. The mousse gets a fun, floral twist with a bit of Earl Grey tea infused into the chocolate. Bergamot and chocolate is one of my favorite flavor combinations, and if you haven't tried it yet, you are in for a real treat.

1. Preheat the oven to 400°F (200°C) with a rack positioned in the center.

2. **Make the crust:** Pulse the graham crackers in a food processor to a fine crumb (see Tip). You should have about 1¾ cups (180 g). Add the butter, cocoa, sugar, and salt, and pulse until the mixture is combined and resembles wet sand.

3. Transfer the mixture into a 9-inch (23 cm) pie plate, and press (a measuring cup is helpful for this) to cover the bottom and all the way up the sides so it just holds together. (You don't want to compact the crust too much, or it will be hard to cut through when serving.)

4. Place the pie plate on a sheet tray, and bake for 8 to 10 minutes, until the crust is aromatic. It should smell toasty and look matte in color. Set aside to cool completely. If your crust happens to slide down slightly in the pan after baking (this sometimes happens with nonstick metal pie pans), press it back up with a measuring cup while it's still hot.

5. **Meanwhile, make the mousse:** Place the tea in a medium heatproof bowl, and add the boiling water. Steep until dark brown and fragrant, 5 minutes. Remove the bag (or strain out the loose tea), squeezing out any excess liquid from the bag, and discard. Add the chocolate.

6. Add 2 inches (5 cm) of water to a small saucepan, set over medium-low heat, and bring to a simmer. Set the bowl with the chocolate and tea on top of the pot (making sure the bottom of the bowl doesn't touch the water) to form a double boiler.

7. Adjust the heat as needed to maintain a soft simmer and let the chocolate melt, 3 to 5 minutes. Remove from the heat, and stir to combine. (Save the saucepan of simmering water!) Set aside the tea-chocolate mixture.

8. Whisk the egg, egg yolk, sugar, vanilla, and salt in a large heatproof bowl. Set the bowl over the softly simmering water (adding more water if needed), and whisk constantly to prevent scrambling until the egg mixture is light in

color, thick, doubled in size, and ribbony, 6 to 8 minutes (see Tip about electric mixers on page 269). Adjust the heat as needed to maintain a soft simmer, and scrape down the sides of the bowl with a spatula occasionally so the eggs don't scramble. Remove from the simmering water.

9. Add the tea-chocolate mixture to the egg mixture, and gently fold with a spatula to combine. Let the mixture cool to room temperature, 10 to 15 minutes.

10. Meanwhile, with a whisk, whip the cream in a medium bowl to form medium peaks, about 4 minutes.

11. When the chocolate mixture has cooled, add the whipped cream in two batches, and gently fold to combine.

12. Add the mousse to the cooled crust, and spread out to an even layer. Cover with plastic wrap, avoiding the top of the mousse as much as possible, and chill for at least 6 hours or up to 24 hours.

13. **Just before serving, make the whipped cream:** Use a whisk to whip the cream, honey, and vanilla in a large bowl to medium peaks, about 4 minutes. Season with a small pinch of salt.

14. Top the pie with the whipped cream, and spread with some swoops and swooshes, leaving a little edge of the mousse exposed. Use a microplane to finely grate some chocolate over the cream to garnish, if using. Cut and serve. Store any leftover pie covered with plastic wrap in the refrigerator for up to 3 days.

Blueberry Pretzel Galette
with Cream Cheese Whip

SERVES 8

Crust

146 grams (1 cup plus 2 tablespoons) all-purpose flour, plus more for dusting

40 grams (⅓ cup) fine pretzel crumbs (see Tip)

1 tablespoon granulated sugar

1 teaspoon kosher salt

141 grams (½ cup plus 2 tablespoons) unsalted butter, cold (refrigerated until ready to use), cut into ½-inch (1 cm) cubes

5 to 6 tablespoons ice-cold water

Pretzel Frangipane

57 grams (4 tablespoons) unsalted butter, softened

50 grams (¼ cup) granulated sugar

1 egg, at room temperature

35 grams (¼ cup, lightly packed) almond flour

30 grams (¼ cup) fine pretzel crumbs (see Tip)

½ teaspoon vanilla bean paste or vanilla extract

¼ teaspoon kosher salt

⅛ teaspoon almond extract

Blueberry Filling

510 grams (18 ounces) fresh blueberries

67 grams (⅓ cup) granulated sugar

2 tablespoons cornstarch

½ teaspoon kosher salt

continued »

I'm a '90s kid who grew up in the Midwest, so inevitably there were many Jell-O-y casserole concoctions at the forefront of every party. They were brightly colored, layered, and almost always more fun to look at than to eat. But there was one I always went for anytime it made an appearance: a layered dessert of strawberry Jell-O, crushed pretzels, and cream cheese. It doesn't necessarily sound good on paper, but I must say it's a stroke of sweet and salty genius. This galette channels all those flavors for a really fun and whimsical dessert. I went with blueberries here for the berry component because they pair so well with the pretzel frangipane that serves as the base of the galette. The cream cheese whip really drives home the nostalgia of this dessert, but some vanilla ice cream on top is also quite perfect.

1. **Make the crust:** Whisk the all-purpose flour, pretzel crumbs, sugar, and salt in a large bowl until combined. Add the cold butter, and toss with your hands to coat the cubes in the flour. Press each piece of butter, one at a time, in between your fingers, and then drop them back into the flour mixture. Toss again with your hands to coat the butter in the flour. The butter pieces should be thin, flat shards.

2. Add the water, 2 or 3 tablespoons at a time, gently mixing with your hands after each addition, to form a shaggy and crumbly dough that sticks together when pressed with your hands. The amount of water needed will vary depending on your kitchen climate and your flour.

3. Transfer the dough to a sheet of plastic wrap, and use the plastic wrap to press the dough into a ball. Flatten into a ¾-inch-thick (2 cm) disc. Refrigerate for at least 1 hour or up to 24 hours.

4. **Meanwhile, make the frangipane:** Using an electric or stand mixer fitted with a paddle attachment on medium, cream the butter and sugar together until light and fluffy, 1 or 2 minutes. Beat in the egg until smooth, and scrape down the bowl with a spatula. Add the almond flour, pretzel crumbs, vanilla, salt, and almond extract, and mix on low to combine.

5. Preheat the oven to 425°F (220°C). Line a sheet tray with parchment paper.

6. **While the oven preheats, make the filling:** Add the blueberries, sugar, cornstarch, and salt to a large bowl, and toss to combine.

7. **Form the galette:** On a floured work surface, roll out the chilled dough to form a rough 15-inch (38 cm) circle, dusting the dough and work surface with more flour as needed to prevent sticking. If the dough is too firm from the refrigerator and starts to crack as you roll, let it sit at room temperature for 5 to 10 minutes and then proceed with rolling it out. I also like to rotate and flip the dough as I roll it out to help with stickage. This dough is delicate but forgiving. If it happens to tear, just gently press it back together. Transfer the dough to the sheet tray.

8. Add the frangipane to the center of the crust, and use an offset spatula to spread it out, leaving a 4-inch (10 cm) border. Pile the blueberry mixture (along with all the sugar mixture) on top of the frangipane, leaving the 4-inch (10 cm) border bare.

For Baking

1 egg

1 tablespoon water

13 grams (¼ cup) mini pretzels, roughly chopped

Demerara sugar, for sprinkling

Cream Cheese Whip

240 grams (1 cup) heavy cream

85 grams (3 ounces) cream cheese, at room temperature

1 tablespoon granulated sugar

1 teaspoon vanilla bean paste or vanilla extract

Pinch of kosher salt

TIP To make the pretzel crumbs, blitz 100 grams (about 2½ cups) of mini pretzels in a food processor to a very fine crumb (with minimal chunks). This will make the right amount of crumb for the entire recipe.

9. Fold the untouched edges of the crust over the blueberries to form the galette. Chill the galette (still on the sheet pan) in the freezer for 10 minutes or in the refrigerator for 20 minutes.

10. While the galette chills, whisk the egg and water in a small bowl until homogeneous. Brush the crust all over with the egg wash, and sprinkle with the chopped mini pretzels and demerara sugar.

11. Bake for 45 to 55 minutes, until the blueberries are bubbly and the crust is deep golden brown. Don't worry if the galette leaks a bit; it's just a sign of a very delicious, flaky crust!

12. **Meanwhile, make the cream cheese whip:** Using an electric or stand mixer fitted with a whip attachment on medium, whip the cream, cream cheese, sugar, vanilla, and salt in a medium bowl to form very soft peaks, about 4 minutes. Transfer to the refrigerator to chill until ready to serve.

13. Let the galette cool for at least 20 minutes before serving. Serve warm or at room temperature with the chilled cream cheese whip on the side.

Roasted Strawberry and Rhubarb Sundae
with Pepita-Sesame Crunch

Strawberry-Rhubarb Mixture

8 ounces (227 g) rhubarb, cut into ½-inch (1 cm) irregular pieces

8 ounces (227 g) strawberries, hulled and halved

⅓ cup (67 g) granulated sugar

3 whole cardamom pods, crushed

1 star anise pod

½ vanilla bean, split and scraped

1 inch (2.5 cm) ginger, thinly sliced

Pepita-Sesame Crunch

½ cup (75 g) pepitas

2 tablespoons sesame seeds

2 tablespoons pure maple syrup

1 teaspoon Espelette (or Aleppo) pepper

Kosher salt, to taste

For Serving

Vanilla ice cream

1 batch Honeyed Whipped Cream (see page 270)

Extra virgin olive oil, for drizzling

Strawberries and rhubarb are such beautiful ingredients in both color and shape. Roasting them together with a touch of sugar is such a nifty way to cook them because they become soft and sweet without totally falling apart, and this also locks in their beautiful pink hue. Serving them with ice cream and a crunchy pepita topping makes for a delicious and elegant sundae that is reminiscent of a cozy crumble or crisp but with a bit more lightness. This is the perfect make-ahead dessert because both the roasted rhubarb and strawberry mixture and the pepita crunch can be made up to 3 days ahead.

1. Preheat the oven to 350°F (180°C) with racks positioned in the upper and lower thirds. Line a sheet tray with parchment paper.

2. **Make the strawberry-rhubarb mixture:** Place the rhubarb, strawberries, sugar, cardamom, star anise, vanilla (pod and all), and ginger in a small baking dish, and toss to combine. Cover with foil.

3. Roast for 30 to 40 minutes, until the rhubarb and strawberries are soft and a beautiful pink syrup forms. Remove the foil, and let the mixture cool to room temperature. Remove and discard the large spices, vanilla pod, and ginger (see Note 1).

4. **Make the pepita-sesame crunch:** Toss the pepitas, sesame seeds, syrup, pepper, and a good pinch of salt in a small bowl. Transfer to the sheet tray, spread into an even layer, and bake in the same oven as the rhubarb for 10 to 12 minutes, until lightly toasted.

5. Let cool fully and then break up the pepita-sesame crunch into small pieces (see Note 2).

6. To serve, divide the strawberry-rhubarb mixture among small serving bowls. Top with a scoop of ice cream, a dollop of the Honeyed Whipped Cream, a drizzle of olive oil, and some of the crushed pepita-sesame crunch.

NOTES

1. You can refrigerate this mixture until you are ready to serve. It will last for up to 3 days in the refrigerator. Bring to room temperature before serving.

2. The pepita mixture will keep for up to 3 days stored in an airtight container at room temperature.

Figgy Tapioca Pudding

SERVES 4 TO 6

Spiced Figs

2 cups (200 g) whole dried mission figs, stems removed and halved

¾ cup (180 ml) boiling water

3 tablespoons brandy

2 whole cardamom pods, crushed

2 whole cloves

1 star anise pod

½ cinnamon stick

1 tablespoon packed dark brown sugar

1 teaspoon kosher salt

Tapioca Pudding

⅓ cup (60 g) small pearl tapioca

2¾ cups (660 ml) whole milk

¼ cup (50 g) granulated sugar

1 teaspoon kosher salt

½ vanilla bean, scraped (see Tip)

3 egg yolks

This classic and comforting vanilla tapioca pudding has an added level of coziness from perfectly spiced figs that also make this dessert scream holiday. That being said, you can easily skip the fig topping and just enjoy the tapioca pudding as is or topped with fresh fruit to make this fitting for any time of year. I prefer serving this pudding warm, but feel free to save any leftovers in an airtight container in the fridge and eat it chilled! Just note that it will have a much thicker—but still equally delicious—texture. Gently reheating the tapioca over low heat on the stove is also an option; just be sure to stir frequently. Soaking the tapioca prior to cooking ensures an even cook, so although it might be tempting, don't skip that step!

1. **Make the figs:** Add the figs, boiling water, and brandy to an airtight container, cover, and let sit at room temperature while you prepare the tapioca.

2. **Make the tapioca:** Add the tapioca to a small bowl, and cover with about 1 inch (2.5 cm) of room-temperature water. Let the tapioca soak at room temperature for 45 minutes.

3. Drain the tapioca through a fine-mesh strainer, and place in a medium pot. Stir in the milk, sugar, salt, and vanilla (pod and all). Bring to a gentle boil over medium-high heat, stirring occasionally, 5 to 7 minutes.

4. Reduce the heat to low, and cook, stirring constantly, until the pudding is thick and the tapioca is cooked, 5 to 7 minutes. The texture should be similar to loose yogurt, and the tapioca should have swelled. Turn off the heat.

5. Whisk the egg yolks in a medium bowl. Slowly whisk about 1 cup (240 ml) of the tapioca pudding into the eggs to temper the egg yolks and prevent scrambling.

6. Using a rubber spatula, quickly stir the tapioca–egg yolk mixture into the pot of tapioca pudding, and return the heat to low. Cook, stirring, constantly, 3 or 4 minutes, to just cook the egg yolks. The pudding will still be about the consistency of loose yogurt but will thicken slightly as it sits. Turn off the heat, cover, and set aside while you finish the figs.

7. Add the cardamom, cloves, star anise, and cinnamon stick to a small pot, set over low heat, and toast the spices until fragrant, 2 minutes.

8. Add the soaked figs and all their liquid, the brown sugar, and the salt to the pot. Bring to a boil, reduce the heat to low, and cook, stirring occasionally, until the figs are even softer and the liquid has reduced to a thin syrup, 10 to 12 minutes. Discard the whole spices.

9. Remove the vanilla bean from the pudding.

10. Serve the pudding warm in individual bowls, topped with some of the spiced figs and a bit of their syrup.

TIP You can substitute 2 teaspoons vanilla bean paste or extract for the vanilla bean.

Index

S

Acknowledgments

To my incredibly patient editor, Olivia: Thank you for envisioning and believing in this book years before I ever thought it was something I could accomplish. For being there through my indecisiveness and my decisiveness. Through my breakdowns and my excitement. Thank you for fixing my many run-on sentences while still capturing my voice through it all. I know you will be editing these acknowledgments as well, so I thank you for that, too.

To Paulina, Christine, Erica, and all of the Portrait Team: Thank you for your never-ending support and encouragement—from helping me stay on track with every deadline to being there with me on every call and meeting.

To the incredible Rebecca Firkser, who meticulously tested every single recipe in this book: You probably grated more pecorino Romano than you ever thought possible! Thank you so much for making each recipe with such care, excitement, and mindfulness. Thank you for every tweak and adjustment to make these recipes more delicious, user-friendly, and beautiful. I'm keeping every single one of your endearing tasting notes forever. They make my day every time I read them.

To Jessica: Thank you for supporting my vision for the design of this book and bringing it to life better than I could have imagined. For every back-and-forth and every change, thank you for bearing with me.

To my dear photographer, Emily Hawkes, who captured every single recipe with such intent and beauty: Thank you for sticking with me through every adjustment and request. Your dedication to getting every shot just right is beyond admirable. From shooting at any hour to get the best beach lighting to directing Gus to getting the coolest picture of a sourdough starter I've never seen. Thank you for bringing my food to life! Thank you as well to Shelby for assisting in making each shot as gorgeous as it is. Truly a dream team!

To Tiffany Schleigh, the incredibly talented food stylist who made every recipe truly shine: It was such a joy to watch even the simplest recipes become such showstoppers. For staying way past wrap hours to prep, building the most beautiful sandwiches, and always appeasing my requests for more black pepper and olive oil, I can't thank you enough. Much love to Max as well for all of his help with prep, for his infectious excitement and positivity, and for frying the prettiest pieces of fish I've ever seen.

To Julia Rose: I am in awe of how beautifully your prop selections brought my vibe to the photography in this book. Your attention to detail and ability to picture each shot, both individually and in terms of the book as a whole, is so amazing to witness. The book really *feels like me*, and every linen, spoon, and platter is a huge part of that. I'll always have fond memories of meeting you for the first time at the prop house ahead of the shoot—me sweating because I'm always so nervous, you with soup spilled in your tote. You assured me everything was going to go smoothly and turn out great. You couldn't have been more right. Thank you as well to Clara and Kayla for helping assist with all things props!

To Maxine McCrann, the incredible artist I had the honor of having illustrate this book: Your art has inspired me for so many years, and it's truly a dream to have your work be such a major part of this cookbook. The way you capture food with such bright and vibrant colors always brings a smile to my face, and I know everyone who gets this book will feel the same way. Thank you for taking all of my random thoughts and ideas I had for the illustrations and creating something truly special. I am so excited for everyone who gets a copy of this book to have a piece of your art.

To all the chefs I've had the pleasure of learning from over the years, but especially Chef Brian, Chef Jen, Chef Ethan and Chef Tony: I have learned so many things from each of you, both about cooking and about life. Your influence has made me the cook I am today.

To my partner, Chuck, probably the only person who truly gets me for me: I never thought I'd meet someone who loves food and cooking as much as I do, and I am elated to say I have met my match. Thank you for cheering me on each and every day and being my shoulder to lean on. From taste testing every recipe multiple times to helping on set every day of the photo shoot, I couldn't have gotten through this process without you.

To my dog, Gus, for being the bestest boy. Every single one of these recipes was tested with Gus at my feet, adorably looking up at me the entire time. My sweetest little sous-chef.

To my parents, Frank and Cindy: I'm not really sure how I can ever truly thank you. Your endless support and encouragement in every aspect of my life have always been at the heart of my successes. Thank you for every pep talk, heart-to-heart, and reality check. Thank you for every food magazine subscription, cookbook, chef's knife, pot set, random kitchen utensil, and special dinner. Thank you for supporting the little hobby I had as a child that turned into my career. Thank you for believing in that young girl's dream.

Thank you to my brother, Mitchell, for always eating any random food experiment I made as a kid and telling me "It's pretty good!" even though I know there is no way it was. Thank you for letting me cook extravagant meals for your friends when they came over and making me feel like a really cool younger sister. Thanks for eating French onion dip with me after school. Love ya, bro.

To all of my aunts and uncles who made every holiday and family meal a masterpiece: Thank you for bringing our family together through food and showing me the importance of breaking bread with your loved ones. A special thanks to my Aunt Cathy and Uncle Craig, who both taught me at a young age what it looks like to be a true chef. You never sugarcoated what working in the industry would be like, but you always encouraged me to follow my dreams. You instilled in me a respect for the food industry way before I even knew what I was getting into.

To my grandparents, Gene, Joyce, Sam, and Tina: You supported my dreams of going to culinary school, created so many of my cherished food memories, and of course are a major part of my culinary inspiration.

To my nephews, Beau and Bradley: Making your birthday cakes every year has kept me brushed up on my baking and pastry skills, and I've loved every minute of it—hope you'll have me every year to come!

To all of my taste testers throughout the years—Katie, Chelsey, Trevor, Risse, Dean, Chester, and Esperanza: Thanks for being some of the first to try my recipes and giving your honest feedback.

Thanks to Palmer's Quality Meats for being the best local butcher a gal could ask for. Special thanks to Doug, for talking me through the best way to call for beef shanks in a recipe, and to Arm, for cutting me some really nice lamb neck bones for my Sunday gravy.

To Matt's Farm Market for always having the most beautiful produce that inspires so many of my recipes. Big shout-out for letting us snap the cutest market pictures for the book as well!

Lastly, I want to thank all of my supporters and followers: Without you, I wouldn't have this amazing opportunity. Your support has given me the chance to do things I would have never imagined possible. I am forever grateful, and I hope I've made something that y'all love as much as I do!

About the Author

Hailee Catalano is a trained chef, former restaurant cook, and recipe developer. Now living with her partner, Chuck, and her dog, Gus, in New Jersey, she takes inspiration from her time in restaurants, her Midwestern upbringing, her Italian American heritage, and her love of seasonal produce to create fun and fresh recipes for home cooks.